'This is a fascinating book and the first to explor
collaborators and assistants in developing relation
them to gain as much as possible from their music th
sees collaborators and assistants participating fully as
that has a significant impact on their music thera|
interesting for music therapists who work with clients who are not able to
participate in a physically or psychologically active way.

Experienced authors write from a clinical and theoretical perspective, intended
to help both practitioners and trainees. All the contributions are written in a very
clear and authentic way. I believe it is good that the material in this book is
available for use in different therapeutic situations.

This is a landmark publication for clinicians and students treating clients who
need assistance and collaboration in their music therapy.'

— *Professor Dr. Jos De Backer, LUCA, School of Arts, campus Lemmens,*
co-author of The Music in Music Therapy; Clinical Applications of
Music Therapy in Psychiatry and Clinical Applications of Music
Therapy in Developmental Disability, Paediatrics and Neurology

'Much has been written about the theory and practice of music therapy, yet an
area of practice not addressed often is the role of carers, staff, assistants, students,
volunteers and family members as collaborators and "skill sharers" in music
therapy sessions. This book, edited by three very experienced therapists and
researchers, fills a large gap in our knowledge of how music therapy works, and
is a very welcome addition to the music therapy literature.'

— *Emeritus Professor Denise Grocke, AO, PhD, Melbourne*
Conservatorium of Music, University of Melbourne

'This thoughtful and elegantly researched volume demonstrates the rich benefits
to be gained by all from collaborative and integrated cross-disciplinary work.
International in authorship, with far reaching content, it will surely emerge as a
go-to reference of music therapy practice for many years to come.'

— *Rachel Darnley-Smith, Senior Lecturer in Music*
Therapy, Roehampton University, UK

of related interest

Music Therapy and Group Work
Sound Company
Edited by Alison Davies and Eleanor Richards
ISBN 978 1 84310 036 2
eISBN 978 1 84642 341 3

Forensic Music Therapy
A Treatment for Men and Women in Secure Hospital Settings
Edited by Stella Compton Dickinson, Helen Odell-Miller and John Adlam
ISBN 978 1 84905 252 8
eISBN 978 0 85700 539 7

Music Therapy with Families
Therapeutic Approaches and Theoretical Perspectives
Edited by Stine Lindahl Jacobsen and Grace Thompson
ISBN 978 1 84905 630 4
eISBN 978 1 78450 105 1

Guided Imagery & Music (GIM) and Music Imagery
Methods for Individual and Group Therapy
Edited by Denise Grocke and Torben Moe
ISBN 978 1 84905 483 6
eISBN 978 0 85700 877 0

Flute, Accordion or Clarinet?
Using the Characteristics of Our Instruments in Music Therapy
Edited by Amelia Oldfield, Jo Tomlinson and Dawn Loombe
ISBN 978 1 84905 398 3
eISBN 978 0 85700 766 7

Collaboration and Assistance in Music Therapy Practice

Roles, Relationships, Challenges

EDITED BY John Strange, Helen Odell-Miller
and Eleanor Richards

FOREWORD BY GRO TRONDALEN

Jessica Kingsley *Publishers*
London and Philadelphia

First published in 2017
by Jessica Kingsley Publishers
73 Collier Street
London N1 9BE, UK
and
400 Market Street, Suite 400
Philadelphia, PA 19106, USA

www.jkp.com

Library of Congress Cataloging in Publication Data
Names: Strange, John (Music therapist) editor. | Odell-Miller, Helen, 1955-
editor. | Richards, Eleanor (Eleanor Gurney) editor.
Title: Collaboration and assistance in music therapy practice : roles,
relationships, challenges / edited by John Strange, Helen Odell-Miller and
Eleanor Richards.
Description: London ; Philadelphia : Jessica Kingsley Publishers, 2017.
Identifiers: LCCN 2016028541 | ISBN 9781849057028 (alk. paper)
Subjects: LCSH: Music therapy--Research.
Classification: LCC ML3920 .C68 2017 | DDC 615.8/5154--dc23

British Library Cataloguing in Publication Data
A CIP catalogue record for this book is available from the British Library.

ISBN 978 1 84905 702 8
eISBN 978 1 78450 223 2

Printed and bound in Great Britain

Contents

FOREWORD BY GRO TRONDALEN   9

ACKNOWLEDGEMENTS   12

Introduction   13
A Well-Trodden Territory in Need of a Map
John Strange, Helen Odell-Miller and Eleanor Richards

1. Assistants as Interaction Partners   22
The Experience of Learning Support Assistants in Group Music Therapy
John Strange

2. Music Therapists' Experiences of Working with Staff in
Sessions   36
Hannah Munro

3. Student Perspectives on Working with Assistants on
Placement During Vocational Music Therapy Training . .   54
Catherine Warner

4. Involving Family Members Who Are Primary Carers
in Music Therapy Sessions with Children with Special
Needs   71
Pornpan Kaenampornpan

5. Exploring the Significance of the Role of Assistants
in Music Therapy Groups in Adult and Older People's
Mental Health Settings   88
Helen Odell-Miller

6. 'Let Them Bring Their Own Song'   99
A Qualitative Study of Developing Relationships Between Care
Staff and Nursing Home Residents with Dementia Through
Music Therapy and Dance Movement Therapy Groups
Ruth Melhuish

7. Caregivers' Dual Role in Music Therapy to Manage
   Neuropsychiatric Symptoms of Dementia 120
   Ming Hung Hsu

8. Psychodynamic Group Music Therapy Facilitates Carers
   to Become Auxiliary Music Therapists 145
   A Case Study and Methodological Analysis
   Anthi Agrotou

9. Supporting the Unplanned Journey 169
   Music Therapy as a Developmental Resource with People with Profound
   and Multiple Learning Disabilities and Their Carers and Staff
   Tessa Watson

10. From Assistance to Co-Therapy 186
    On the Role of the Co-Therapist in Nordoff Robbins Music Therapy
    Jörg Fachner

11. Music and Attuned Movement Therapy 200
    How the Facilitator Mediates Between Client and Therapist
    John Strange, Mary-Clare Fearn and Rebecca O'Connor

12. 'Music and Movement' 227
    Integrated Music Therapy and Physiotherapy for People with Severe
    Physical Disabilities at Risk of Developing Fixed Deformities
    John Strange and Lyn Weekes

13. Improvised Music to Support Client–Assistant
    Interaction 235
    The Perceptions of Music Therapists
    John Strange

14. Who Knows Me Best? 253
    Exploring the Collaborative Roles of Transient Practitioners
    and Constant Practitioners in Music Therapy
    Sarah Hadley

15. An Inclusion Group for Primary School Pupils With and
    Without Profound Learning Disability 275
    Motoko Hayata and John Strange

16. Building Musical Bridges in Paediatric Hospital
    Departments 285
    Tone Leinebø and Trygve Aasgaard

17. Someone Else in the Room: Welcome or Unwelcome? . . 304
An Attachment Perspective
Eleanor Richards

18. Valuing Human Resources 314
Training, Service Development, Research: The Way Forward
John Strange, Helen Odell-Miller and Eleanor Richards

APPENDIX 320

CONTRIBUTORS 323

SUBJECT INDEX 329

AUTHOR INDEX 333

Foreword

Musical relationship: An act of trust

To be seen is crucial to every human being. To be recognised as a human being with personal will and subjectivity is vital, no matter what one's role or position in life. As *homo communicans* we are seeking each other through different dimensions, while striving towards meaning and fulfilment in daily encounters – not least through musical experiences in a music therapy practice. Music is a way of communicating through an art form. Music is an agent in itself. Additionally, music re-makes anew in the moment.

However, interacting and playing through music involves a risk:

> Improvising is experimenting, and, as such, it is a trial and error undertaking that involves considerable risk. At every moment, something can go in an unwanted direction... The improviser is constantly confronted with the risk of failure and the limits of his capacity. In addition, there is always a risk of meaninglessness. (Bruscia 2014, p.145)

Allowing oneself to be involved in a musical encounter always involves uncertainty. Interestingly, these life conditions apply equally to the client and the music therapist and also to significant others in music therapy such as 'carers, family members, custodians, members of the community, volunteers, key workers, case managers and many who are collaborators with music therapy participants attending music therapy' (this volume, Introduction). Such an ambiguous position, though, affords new possibilities of musical interaction and, hence, a potent space for development and change. Winnicott (1971, p.50) stated, 'Playing is an experience, always a creative experience, and it is an experience in the space–time continuum, a basic form of living.' I suggest such a creative experience is *an act of trust*. From a philosophical point of view, such an act of trust is not dependent on the different positions or roles in music therapy practice. Within a relational paradigm, we are all in the world together and therefore fellow travellers (Yalom 2001).

A musical relationship in therapy also involves different positions and authorities by virtue of qualifications. In addition, one person is most often seeking help and another is defined as helper. The participants are bringing a variety of resources (and constraints) into the setting. Participation in a professional music therapy practice as a significant other also involves some power, while still possessing an in-between position encircled by the therapist and the client. There is always a mutual influence within a music therapy relationship, be it in an individual setting or in a group. Culture, personal qualities and context in a broad sense influences the power structure of a music encounter. The overall aim, however, is to allow for a relational experience with the other. A respectful and attentive presence, attuned in the here-and-now, empowers the other as the outstanding and irreducible creation that she or he is.

In *Playing and Reality*, Winnicott (1971, p.51) drew attention to significant moments in therapy. He argued that psychotherapy can dig deeply without interpretive work: '…the point that I make in reporting what I call "therapeutic consultations" [is] that the significant moment is that at which *the child surprises herself or himself.* It is not the moment of my clever interpretation that is significant' (emphasis in original).

Transferred to music therapy, such a surprising act may be as evident to the significant other and to the music therapist as it is to a client herself. Involving oneself in a musical relationship allows for a variety of experiences at different levels while supporting the creation of new life stories. 'The phenomenal music therapy relationship then emerges as an art form – a field of relational lived experiences – emerging from an inborn, communicative musicality' (Trondalen 2016, p.89). In music therapy, which is a cultural experience, the client(s), the significant other(s) and the music therapist(s) play together as they direct and attune themselves toward the music and the musical participation. Playing deals with joy and fun as deep existential themes are seriously played out during musical playing in different modes. Playing is for real.

Collaboration and Assistance in Music Therapy Practice addresses a myriad of impacts of assistants and collaborators in the music therapy room. The contributors write from a clinical, narrative and/or research perspective, while exploring both the roles of different professions co-working on an equal basis with music therapists, and those of parents or other family members present in the therapy room. A historical reflection on assistants and co-therapists in music therapy groups in adult mental health is included, as well as a suggested way forward in training, service development and research.

This volume is a valuable resource as it documents a wide variety of possible ways of involving assistants and collaborators to gain as much as possible from the music therapy group or individual session. Whatever roles the different assistants and collaborators in music therapy perform, they will always influence the session. As the book clearly states, 'It is not possible to be simply a "fly on the wall"' (Introduction).

As human beings, those collaborating and assisting in music therapy practice are always present as existential soundboards to each other's life. The meaning of music therapy, then, is the meaning of a shared experience. As long as it is something that we can open up for and share with each other, such a shared life world experience offers new competencies for life.

Gro Trondalen,
Professor of Music Therapy,
Norwegian Academy of Music

References

Bruscia, K.E. (2014) *Defining Music Therapy* (3rd ed.). University Park, IL: Barcelona Publishers.

Trondalen, G. (2016) *Relational Music Therapy: An Intersubjective Perspective.* Dallas, TX: Barcelona Publishers.

Winnicott, D.W. (1971) *Playing and Reality.* London and New York: Tavistock/Routledge.

Yalom, I.D. (2001) *The Gift of Therapy: Reflections on Being a Therapist.* London: Judy Piatkus.

Acknowledgements

This book emerges from a collaboration of the three editors at Anglia Ruskin University (ARU) when John Strange was a PhD student and Helen Odell-Miller and Eleanor Richards were his supervisors. We are grateful to ARU and to all students, participants in music therapy and those assisting in music therapy, and to the therapists contributing chapters, for the range and depth of their contribution to our work. We thank our families, friends and colleagues for their consistent support of, and interest in, this project. We also thank Sage Publications for permission to reproduce tables and selected verbatim quotations from interviews.

Introduction

A Well-Trodden Territory in Need of a Map

John Strange, Helen Odell-Miller
and Eleanor Richards

Music therapists' practice regularly includes working with significant others in the lives of participants in music therapy. These significant others are carers, family members, custodians, members of the community, volunteers, key workers, case managers and many who are collaborators with music therapy participants attending music therapy. Although this is common practice, and music therapists work to engage these significant others musically within the relationship they have with the main participants in music therapy, there is little literature which emphasises the importance of the attendees in facilitating the developing relationship with the participants, and in enabling the participants to gain as much as possible from the music therapy group or individual session. In case studies these significant others or non-music therapist attendees often receive only a passing reference, with little indication of what role they played or even of why they were present. Occasionally, as in many of the chapters on the theory and practice of group work in particular clinical settings edited by Davies and Richards (2002), the nature and purpose of the participation of assistants are clearly set out. Nevertheless, writing with a specific focus on the role of the assistant and the relationships between clients and assistants has been rare. A fresh exploration of the field is therefore necessary. We hope this book will not only throw new light on the broad topic of collaborators and assistants, but also point readers towards existing writing, relevant to the topic, of which they are unaware, and encourage others to write about it.

We define assistance and collaboration as broadly as possible. Others besides the music therapist and the clients may be present in music therapy sessions for a variety of reasons: to transport or escort clients to and from sessions; to monitor medical and security issues; to observe and give verbal feedback; to provide physical or other practical support to help clients to participate; to share in the management and perhaps also the planning of group therapy; to participate fully as group members; and so on. Whatever their role, they will have a significant impact upon therapy. This must be understood and managed in order to derive the most advantage. An assistant's role may range from one of active participant to one of non-participant observer, but everyone present in a music therapy session will influence it in some way. It is not possible to be simply a 'fly on the wall'.

There are two groups who might be considered collaborators, and who certainly contribute significantly to music therapy, whose roles this book does not explore because they have been treated thoroughly in other recent publications. The first group consists of members of other professions co-working on an equal basis with music therapists, whose contribution was thoroughly surveyed by Twyford and Watson (2008). The second group consists of parents or other family members present in the therapy room because an important focus of the therapy is their relationship with the child and its impact upon health and well-being. Parents and other family members are covered in recent volumes by Oldfield and Flower (2008) and Edwards (2011). We do, however, include Kaenampornpan's study, in Chapter 4, of work in Thailand in which family members assisted and facilitated therapy, and then continued some of the therapeutic activities at home. Here the family members' relationship with their child and the improvements seen in this was the focus of the work.

The relationship of therapist and co-therapist which Paul Nordoff and Clive Robbins pioneered in the 1960s (see Chapter 10) highlights the therapeutic potential of collaboration. Nordoff and Robbins stipulated that the co-therapist must be a second fully qualified music therapist, whereas none of the assistants and collaborators discussed in all other chapters of this book are music therapists.

As the title indicates, assistants and collaborators are considered in terms of their roles, the responsibilities that they entail and the challenges encountered. Factors determining the nature of their roles include the theoretical model guiding the therapy, the needs of the clients and the available resources – human, institutional and environmental. By responsibilities we refer both to specific tasks, for example providing nursing oversight, security or record keeping, which may be partially or completely delegated to the assistant, and also to the attitudes and standards of behaviour required when assisting or collaborating in music therapy. We also consider the unconscious processes involved in these relationships, where roles may mirror those of family members, for example, and we are concerned with the psychoanalytic and psychodynamic implications of the nature of these relationships. Challenges encountered by music therapists working collaboratively may be either inherent in the model and process of collaboration itself or the result of professional or institutional resistance to such work.

This is a 'reader' rather than a 'handbook'. Authors write from a clinical, narrative and/or research perspective, and the book is intended to help practitioners and trainees in their practice. Three recent research studies (Schmidt-Robyn 2008; Munro 2011; Strange 2014) have focused on the use of assistants in music therapy. Schmidt-Robyn (2008, p.15) states that 'the assistant's presence will almost always challenge our conventional ideas about music therapy and the therapist's role'. She found that music therapists were roughly equally divided between those who regarded assistants as partners in the therapy, those who regarded them as observers and those who adopted either view according to circumstances. Some interviewees would allow assistants to play instruments or contribute in other ways, but very few would actually encourage such participation, and two did not believe the therapist should acknowledge an assistant's presence in any way. Munro's (2011) study (see Chapter 2) gave equal weight to both the benefits and the potential problems for client, therapist and assistant, and considered work with non-professional assistants in the broader context of other circumstances in which a third person may be present.

Strange (2014, pp.96–109) surveyed the experiences and attitudes of music therapists who had worked with profoundly disabled clients of any age, an area of practice where the use of assistants is probably most prevalent. The final survey question invited suggestions as to why such scant attention is usually given to assistants in the literature. Some respondents suggested that the topic was not central to music therapy, or at least not a priority, and one said the use of assistants is rare (a view not borne out, at least in the field of profound learning disability, by the fact that 49 of 50 respondents reported using assistants). Other explanations offered were that work with assistants was too disparate to be generalised, that music therapists might be reluctant to publish accounts of work they felt was compromised by a failure to manage the challenges of using assistants, and finally that writing about the role of assistants might generate tensions or damage the image of the profession.

We had no difficulty, however, finding authors keen to explore the topic. We hope the book will prove instructive in several ways: by documenting the wide variety of possible ways of involving assistants and collaborators, and the benefits to clients from doing so; by giving those responsible for commissioning, planning or delivering music therapy some idea of how best those benefits may be secured; and by showing that there are many ways of studying and writing about the topic, thus encouraging others to do so.

Statutory regulation, in countries which have achieved it, and professional self-regulation, which is more widespread, both perform the essential function of ensuring that only appropriately trained, skilled and ethically responsible persons practise as music therapists. However, there is a growing call for 'skill sharing' – the exercise of elements of music therapy practice beyond the boundaries of the regulated profession when it is safe and ethical to do so. Several charitable organisations, notably Music as Therapy (Quin 2014), have successfully extended many of the benefits of music therapy to countries, regions and situations where an affordable professional service commensurate with need would be a pipe dream. Sarah Hadley (Chapter 14) tells how a similar skill-sharing initiative was established in a London National Health Service (NHS) Trust when it became clear that demand for music therapy far exceeded supply. Rather than undermining the status of music therapists, the decision to train non-professionals to offer a carefully tailored derivative of developmental music therapy, intended for children at moderate risk, actually led to greater recognition of music therapists as expert trainers, open to innovation and responsive to the financial pressures on public services.

In bringing this book to fruition, we have been excited to discover how authors have developed their initially agreed abstracts. We do not aim to promote one particular view of the role of assistants and collaborators; indeed, the great variety of approaches and theoretical positions presented demonstrates that no one-size-fits-all model could or should be sought. Chapters which include musical transcriptions range from a more 'music-centred' theoretical stance to chapters without such a focus.

In Chapter 1, John Strange describes clinical work with profoundly learning-disabled teenagers, which in learning support assistants became the teenagers' primary interaction partners, supported by musical improvisation rather than verbal guidance or modelling. Semi-structured interviews in which learning support assistants responded to video clips of the work reveal a striking unanimity in their perceptions of the approach and its value as a way of fostering clients' development.

In Chapter 2, Hannah Munro investigates the role of assistants through interviews with five music therapists from different training backgrounds, working in diverse clinical areas. She explores when and why additional staff may be present, how their presence may affect the client/therapist relationship, and the benefits and challenges of working with staff in sessions, for client, therapist and assistant. Her concluding guidelines for good practice cover the management of the whole therapist–assistant relationship – what is expected of the therapist as well as of the assistant.

In Chapter 3, Catherine Warner investigates how music therapy students construct their experiences of working with assistants on training placements in a range of settings, by interviewing Master of Arts students undertaking different UK music therapy trainings. She illuminates how students construct their learning experiences and the notion of 'assistant', and explores differences between student learning in institutional or community settings. She considers how the values and perceptions articulated by the students might relate to their developing identities as therapists.

In Chapter 4, Pornpan Kaenampornpan describes music therapy work at a special education centre in Thailand, where her doctoral research took place. She explains how she involved family members in the therapeutic process and examines how their involvement helped the children's development and strengthened the relationships between the children and their families. She offers guidance on how to work with parents or other family members, and how to help them to use music with their children in the home environment.

In Chapter 5, Helen Odell-Miller offers a historical reflection on assistants and co-therapists in music therapy groups in adult mental health. She examines the roles of co-therapists and assistants and their working relationships within the multidisciplinary team, as group music therapy has evolved over the years in a wide variety of NHS and other adult mental health settings. She considers how the dynamics of these relationships can be used to develop the group process and enhance participants' experiences in groups. Evaluation and in-depth written and verbal review of each group process is discussed, drawing upon evaluation processes developed or adapted by the author.

In Chapter 6, Ruth Melhuish describes a qualitative study in a care home for people with dementia. Nursing home staff who participated regularly in both music therapy and dance movement therapy groups explore in interviews the experience and perceptions of working with residents, and identify whether and how this experience had an impact on their own work. Melhuish concludes by considering the relevance of the results of the study to contemporary approaches to dementia care.

In Chapter 7, Ming Hung Hsu describes a clinical trial conducted in dementia care homes, exploring the dual role of caregivers in both supporting music therapy sessions and extending the effects of music therapy into the daily management of dementia symptoms. He asks how carers can be effectively involved in music therapy, how they can facilitate care home residents' access to therapy, what they themselves gain from their involvement in music therapy, how the influence of music therapy reverberates in their day-to-day care practice and whether there are limits to their involvement.

In Chapter 8, Anthi Agrotou presents a pioneering group music therapy project in a state institution for profoundly learning-disabled people in Cyprus. Carers with no professional training in either music or learning disability acquired therapeutic skills through forming attachment bonds with three residents who were functioning in an autistic type of isolation. The therapeutic methodology facilitated residents' evolving ability to express their needs for human intimacy, creative expression and autonomy, and enabled carers to gain insight and develop from emotionally unresponsive onlookers into effective auxiliary music therapists.

In Chapter 9, Tessa Watson describes an approach, developed over many years of clinical experience, with people with profound and multiple learning disabilities, using a music therapy and sensory interaction group involving pre-composed and improvised music as well as physiotherapy exercises. The function of the group for service users and staff is explained. Theories underpinning the group are discussed, particularly the relevance of attachment theory to the way the group encourages new, creative and healthy ways of relating between staff and service users.

In Chapter 10, Jörg Fachner reports on a research study in which prominent exponents of Nordoff Robbins creative music therapy gave semi-structured interviews to which a qualitative analysis was applied in order to reconstruct the contemporary role of the co-therapist and to investigate how far the original Nordoff Robbins approach developed from the circumstance that Clive Robbins was at the beginning an assistant but then developed into a co-therapist.

In Chapter 11, John Strange, Mary-Clare Fearn and Rebecca O'Connor describe 'Music and Attuned Movement Therapy', an approach involving the specialised role of the hands-on facilitator, developed in work with children having profound physical disabilities. They explain how in this triadic relationship the facilitator, working intuitively, responds simultaneously to bodily signals from the child and musical signals from the therapist, supporting the child to perform self-expressive movements of her own volition which she cannot manage independently.

In Chapter 12, John Strange and Lyn Weekes relate the development in a large mental handicap hospital of a collaboration between music therapy and physiotherapy which became known as 'Music and Movement'. Groups of patients at risk of developing fixed deformities experienced a planned sequence of movement and stretching exercises, modified according to their individual needs, supported by one-to-one facilitators. A sequence of motivating music structured and guided the work, creating an enjoyable group experience with specific clinical focus.

In Chapter 13, John Strange outlines the challenges of researching outcomes of improvisational music therapy, particularly the question of how to analyse the music and assess its clinical influence. He describes how continuous responses by a panel of music therapists to video recordings from sessions were recorded using 'video on video' and then collated with musical transcriptions, to stimulate group discussion and comparison of their perceptions of the musical-clinical process.

In Chapter 14, Sarah Hadley explains the nature and origins of 'Interactive Music Making' and its role in a community music service for children alongside traditional music therapy, modelled on earlier pioneering work with care staff in Romanian orphanages.

Music-based tools to establish positive relationships, long familiar to music therapists, are imparted to Interactive Music Makers to equip them to offer a developmentally based service to children with less complex difficulties than those offered traditional music therapy.

In Chapter 15, Motoko Hayata and John Strange outline the evolution of attitudes to inclusion and describe a voluntary-sector music therapy service's pragmatic response to the inclusive ethos of a particular primary school and local education authority. They examine the benefits to both the disabled and the non-disabled pupils in 'inclusion groups' and also to the staff involved, using case studies, and they explore the web of 'helping' relationships between music therapist, specialist teacher, teaching assistants and pupils.

In Chapter 16, Tone Leinebø and Trygve Aasgaard present a variety of joint music therapy activities and interventions in a university hospital paediatric department in which music therapists collaborate with nurses, medical staff, physiotherapists, parents and siblings of young patients. Common therapeutic aims are related to fostering enjoyable and pleasant experiences, and to reducing discomfort for both patients and families whose lives are marked, temporarily or permanently, by illness, treatment procedures and uncertainty. The chapter demonstrates how elements of musicking build bridges between people and help patients to maintain access to some good aspects of life.

In Chapter 17, Eleanor Richards considers how insights from contemporary attachment theory are consciously employed in the work described in a number of chapters and, more broadly, how the experience of shared music-making itself may play a part in fostering more secure and therefore creative attachments between all involved in the therapeutic encounter. She also draws attention to the need for professionals to examine their own attachments, emotionally rooted and not always conscious, to particular ways of working.

In Chapter 18, we draw general conclusions concerning how the most effective use may be made of assistance and collaboration in music therapy practice and how the development of professional training and workforce planning may facilitate this process. The case is made for further research and writing to raise awareness of the role and potential of assistance and collaboration in music therapy and to advance understanding of the issues raised.

References

Davies, A. and Richards, E. (eds) (2002) *Music Therapy and Group Work: Sound Company.* London: Jessica Kingsley Publishers.

Edwards, J. (2011) *Music Therapy and Parent–Infant Bonding.* Oxford: Oxford University Press.

Munro, H. (2011) 'Music Therapists, Clients and Support Staff: Using Framework Analysis to Investigate the Experiences of Music Therapists Who Have Worked with Support Staff in Music Therapy Sessions, with a View to Developing Guidelines for Good Practice.' Unpublished MSc thesis, Queen Margaret University, Edinburgh.

Oldfield, A. and Flower, C. (eds) (2008) *Music Therapy with Children and Their Families.* London: Jessica Kingsley Publishers.

Quin, A. (2014) 'Embedding Innovation into the Counterpoint of Music Therapy Practice Today.' Keynote address. In G. Tsiris, C. Warner and G. Watts (eds) *Counterpoints: Music Therapy Practice in the 21st Century.* BAMT Conference, Birmingham, 21–23 February 2014. London: BAMT.

Schmidt-Robyn, B. (2008) *Two's Company but Three's a Crowd?* Norderstedt: Books on Demand.

Strange, J. (2014) 'Improvised Music to Support Interaction Between Profoundly Learning-Disabled Teenagers and Their Learning Support Assistants.' PhD thesis, Anglia Ruskin University, Cambridge. Available at http://hdl.handle.net/10540/314588, accessed on 30 April 2016.

Twyford, K. and Watson, T. (eds) (2008) *Integrated Team Working: Music Therapy as Part of Transdisciplinary and Collaborative Approaches.* London: Jessica Kingsley Publishers.

Chapter 1

Assistants as Interaction Partners

The Experience of Learning Support Assistants in Group Music Therapy

John Strange

Introduction

Much of the literature on group music therapy prioritises the role of client–therapist and client–client relationships. Writing with a specific focus on the role of the assistant and on relationships between clients and assistants has been rare and mostly found in descriptions of music therapy practice in particular settings and circumstances (Carter and Oldfield 2002; Durham 2002; Sutton 2002; Watson and Vickers 2002) rather than in writing focused on outcomes or theoretical issues. The present chapter and Chapter 13 describe two stages in my doctoral investigation of a specific approach in group music therapy for profoundly learning-disabled teenagers in which the role of assistants as interaction partners was central.

Education and therapy

Most of my clinical work has taken place in schools; around half has been with groups, and about half of those groups have included assistants. Often they have made a valuable contribution and sometimes they have been indispensable. Occasionally my relationship with assistants has been tense and problematic because of the different expectations of the assistant in the classroom and the therapy room. Sutton (2002) observes:

> Our approach and theoretical training can be at odds with the ways that children's educational progress is measured. While able to think developmentally and in terms of types of behaviour, we focus on the

psycho-emotional aspects of a child's life. This is not the focus of a school curriculum. (p.192)

Classroom teaching has changed since the 1960s. The emphasis has shifted away from what the teacher does to bring the curriculum to life, to the provision of a sequence of varied learning and self-monitoring activities for the pupils. A typical modern lesson, in our technology-dominated world, moves at a hectic pace, leaving little room for free discussion or the 'potential space' which Sutton tells us is needed in order to explore the psycho-emotional aspects of a child's life.

Specific difficulties experienced by assistants

Despite their different aims and approaches, teachers and music therapists, as fellow professionals, can usually find at least a *modus vivendi* and often a fruitful collaboration, provided there is mutual respect and regular communication. It is more complicated for support staff. They can easily feel they are 'serving two masters', one of whom (usually the therapist) may seem to be perplexingly off message. To remedy this situation, music therapist and assistant(s) should meet in advance and explore how the latter see their potential role. Then their understanding can be developed as necessary through experiential learning such as role-playing a therapy situation and by showing video examples. But suppose such preparation is not possible: What, then, is the alternative?

Triadic support of interaction by improvisation: Background

I have discussed elsewhere (Strange 2012) a body of work in a mainstream further-education college with teenagers with profound and multiple learning disabilities (PMLD) from three special schools. I shall refer to these teenage clients as 'the students'. Most students were accompanied by personally assigned learning support assistants (LSAs) responsible for all aspects of their care, who also supported them in many other contexts and were therefore familiar with their idiosyncrasies. Many of the LSAs assisting in the groups had been unable to attend the training I had provided, and the timetable of the day in college did not allow for either briefing or debriefing. Yet if

I had relegated all these support staff to the role of mere observers, I would have forfeited the potential gains from combining elements of psychodynamic and educational approaches (Nicholls 2002, p.235) offered by working with assistants. If I assigned a more active role to assistants, they might initially lack some of the skills needed, but I was confident they could soon acquire them experientially by learning on the job. A major contribution to this learning was made by an approach I developed for use at intervals during sessions according to clinical need. I now call it 'triadic support of interaction by improvisation' or TSII (Strange 2014, p.8).

The rationale for TSII – supporting the client–assistant relationship by improvising music, rather than by engaging socially with either partner – is that interpersonal interaction is crucial to developmental learning for those with PMLD (Nind and Hewett 1994). The students habitually sought such interaction from the assistants rather than from peers. TSII evolved by the accumulation of spur-of-the-moment pragmatic-intuitive decisions to 'go with the flow' and support student–assistant interactions. Other music therapists most probably work in a similar way in similar circumstances, but I believe I am the first to single out the approach for a research investigation.

A comparable approach developed for children with autism and their mothers

The closest parallel to TSII described in the literature is 'musical interaction therapy', developed to support social interaction between an autistic child and a parent. Wimpory and colleagues write of a 3-year-old autistic girl interacting with her mother:

> The musician's role was similar to that of the pianist accompanying silent films. The music reflected the mood, timing and meaning of the dyad's activities...the (harp) music became quieter if the child avoided her mother and more exciting if she approached her – gradually reaching a crescendo with the climax of dramatic games... Support for the timing of interaction may...highlight maternal behaviour, making it more predictable and thereby facilitating, but not training, social participation... (Wimpory, Chadwick and Nash 1995, p.543)

People with autism have a specific difficulty in processing social information, which severely compromises their ability to interact with others, but non-autistic people with profound and multiple impairment have similar difficulties. They often lack both language and many non-verbal skills of communication, and may as a result experience an impoverished, purely functional style of communication with their carers. TSII is intended to help both client and carer by facilitating interaction, encouraging joint attention, structuring dialogue, and conveying and reflecting feelings. These are all familiar music therapy aims, but most accounts of music therapy to foster interpersonal interaction describe the development of communication between client and therapist (Holck 2004) or, in the case of a group, between client and group (Nicholls 2002; Stewart 2002). TSII, like musical interaction therapy, focuses specifically on interaction between client and assistant, and requires the music therapist to enter that interaction musically rather than socially.

The development of TSII

Realising that the students' emotional and developmental needs were best fostered through interpersonal interaction, I encouraged and supported the interactions already occurring between students and LSAs. These interactions taught me more about the students' interactive abilities than I could have discovered by only interacting with them myself. I also became more aware of the interactive skills of the LSAs. In supporting student–LSA interactions I was developing not only the students' interactive skills but also those of the LSAs, so that they might become more effective interaction partners, both in music therapy and beyond.

I supported student–LSA interaction by means of improvised musical accompaniment, from a keyboard in the corner of the room at some distance from the interacting dyads. My aim was to encourage, develop and consolidate any interactions that met the student's emotional and developmental needs, but also to encourage and facilitate change when interactions did not seem to be meeting those needs. Even when an LSA's interaction with a student seemed unhelpful to the student, I tried to avoid taking over from the LSA as the student's interaction partner. To have done this would not have addressed the underlying causes of the unhelpful interaction, and might have conveyed doubts as to the partners' ability to tolerate and contain any difficult feelings about being together. Stern (1998), describing various schools of mother–infant psychotherapy, explains how, in McDonough's 'Interaction Guidance':

> The therapist does not interact with the baby to model behaviours for the mother; this could sabotage the mother's self-confidence and destroy her view of the therapist as her ally, making him her successful competitor or a better or more expert caregiver. (p.141)

Confining my intervention to a musical one, even when I hoped to modify the LSA's behaviour, avoided sabotaging the self-confidence of the LSAs.

There were two kinds of situation in which I was most likely to use TSII. The first was when I had decided to focus my therapeutic intervention, and the group's attention, on one student for a while. This often arose during a series of student solo 'spots', interspersed with a pre-composed chorus in which all were invited to play. During each student's solo spot, other students would be encouraged to pay attention and listen, but not discouraged from spontaneously joining in. The LSA allocated to the student in the spotlight might play an instrument or encourage the student in other ways, without needing to be asked. She might do this when the student seemed unresponsive, or appeared to be having difficulty in playing an instrument, but equally she might respond musically or socially when the student was already musically or socially more active. At other times she might simply act as a watchful, caring presence, conveying her interest and encouragement to the student by subtle social or musical signalling. I would relate my musical support to what both partners were doing, rather than only to the student's responses. As well as playing, I might sing about what was occurring, giving voice to what I imagined either partner might be thinking or feeling, while usually avoiding addressing them directly.

The second circumstance when TSII was often used was when, either during a group improvisation or during a lull between activities, I noticed an interaction developing spontaneously between a student and an LSA. Again I would relate my musical support to the contributions of both partners. My music would draw the attention of the rest of the group to the interaction by echoing and perhaps amplifying its key musical features. If other group members were playing, the structure and mood of my playing, attuned to the behaviour of the dyad I was supporting, could draw others' music into a closer relationship with that of the focus dyad. This met an important clinical aim for group members, that they should become more aware of, and responsive to, their peers' actions and the moods they expressed, and also more aware of other group members' interest in, and reactions to, their own communicative behaviour.

An approach distinct from TSII but with certain similarities is Music and Attuned Movement Therapy, developed by Fearn and O'Connor (2008) for young children with profound disability including limited movement ability (see Chapter 11). In this model the facilitator working with the music therapist may be a teacher, physiotherapist, occupational therapist or nurse, or sometimes the child's parent. She or he aims 'to reflect and facilitate the child's breathing and movement patterns…and…hasten the child's development of awareness of self and self in relation to others' (Fearn and O'Connor 2008, pp.57–58). While assisting the child in this way, the facilitator, who is thoroughly briefed and debriefed to support her role, is also assisting the music therapist, because she is able to detect and physically facilitate movement intentions the therapist might not otherwise notice. The LSAs with whom I developed TSII were much less thoroughly briefed than facilitators in Music and Attuned Movement Therapy, but those who worked with the two most physically disabled students in the study were nevertheless both diligent and skilled at detecting and facilitating their incipient movements rather than imposing their own.

Researching the experience of LSAs assisting in TSII

I recruited two groups of research collaborators to evaluate clips from the video archive of the groups. The first were the LSAs themselves, whose contribution is described in this chapter. Watching video clips of the therapy in which they had been involved, they often showed surprise at the level of functioning and capacity for interaction shown by the students whose abilities they had thought they knew so well. Such judgements might perhaps count as outcomes of therapy but should be viewed with caution because the video excerpts were purposely selected to show the effective use of TSII, and no negative examples were included. Thus, although the potential for TSII to foster and develop interaction was demonstrated, one could not know how often this potential was actually realised.

I showed each LSA a clip of her own interaction with a student, supported by my improvised music, and asked her to comment on the student's observable behaviour and possible mental processes, her own behaviour and mental processes, and finally my keyboard music. Henry and Fetters (2012), in describing 'video elicitation interviews' in which interviewees view video recordings of their own interactions with another person, state:

> [I]nterview participants have 3 distinguishable kinds of experiences. First, participants typically recall the thoughts, beliefs, and emotions they experienced during the interaction. Second, participants frequently re-experience or relive the interaction while watching themselves on video and may even display physiologic or emotional changes in response to the events in the video recording. Finally, participants often reflect on their thoughts and actions or those of their interaction partner. (p.119)

In my research, however, there was a gap of over a year between involvement in the therapy and viewing the video clip (in contrast with a gap of between a few hours and 2 weeks recommended for video elicitation interviews). The LSAs' direct recall of their experience at the time had therefore faded, but they certainly seemed to relive those experiences as they watched and were eager to reflect on what they saw and what it meant. Since it is the dyadic interaction which TSII addresses, the LSAs' experiences are as important as those of the students, despite their not being clients nor seeing themselves as such. They could also speak on behalf of the non-verbal students and interpret the meaning of their behaviour. Precedents for such expression by proxy may be found in other qualitative studies (Aigen 1997; Nowikas 1999).

The complete methodology can be seen online (Strange 2014), and what follows is only a summary. During the interviews, in which three viewings of the video clip punctuated the 30-minute discussion with each LSA, a video camera was positioned so that it re-recorded the video and soundtrack from the video clips, together with the voices of the LSA and myself as we watched. Viewing this new composite recording of the interview, I annotated musical transcriptions of the therapy excerpt with the LSAs' comments, indicating the precise point in the clip to which each comment referred. The entire interviews were transcribed *verbatim*, apart from substituting aliases, and complete transcripts were sent by email to the LSAs for checking.

The interview transcripts were analysed using interpretative phenomenological analysis (Smith, Flowers and Larkin 2009) as a way of understanding the LSAs' experience of TSII. This analysis revealed that all the LSAs had shown a commitment to the students' welfare and best interests, a good knowledge both of individual needs and the needs shared by the whole client group and, importantly, keen powers of observation. No LSA had difficulty in describing either the student's behaviour or her own, although comments on specifically musical behaviour tended to be simple and factual rather than addressing its expressiveness and possible meaning. This limitation may have been due partly to lack of familiarity with musical terminology and partly to prioritising the intention and meaning of observable actions, rather than musical subtleties which LSAs may not have considered relevant. Thus, although LSAs attributed to students feelings and intentions, such as happiness, pride or an inclination to tease, they did not usually evidence these feelings and intentions by reference to the students' music. Music was spoken of in mundane terms as being loud, soft, fast, slow, repeating or varying, rather than as expressing or reflecting feelings or intentions. Interestingly, however, purely musical *interactions* were sometimes described as communication.

In speaking about the students, all the LSAs readily moved unprompted from discussing what could be observed to suggesting possible underlying mental processes, drawing on their knowledge of the students' character traits. It was striking how often the students' mental processes were expressed in terms equally appropriate for people without a learning disability. This seemed to indicate an awareness of the students' potential for a rich mental life. When LSAs spoke of their own mental processes it was mainly to explain the intentions of their behaviours towards the students and the general principles which had guided them, although several also mentioned their feeling reactions to how a student behaved or had progressed. A meta-analysis of all seven interviews revealed that the seven LSAs, despite having watched strongly contrasting video clips, broadly agreed on five major themes.

Five major themes on which the seven LSAs agreed

Theme 1: The students have a right to self-determination and self-expression

All LSAs showed an empathic and respectful attitude towards the students. They sometimes spoke of their musical and other behaviours in terms familiar from an educational context, such as 'work', 'motivation', 'attention', 'achievement' and 'independence', but they all seemed aware that music therapy is different from education, and attached great importance to the students' right to self-expression and self-determination. They saw their own role as supporting and facilitating what the students wanted to do and discovering and evoking what else they were capable of doing, providing only the level of help needed and allowing the students to retain control. The students' enjoyment and fulfilment were seen as paramount.

LSA 1 spoke of allowing students to 'do their own thing' and explained that, despite appearances to the contrary, her student 'was actually doing all the movements'. LSA 3 said it was nice for her student 'to be able to express himself through me' and imagined him thinking 'I can do this...I don't need anybody else'. Rather than interfere too much, she 'just let him get on with it'. LSA 4 had a student with a profound physical disability and commented that it was 'hard to sit there and just wait to let him do it' but that he should be allowed to do as much as possible himself because this was 'an added bonus'. LSA 5, despite a wish to explore her student's understanding of imitation, explained that it was 'not that I'm saying "Zeb, right, you must do this now"'. LSA 7 said, 'The whole idea is to encourage students to be as independent as they possibly can', and stressed that it was important 'to know [that] when she's saying "I've finished" that she's not being naughty'.

Theme 2: A student's pleasure and pride in success give the LSA pleasure

LSA 1 deduced that her student was enjoying playing with assistance because 'she was sort of looking at me' and 'if she didn't want to do it she wouldn't hold the stick'. LSA 2 felt her student was 'probably very pleased with herself, what she's doing', and tried to encourage this by 'smiling at her and...sort of nodding towards her and...you know sort of trying to give her that encouragement'. LSA 3 said her student 'just seemed to really come out of himself' and felt that he 'arose, blossomed, you know' in 'his moment of glory'. LSA 4 thought her student was enjoying playing with assistance and also enjoying the playing of others, because of 'the reactions on his face, the smiles'. LSA 5 felt both she and her student equally liked to see the other enjoying themselves: 'He could probably see that I was enjoying it too, and he does…feed off of that, Zeb, you know, if you're enjoying it he gets quite…he enjoys it even more.' LSA 6 spoke of her student wanting his achievement to be recognised: 'He was also looking around to see if people were actually watching him…as if to say, "Look, I've done it!"' LSA 7 thought her student 'felt really…proud, happy with herself', while she herself was 'just sitting there thinking, "You've done really well, girl!"'

Theme 3: The turn-taking, imitation, non-verbal communication and understanding were impressive

LSA 2 noted that her student 'was giving good eye contact, she's initiating that interaction with me', and LSA 3 imagined her student saying 'I want you to join in with me'. LSA 5, who 'tried to see whether he would actually copy me', also wondered if 'maybe he was waiting to see if I would actually copy *him*'. LSA 6 said, 'It's what Hamid wanted, to interact, you know', and felt that the quality of the interaction between the student and herself indicated a deep mutual understanding: 'You can see just how much we did know one another…and what we were thinking…you know, and feeling.'

Theme 4: The therapist's music influenced the students

Although the LSAs sometimes said they had helped students to be aware of my music and join in or respond to it, only one ever spoke of having responded to it herself, or being influenced by it in any way. Thus, LSA 1, although her student turned towards the keyboard music, felt that for herself the music was merely 'in the background, it's part of that'. LSA 3 felt the music not only attracted the student's attention but triggered his interaction with her: 'He actually tuned in to you and that is when he got hold of my hand and started with the clapping.' He then actively invited the therapist into the turn-taking:

'He's waiting for your reaction to start, and you come in, and every time I clap he looks round to you as if to say, "Well, it's *your* turn."' He enjoyed parallel playing – 'He's getting faster...as though he's going with you' – and it was hard to identify leader and follower: 'Some of it I think he's going with you, and other times I think you're waiting for Cameron and you're going with *him*.' At no point, however, did LSA 3 suggest that the keyboard music had guided or supported her own interaction with the student. LSA 4 also saw the keyboard as helping to start the student's assisted playing, because 'sometimes they're waiting for someone else to start', and as providing a rhythmic framework – 'It keeps the beat, it gives them something to react to' – but she did not see it as supporting or guiding her own contribution. LSA 5 said her student noticed the keyboard 'mimicking what we were doing with the beats...Zeb obviously can hear that', but later she spoke of the keyboard as 'just following us'. LSA 6 felt the keyboard music was intended 'to see if they were actually listening to a beat' and to 'stimulate their...senses'. LSA 7 was the only one to say that the music had influenced her as well as her student: 'She was responding to the music the same as I was...we're quite, you know, swaying and...I think subconsciously...the music that you was hearing on the keyboard, it was that kind of rhythm and you'd...[sway].'

Theme 5: Music therapy was a valuable resource and the interviews were interesting and enjoyable

Several LSAs made positive evaluations of music therapy. There was general agreement that the students enjoyed music therapy, and some LSAs spoke of students making progress, contrasting present with past, music therapy with other activities and contexts, and in one case comparing the end of the clip with the beginning. Other activities that had featured in sessions were also mentioned, and the absence of specific references to the approach I have entitled TSII suggested that for them it had become a familiar ingredient of therapy and well integrated into the whole. LSAs found seeing the clips interesting and informative, and suggested that reviewing video could be a valuable way to improve their skills through reflection on their own contribution and sharing of best practice.

Discussion: Viewing the findings in terms of attachment theory

The LSAs' skills as seen in the clips, and the attitudes revealed in their interviews, were influenced by the experience not simply of TSII but of the whole course of music therapy in which they had been involved. Their relationships with the students may be understood through the lens of attachment theory. Stern's (1998) concept of representation and enactment focuses attention on the formative relationship in which an infant and a mother accumulate a store of implicit knowledge throughout the history of their relationship, which they unconsciously draw upon as they relate to each other in the present moment. Wallin (2007) explains the concept of attachment style, a way of managing significant relationships which has its roots in infancy but continues to guide a person throughout life. Just as a parent's attachment style influences the quality of attachment developed by the infant, so does the attachment style of a therapist influence the quality of attachment that develops in the therapist–client relationship (Wallin 2007). The triadic relationship in TSII is a complex field in which such influences are at work, not only between the LSA and the student but also between the music therapist and the LSA. Thus, the attachment style of the music therapist plays a role in shaping the relationship the LSA forms with the therapist, which in turn influences her relationship with the student.

The music therapist may not influence an LSA's attachment style beyond the therapy room. However, attachment style is more a repertoire of styles than a fixed entity (Wallin 2007) and different parts of the range may be evoked by different relationships and situations. Thus, Stern (1998, p.13) includes, in his diagrammatic representation of the triad of mother, baby and psychotherapist, two distinct versions of the mother's representation of her relationship with the baby. The second of these versions, which Stern labels Mrep2, is the way she views that relationship when the therapist is present. It is, of course, not the mere fact of his presence but rather the *quality* of that presence and of his interventions which determine how Mrep2 differs from the mother's view of the relationship with her baby when the therapist is not present, which Stern terms Mrep1. Thus, my attitudes and actions may have led LSAs to view their relationships with students differently during music therapy from how they had viewed those relationships previously in other contexts, and it is possible that some of these changes could have proved more durable and influenced their future relationships.

Conclusions

A quantitative study of the effectiveness of the approach has yet to be undertaken. 'TSII' was a term invented to describe an approach which had evolved in a particular setting, rather than a pre-defined procedure for use in response to prescribed indications. It did not follow a treatment manual, as would be necessary in any clinical trial of the approach. However, the qualitative study of LSAs' experience of participating in TSII in the present chapter is a first step towards establishing it as a valid approach in work with profoundly disabled clients. The testimony of the seven LSAs, who did not confer – that the responses of students in music therapy contrasted favourably with what they knew of them in other settings – suggests that TSII is effective. The investigation of the same clinical material in collaboration with a panel of music therapists, to be described in Chapter 13, augments and enriches our understanding of the musical-therapeutic process and concludes with suggestions as to how TSII might be further explored.

Both parts of the study, however, suffer from limitations. The clinical extracts studied were selected as examplars of TSII, consisting of about 2 minutes of therapy with each of seven student–LSA pairs, from a single client group and setting and with a single therapist, from which it would be risky to generalise. There may also have been a 'demand effect' arising from the fact that the interviewer was himself the therapist. A study which fully addressed these limitations would be a much more complex undertaking, but well worth the effort.

References

Aigen, K. (1997) *Here We Are in Music: One Year with an Adolescent Creative Music Therapy Group*. Gilsum, NH: Barcelona Publishers.

Carter, E. and Oldfield, A. (2002) 'A Music Therapy Group to Assist Clinical Diagnoses in Child and Family Psychiatry.' In A. Davies and E. Richards (eds) *Music Therapy and Group Work: Sound Company*. London: Jessica Kingsley Publishers.

Durham, C. (2002) 'A Music Therapy Group in a Neurological Rehabilitation Ward.' In A. Davies and E. Richards (eds) *Music Therapy and Group Work: Sound Company*. London: Jessica Kingsley Publishers.

Fearn, M. and O'Connor, R. (2008) 'Music and Attuned Movement.' In K. Twyford and T. Watson (eds) *Integrated Team Working: Music Therapy as Part of Transdisciplinary and Collaborative Approaches*. London: Jessica Kingsley Publishers.

Henry, S.G. and Fetters, M.D. (2012) 'Video elicitation interviews: a qualitative research method for investigating physician–patient interactions.' *Annals of Family Medicine 10*, 2, 118–125.

Holck, U. (2004) 'Turn-taking in music therapy with children with communication disorders.' *British Journal of Music Therapy 18*, 2, 45–54.

Nicholls, T. (2002) 'Could I Play a Different Role? Group Music Therapy with Severely Learning Disabled Adolescents.' In A. Davies and E. Richards (eds) *Music Therapy and Group Work: Sound Company*. London: Jessica Kingsley Publishers.

Nind, M. and Hewett, D. (1994) *Access to Communication: Developing the Basics of Communication with People with Severe Learning Difficulties Through Intensive Interaction*. London: David Fulton Publishers.

Nowikas, S. (1999) 'Discovering Meaning in Kelly's Non-Verbal Expressions.' In J. Hibben (ed) *Inside Music Therapy: Client Experiences*. Gilsum, NH: Barcelona Publishers.

Smith, J.A., Flowers, P. and Larkin, M. (2009) *Interpretative Phenomenological Analysis: Theory, Method and Research*. London: Sage.

Stern, D.N. (1998) *The Motherhood Constellation: A Unified View of Parent–Infant Psychotherapy*. London: Karnac.

Stewart, D. (2002) 'Psychodynamic Group Music Therapy as Facilitating Environment, Transformational Object and Therapeutic Playground.' In A. Davies and E. Richards (eds) *Music Therapy and Group Work: Sound Company*. London: Jessica Kingsley Publishers.

Strange, J. (2012) 'Psychodynamically Informed Music Therapy Groups with Teenagers with Severe Special Needs in a College Setting: Working Jointly with Teaching Assistants.' In J. Tomlinson, P. Derrington and A. Oldfield (eds) *Music Therapy in Schools: Working with Children of All Ages in Mainstream and Special Education*. London: Jessica Kingsley Publishers.

Strange, J. (2014) 'Improvised Music to Support Interaction Between Profoundly Learning-Disabled Teenagers and Their Learning Support Assistants.' PhD thesis, Anglia Ruskin University, Cambridge. Available at http://hdl.handle.net/10540/314588, accessed on 15 November 2014.

Sutton, J. (2002) 'Preparing a Potential Space for a Group of Children with Special Needs.' In A. Davies and E. Richards (eds) *Music Therapy and Group Work: Sound Company*. London: Jessica Kingsley Publishers.

Wallin, D. (2007) *Attachment in Psychotherapy*. New York, NY: Guilford Press.

Watson, T. and Vickers, L. (2002) 'A Music and Art Therapy Group for People with Learning Disabilities.' In A. Davies and E. Richards (eds) *Music Therapy and Group Work: Sound Company*. London: Jessica Kingsley Publishers.

Wimpory, D.C., Chadwick, P. and Nash, S. (1995) 'Brief report: Musical interaction therapy for children with autism – an evaluative case study with two-year follow-up.' *Journal of Autism and Developmental Disorders 25*, 5, 541–552.

Chapter 2

Music Therapists' Experiences of Working with Staff in Sessions

Hannah Munro

Introduction

This chapter describes research which investigated the experiences of music therapists who had worked with staff in sessions (Munro 2011). The research aimed to investigate when and why staff were present in sessions and the effect (if any) this might have on the therapeutic process. The research was also generative (Ritchie 2003) in that I hoped to put forward suggestions or strategies for good practice when working with other staff in sessions. The main research questions were:

- What are the experiences of music therapists who have worked with staff in sessions?

- What recommendations could be made to facilitate effective teamwork with staff in sessions?

My motivation to undertake this research arose from practical experiences as a student on placement, as clients were often accompanied by key workers in sessions. Questions arose, such as what happens to key therapeutic tenets such as confidentiality, transference and boundaries when another person is present in the session. On a practical level, I was unsure if support staff should remain as onlookers or if I should directly involve them in the session. The area did not seem to have received a great deal of investigation in the literature and thus appeared to be a relevant subject for further research. For the purpose of the study, the term 'staff' included any non-music therapist present in sessions, including professionals, para-professionals and non-professionally aligned staff.

Literature review

The book which had greatest relevance to my subject, *Two's Company but Three's a Crowd?* (Schmidt-Robyn 2008), looked at the role of assistants in music therapy sessions. Schmidt-Robyn found that assistants were frequently present in music therapy sessions. She explored why assistants were present and how this affected the unfolding of the therapeutic process. Her findings and reflections were useful to compare with the results of my own research.

Integrated Team Working (Twyford and Watson 2008) was also relevant to my subject, along with other literature in the realm of collaboration and teamwork. Individual chapters in other music therapy texts (Carter and Oldfield 2002; Nicholls 2002; Sutton 2002; Pavlicevic 2003; Watson 2007) provided insight into work with others present in sessions in addition to the music therapist, and clearly showed the significance and importance of their presence.

Another area with parallels to my study was the involvement of parents in sessions. This area was more fully represented in the literature (Müller and Warwick 1993; Oldfield and Bunce 2001; Woodward 2004; Allgood 2005; Procter 2005; Oldfield 2006). There appeared to be many benefits of involving parents in their child's therapy, and it was interesting to consider if involving key workers in sessions might bring similar benefits to clients. A further area relevant to my study was the relationship between therapist and co-therapist in Nordoff Robbins creative music therapy. (This approach is considered in Chapter 10.) Reviewing the literature revealed that the issue of working with other staff in sessions was relevant to most clinical areas and was, thus, an appropriate subject for further research. As Strange (2014) also concluded, the topic had been little studied in its own right. Only one study (Schmidt-Robyn 2008) was found which looked specifically at the impact upon the therapeutic process of having an assistant in sessions.

I decided to address the principal research question by way of four subsidiary questions:

1. When and why are staff present in music therapy sessions?

2. Does the presence of staff change the nature of the client–therapist relationship?

3. What are the benefits and challenges of working with staff?

4. What recommendations could be made for facilitating effective teamwork with staff in sessions?

Methodology, methods, analysis and trustworthiness

Methodology

The epistemological approach taken could be described as 'interpretivism' which acknowledges that 'the researcher and the social world impact on each other' (Snape and Spencer 2003, p.17) and does not regard quantitative methods derived from the realm of the natural sciences as being appropriate for investigating social phenomena, because the social world is not governed by fixed laws. I wanted to examine music therapists' experiences of working with non-music therapists in sessions and, as Bruscia (2005) recommended, 'if the purpose is to explicate, describe and understand a phenomenon in all its wholeness...then a qualitative approach is indicated' (p.75).

Methods

I used semi-structured interviews to gather data and chose five music therapists through purposive sampling (Ansdell and Pavlicevic 2001). To broaden the applicability of my findings I interviewed music therapists with different training backgrounds who had worked with children and adults in a variety of clinical settings with varying years of experience (from 6 months to 25 years). I gave the therapists the pseudonyms Paul, Mike, Alison, David and Joan, rather than numbers, in order to preserve the impression of a real person speaking, while protecting their identity. Interviewees were given much freedom to talk about their experiences but were also given some questions beforehand to consider. The interviews were transcribed verbatim.

Analysis

I subjected the interview transcripts to framework analysis, described by Ritchie and Spencer (1994) and first developed for conducting applied qualitative research which aimed 'to meet specific information needs and provide outcomes or recommendations' (p.173). As I wanted to address specific questions and hoped to generate guidelines for good practice, framework analysis was an appropriate method to adopt.

Framework analysis is a two-stage approach. First, information from the interview transcripts is indexed and clustered into thematic charts. This provides a well-organised data set, making the second stage of interpretation, in which the analyst increasingly refines and interprets the data, much easier. For interpretation of the data, the thematic charts are investigated through cross-case analysis and within-case analysis. From analysing the data, six main themes or categories emerged, as shown in Figure 2.1. (The subcategories are not shown.)

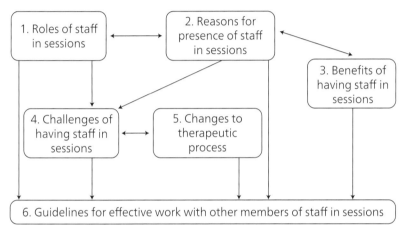

Figure 2.1 Interrelated categories emerging from interpretation and analysis of data

Trustworthiness

I tried not to ask leading questions (Robson 2002) during the interview and I also monitored my own responses to the data emerging by noting them in a reflective diary. In the analysis and reporting of the data I attempted to avoid quoting from one respondent more than another. Lincoln and Guba (1985) refer to the usefulness of member checking as a means of external validation. To this end I sent all manuscripts back to the interviewees. I also incorporated triangulation by asking my research partner to check the data entry of two transcripts into the framework. I also gave excerpts of coding to my research partner in order to increase reliability of the interpretative stage of the process. A visual audit trail is also traceable in framework analysis. Full details of methodology, methods and design are available in Munro (2011).

Findings

When and why are staff present in music therapy sessions?

In order to answer this question, data from two categories were used: the first category contained codes pertaining to 'roles' and the second category contained codes relating to the 'reasons for the presence of other staff in sessions'. Although there was inevitable overlap between the two categories, it seemed appropriate to distinguish them for analysis. The question of why staff were present in sessions was partly answered by addressing the following question: 'What do staff do in sessions?' – that is, 'What are their roles?' From the data, staff appeared to be in sessions in one or more of three roles, namely those of observer, assistant or co-therapist.

David used the terminology of a 'spectrum' to aptly explain the different roles of an 'extra' person in therapy:

> If we take the spectrum as defining the presence of another member of staff I would tentatively place being a co-therapist at one end of the spectrum, being a supporter or facilitating the work around the middle, and then at the other end of the spectrum I would look at a member of staff being there to assess somebody's responses by observing.

This concept is illustrated in Figure 2.2.

Figure 2.2 The spectrum of roles which staff may adopt in sessions

Data from the other four interviewees appeared to substantiate David's theory that staff could be present in the different capacities of observer, assistant or co-therapist. However, all five therapists stated or implied that staff were *usually* present in the role of assistants; alternative terms used were 'supporters' or 'helpers'. Mike stressed that, when staff were present in sessions as assistants, the therapist remained 'responsible for being the container of the therapy and for everyone's safety'. This was corroborated by the other interviewees: the therapist always appeared to lead, direct and remain responsible for the staff member when they were present in the role of an assistant.

In considering the role of observer, Joan said that they 'don't interact', seeing their role in sessions as a passive one. However, the role of observer seemed much less common. Those present as observers were usually other professionals (David and Mike) who were sitting in to assess someone's responses and behaviours; or were support staff who had to be present (Alison) when there was a requirement for clients to have two-to-one support for behavioural reasons; or were nurses (Joan) who had to be constantly present for the client's health needs.

At the opposite end of the spectrum to observers were co-therapists. Co-therapists were felt to have equal responsibility to the music therapist for the therapeutic process and would be involved in planning, aims and reflection after sessions. Interviewees had differing views on whether other staff could become co-therapists. David referred to long-term work in UK National Health Service settings where he had jointly run groups with adult mental health nurses, and felt that such work could be described as co-therapy. He explained how he would plan sessions, develop aims, run sessions and reflect on them with his colleague. He felt that if the 'other person' had had therapeutic training themselves and relevant experience, then they could be a co-therapist. Similarly, Joan described work she did with a psychologist as evolving into co-therapy; again, a fundamentally important part of this work was the close joint analysis of sessions as part of a research project. Mike also thought that a co-therapist would have to be 'someone with a therapeutic background, so someone with therapeutic training'.

Alison thought that if there was time for 'close liaison' it was possible for staff (including care/support staff) to become co-therapists, but in practice she found working with staff had 'a very different dynamic' compared with her work with another music therapy student, acting as co-therapist, while on placement. Mike felt that it was vital to work collaboratively at all times, but when asked if he felt his work with support staff could be described as co-therapy, he replied:

> I think there is a difference because ultimately I am in charge of the safety of the group, of the client, of the SLA (support-for-learning assistant),

so ultimately it's me that is the container of the vessel, of the therapy. It would be unfair of me to expect an SLA...they can become more in tune to the actual process of what is happening...[but not as a co-therapist]...I am in complete agreement with therapeutic music-making, but clinical music therapy...is something different. That is why there is a 2-year training in order to do it.

Thus, the general consensus seemed to be that it was unusual for staff to be in the role of 'co-therapist' unless they had the necessary professional therapeutic training and experience themselves. With hindsight, perhaps I should have introduced the term 'co-worker', as this may have reflected the role support staff may take on with experience and when time was available for close collaboration. Nevertheless, music therapists *usually* worked in sessions with staff who were in the role of assistant, and much less frequently with staff who were present in the role of observer. However, the idea of a 'spectrum' (see Figure 2.2) allows for roles to overlap and develop in the course of therapy.

Having considered the various roles that staff may undertake in sessions, information from category 2 provided further reasons why staff were present in their various roles. All five interviewees were unanimous that the request for the presence of support staff either came from the therapist or was supported by the therapist. In the case of group work all said they always, or nearly always, had assistants present and were emphatic about the advantages of doing so (see the next category, 'benefits').

It was a more complex picture when considering why staff might be present in individual sessions. For three of the five therapists interviewed, it did not appear to be common for support staff to be involved in individual work. In 26 years of work, David had very rarely worked with another member of staff in individual sessions, and when staff had been present they had been there to observe clients in a professional capacity (e.g. as social workers). In the case of Alison and Paul, when staff were present in individual sessions it tended to be for very specific reasons such as the extreme health needs of children, behavioural issues or a client preference for attending with a key worker.

In contrast, Joan always had a member of staff present when working in individual sessions in music interaction therapy

(Wimpory, Chadwick and Nash 1995), as in this approach the role of the music therapist is specifically to support the interaction of child and key worker with each other. Likewise, Mike always chose to have a member of staff present in individual sessions. A significant reason Mike gave for always having staff present was in order to avoid any false allegations. There may indeed be a wider gender issue here as Paul had also spoken about the 'expectations' of the involvement of another member of staff being present in his work with very young children. However, Mike also felt that having another member of staff present enriched the experience for clients, which was another reason why he always chose to work with another member of staff even in individual sessions.

What are the benefits of working with staff in sessions?

Data from category 3 were analysed in order to answer this question. Three subcategories emerged: benefits for clients, benefits for staff and benefits for the music therapist.

Benefits for clients

In this first subcategory there appeared to be many advantages for clients having their key worker, support assistant or nurse accompany them in sessions. This was particularly the case in group work as it enabled clients with significant physical impairments to participate who would otherwise have been unable to do so. It also enabled clients' own relationships with their key workers to develop as the staff members discovered new ways of working, and also as they saw what Joan described as 'hidden abilities' emerging in clients. Paul and Mike also referred to the significance of the child being able to watch the adult's behaviour, and Paul explained how staff members could model music-making, 'taking pressure off the child in the moment but giving them the chance to see what *could* happen'. Joan also compared the effect of sympathetic observers in sessions to musicians playing to a receptive audience and explained how both client and therapist felt encouraged by having someone witness the work. The importance of 'witnessing' was also highlighted by Paul and Mike.

Benefits for staff

All interviewees felt that by attending sessions staff could see clients' potential, and their relationship with the clients could be enhanced through the interaction in the music. David also claimed that staff became 'more skilled' as a result of being exposed to a different approach, and Alison felt that the staff who had assisted in music therapy could, as a result, 'use a different approach' in the classroom. Mike pointed out that staff often really enjoyed coming to sessions, and Alison used the term 'thrilled' to describe the reaction of staff witnessing the involvement and concentration of the clients.

Benefits for the music therapist

There appeared to be many advantages for music therapists in involving staff in sessions. Group work could be difficult without their aid, and all interviewees found their practical assistance invaluable. This included bringing clients to and from sessions and fetching instruments for clients, and also modelling playing instruments for children. Mike gave the example of a staff member moving around a group, giving each client a turn on the drum while the therapist was at the piano. Alison also suggested that, for larger groups, staff could help keep clients focused, especially if there was 'too much going on for one person to contain'. All therapists were emphatic about the importance of support staff in group work as it appeared that this enabled the therapist to maintain the musical flow of the work, and the overall responsibility of the therapeutic process, while others could help out with practical matters.

Joan and Paul spoke also about the personal encouragement of working with enthusiastic staff. The day-to-day knowledge of clients held by key workers, as well as their understanding of the history of the clients, was found useful by all interviewees. Paul found their understanding of clients' physical conditions very helpful. David claimed that the insight and perspective of other members of staff in sessions often informed his work: he compared this dual perspective with supervision. Mike explained how knowledge of home circumstances could be quickly passed on to him by staff, and this enabled aims in sessions to change from week to week so as to be relevant to what was currently happening in a client's life.

What are the challenges for music therapists of working with staff in sessions?

Category 4 provided data about the challenges experienced by music therapists when others were present in sessions. The main challenge (Mike) for the therapist appeared to be the careful setting up of the therapeutic space. David felt that the biggest challenge for therapists was in 'defining roles and the evolution of roles', and Paul said, 'It is key isn't it…[that] we know what our role is?' I had not prompted any of the therapists to use the term 'role' in relation to the question about 'challenges', but it cropped up in three interviews.

Furthermore, staff often seemed to find it hard to allow sessions to be client led and were described as sometimes being, in Alison's words, 'overly helpful' or coercive in making clients participate. Largely this was a result of misunderstanding what music therapy was about. She said, 'The general perception about what music therapy was, was quite a long way from my idea.' Therapists also spoke about the personal feelings of being judged when another person was present in the room.

There appear to be many more practical challenges of involving a member of support staff in sessions; in particular, most therapists felt there was never enough time for liaison, and two therapists interviewed felt there were no opportunities given for staff training. As a result, staff could sometimes be inattentive, for example looking at their mobile phone or talking in sessions. More seriously, four of the five therapists claimed that there had been rare occasions when the personal or cultural prejudice of staff appeared to create unresolvable problems and the work could not continue.

Does the presence of staff change the nature of the client–therapist relationship?

Data from category 5 provided the material to answer this question. There was general consensus that this was less of an issue in group work, but change to the therapeutic relationship in individual therapy appeared more significant and was perceived in various ways. If a client was totally unaware of the presence of a third person, one interviewee felt that person's presence had no effect on the therapy. Joan suggested that if the client was, for example, very ill or unable to take in more than one channel of communication, then the client–therapist relationship could develop as usual. Two other therapists felt that there was inevitably an impact, but provided the staff member was experienced and sensitive, the therapist–client relationship could develop with no significant impediment. However, the work could also take on 'a group ambience' if the staff member was 'attentive and open' and involved where appropriate. Another perspective was described by Mike, who used the word 'triangulation' to explain how a 'containing parental forum' was created when he worked alongside a member of staff, and he believed this enhanced the client's therapeutic experience. Similarly, Alison suggested that the therapeutic dyad became 'more of a triad', and this was also implied by Paul.

Two other changes to the therapeutic process were identified: the effects of staff presence on boundaries and on confidentiality. Mike and Alison spoke about the issue of boundaries, usually in the context of staff not understanding the difference between acceptable behaviours in the classroom and those of the therapy room. Mike said he often came up against a response such as, 'We don't let them do that in the class, so why do you let them do it here?' Mike and Paul referred to the way the presence of a member of staff could also potentially prevent authentic behaviours from emerging.

Confidentiality is another important element of the therapeutic alliance, and it is interesting that only two therapists spoke about this – and even then, this was usually after prompts in interview. Mike explained that there was greater need for confidentiality in work with some client groups, for example in psychiatry where clients had experienced abuse or neglect. In these cases he described the boundaries as becoming tighter, and he would insist that he needed to be supported by the same member of staff each week. He also ensured that the staff and client were fully aware of the confidentiality of sessions in order for the client to feel reassured and for the work to progress. Alison also stressed the importance of support staff being fully cognisant with matters of confidentiality, but even when this was the case she felt that there were times when clients benefited from working with the therapist alone. She referred to a particular situation where she decided against involving a member of staff precisely because of the issue of confidentiality – 'It felt like having somebody else in might take away from the whole confidentiality of the session'

– and she felt this particular client needed 'this one-to-one quite intense line of communication'.

Thus, confidentiality and boundaries are areas which are affected by the presence of other staff, but through good communication and understanding, these difficulties can usually, though not always, be minimised so that they do not compromise the therapeutic process.

What are the emergent themes?

In common with most qualitative research, unanticipated themes can arise which seem to be significant and deserving of further investigation. In this research one such theme was the importance of training for music therapy students in order to prepare them for work with staff in sessions. All three Nordoff Robbins-trained music therapists made reference to the usefulness of student experiences of working in co-therapy teams. Alison also felt that it was important that students were made aware of the challenges and benefits of working with support staff, feeling that there was perhaps something of a gap in training in regard to this, although she also acknowledged that knowing what to say and how to work with staff was part of the learning curve of becoming a music therapist. (Chapter 3 investigates trainee music therapists' experiences of work with assistants in sessions when on clinical placement.)

What recommendations could be made for facilitating effective teamwork with support staff in sessions?

Guidelines for working in music therapy sessions with non-music therapists were drawn from data in category 6 and are presented in the appendix at the end of this book.

Discussion

Miles and Huberman (1994) describe the final stages of qualitative research as linking the findings from the data analysis into a formalised body of knowledge (in this case, the literature reviewed) in order to outline and formulate constructs or theories.

The concept of a spectrum of roles for the 'other' in the therapy room

David's idea about 'the spectrum' of observer, assistant and co-therapist (see Figure 2.2) appears to be a useful concept to explain the various roles of any 'extra' person in sessions. The idea of a spectrum suggests that there is a continuum of roles. Similarly, adaptability is also required in the Nordoff Robbins approach (Nordoff, Robbins and Marcus 2007), where the co-therapist sometimes may be quietly watching the session and other times may be actively involved.

Nevertheless, all interviewees felt that it was important, at the outset of work with a client or a group of clients, for music therapists to explain to staff what role and task they would be expected to undertake. This delineation of roles and understanding of the spectrum is significant, as the literature indicates that role ambiguity is not conducive to effective work or job satisfaction (Tubre and Collins 2000). Twyford and Watson (2008), in advice about team working, similarly write that 'individual roles should be meaningful, intrinsically rewarding and clearly defined' (p.19).

Group work

Most of the examples in the literature review of co-working in sessions with non-music therapists came from an edited compilation on group work (Davies and Richards 2002). There are fleeting references to the significance of assistance in group work elsewhere: for example, Alvin, in running groups with autistic children, always had assistants at the ratio of at least one to two children and wrote that 'the success of the activity was very much due to the dynamism of the assistants' (Alvin and Warwick 1991, p.28). However, this research suggests that the involvement of assistants in group work appears to be a significant area of practice deserving more attention than it has hitherto received.

Teamwork

There appear to be many benefits from involving staff if their presence is prepared for carefully. Although there is sufficient evidence in the literature (Hills, Norman and Forster 2000; Twyford and Watson 2008; Darsie 2010) to indicate that interdisciplinary work between music therapists and other professionals is important, the present study suggests that 'multi-agency' teamwork with care workers and para-professionals is probably equally as important, although such groups are under-represented in the literature on teamwork in music therapy. As Pavlicevic wrote, 'staff members on the ground can be music therapists' best allies' (2003, p.38).

All therapists interviewed in this study felt that staff knowledge of clients could inform their work. Other authors (Graham 2004; Saul 2007) have similarly stressed the benefits of music therapists learning about their clients from clients' key workers. Schmidt-Robyn (2008) also felt that assistants could be 'a bridge between therapy and the outer world' (p.99).

Benefits for staff

The positive changes to staff practice which all interviewees spoke about witnessing as a result of involvement in music therapy are also reflected in the literature (Graham 2004; Saul 2007; Watson 2007) and are a key area explored in many other chapters in the present volume.

The therapeutic process

The importance of staff 'witnessing' sessions was highlighted by Paul, Mike and Joan. In a psychotherapeutic intervention with parents and young children, Muir and Thorlaksdottir (1994) claim that attentive listening is the first strand in the therapeutic process. Nordoff and colleagues (2007) also stress the significance of the co-therapist remaining 'completely attentive' (p.196) throughout the session.

Mike used the word 'triangulation' to explain how a 'containing parental forum' was created when he worked alongside staff in sessions. This is reminiscent of Procter's (2005) reference to the parental model created when two adults work in a session with a child. Other authors have also found that music therapists speak about triangulation in reference to the relationships which develop between parent, child and therapist (Bignold 2009). Joan described how at times the presence of an assistant could have the effect in individual therapy of creating a 'group ambience', and Bignold (2009), in her research with therapists working with children and parents, also found that there were parallels with group work.

Challenges of working with staff in sessions

The interview data clearly showed that working with a member of staff did not come without challenges. Personal dynamics between support staff and therapist which had to be managed ranged from working with support staff who appeared to have an aversion to music therapy, to staff who had a cultural prejudice against the therapist, to dealing with issues of envy and ego or simply misunderstanding. Strong feelings could be evoked on the part of the music therapist. Hills and colleagues (2000) found that envy and rivalry were common problems among music therapists in collaborating with other professionals in teams. Nowikas (1993) wrote that understanding the dynamics of teamwork was important for effective work in Nordoff Robbins co-therapy teams. Schmidt-Robyn (2008) similarly thought that it was important that therapists have an awareness of subconscious dynamics, such as ego, jealousy and pride, which could arise when working with assistants (p.61). She found that many of her respondents cited behaviour management as a major reason for the presence of an assistant in sessions. However, findings from the present research suggest that this is a potentially difficult area for music therapists. Paul said that, particularly in one-to-one sessions, 'It becomes difficult to know who is supporting who to do what!' Both Paul and Mike felt that there could be a tendency for behaviours to be either 'put on' or repressed because of the presence of support staff, and certainly this corroborated Schmidt-Robyn's finding of the disappearance of the neutral space when assistants were involved in therapy, as evidenced by her own experience that the assistant's presence actually provoked the very challenging behaviour that it had been intended to prevent. The implication of this finding is that music therapists should think very carefully before accepting assistance for behavioural issues, particularly in individual sessions, and be aware, if an assistant is to be present, of the complexities of the situation.

Conclusion

Now we return to our first main research question: 'What are the experiences of music therapists who have worked with staff in sessions?' On the whole, interviewees related positive experiences of work with support staff. Although all mentioned some negative experiences, these were, as David said, 'exceptions which proved the rule'. The work of support staff was found to be particularly significant in group work, and this has not been previously investigated in the literature. The concept of the 'spectrum of roles' generated in this research also provides a different lens through which to explore the subject of staff presence in music therapy sessions.

Considering the second main research question – 'What recommendations could be made to facilitate effective teamwork with staff in sessions?' – many benefits of having support staff present in sessions were identified, but this study found that working with another member of staff also brought challenges. This underscores the relevance of guidelines for music therapists, especially for students on placement and for those setting out in work. Hopefully the recommendations for good practice found in the appendix (at the end of the book) will be helpful. This study also confirmed the benefits of working in co-therapy teams during student training in relation to later work with assistants and noted a possible gap in student training regarding exploration of the issues which arise as a result of working with other staff in sessions.

In conclusion, successful collaborative work in sessions appears most likely to be achieved when staff understand that music therapy is client led, and when they themselves feel valued and affirmed, and secure in understanding what their role and task will be. The music therapist needs to be aware of the impact of the presence of staff on the therapeutic process, but with preparation and ongoing communication such collaborative work appears to be a very positive way of working for the benefit of a wide range of clients.

References

Allgood, N. (2005) 'Parents' perceptions of family based group music therapy for children with autism.' *Music Therapy Perspectives 23*, 2, 92–99.

Alvin, J. and Warwick, A. (1991) *Music Therapy for the Autistic Child* (2nd ed.). Oxford: Oxford University Press.

Ansdell, G. and Pavlicevic, M. (2001) *Beginning Research in Arts Therapies: A Practical Guide*. London: Jessica Kingsley Publishers.

Bignold, K. (2009) 'Three in the Music Therapy: Company or a Crowd? An Exploration of the Impact of Involving Parents in Their Children's Music Therapy.' Unpublished MA thesis, Guildhall School of Music and Drama, London.

Bruscia, K.E. (2005) 'Research Topics and Questions in Music Therapy.' In B.L. Wheeler (ed) *Music Therapy Research* (2nd ed.). Gilsum, NH: Barcelona Publishers.

Carter, E. and Oldfield, A. (2002) 'A Music Therapy Group to Assist Clinical Diagnoses in Child and Family Psychiatry.' In A. Davies and E. Richards (eds) *Music Therapy and Group Work: Sound Company.* London: Jessica Kingsley Publishers.

Darsie, E. (2010) 'Interdisciplinary team members' perceptions of the role of music therapy in a pediatric outpatient clinic.' *Music Therapy Perspectives 27,* 1, 48–54.

Davies, A. and Richards, E. (eds) (2002) *Music Therapy and Group Work: Sound Company.* London: Jessica Kingsley Publishers.

Graham, J. (2004) 'Communicating with the uncommunicative: music therapy with pre-verbal adults.' *British Journal of Learning Disabilities 32,* 24–29.

Hills, B., Norman, I. and Forster, L. (2000) 'A study of burnout and multidisciplinary team-working amongst professional music therapists.' *British Journal of Music Therapy 14,* 1, 32–40.

Lincoln, Y.S. and Guba, G.E. (1985) *Naturalistic Inquiry.* Beverly Hills, CA: Sage.

Miles, M.B. and Huberman, A.M. (1994) *Qualitative Data Analysis: An Expanded Sourcebook.* London: Sage.

Muir, E.E. and Thorlaksdottir, E. (1994) 'Psychotherapeutic intervention with mothers and children in day care.' *American Journal of Orthopsychiatry 64,* 1, 60–67.

Müller, P. and Warwick, A. (1993) 'Autistic Children and Music Therapy: The Effects of Maternal Involvement in Therapy.' In M. Heal and T. Wigram (eds) *Music Therapy in Health and Education.* London: Jessica Kingsley Publishers.

Munro, H. (2011) 'Music Therapists, Clients and Support Staff: Using Framework Analysis to Investigate the Experiences of Music Therapists Who Have Worked with Support Staff in Music Therapy Sessions, with a View to Developing Guidelines for Good Practice.' Unpublished MSc thesis, Queen Margaret University, Edinburgh.

Nicholls, T. (2002) 'Could I Play a Different Role? Group Music Therapy with Severely Learning Disabled Adolescents.' In A. Davies and E. Richards (eds) *Music Therapy and Group Work: Sound Company.* London: Jessica Kingsley Publishers.

Nordoff, P., Robbins, C. and Marcus, D. (2007) *Creative Music Therapy: A Guide to Fostering Clinical Musicianship* (2nd ed.). Gilsum, NH: Barcelona Publishers.

Nowikas, S. (1993) 'A Qualitative Investigation of Teamwork in Nordoff–Robbins Music Therapy.' Unpublished MA thesis, New York University, New York, NY.

Oldfield, A. (2006) *Interactive Music Therapy in Child and Family Psychiatry: Clinical Practice, Research and Teaching.* London: Jessica Kingsley Publishers.

Oldfield, A. and Bunce, L. (2001) 'Mummy can play too: short term music therapy with mothers and young children.' *British Journal of Music Therapy 15,* 1, 27–36.

Pavlicevic, M. (2003) *Groups in Music: Strategies from Music Therapy.* London: Jessica Kingsley Publishers.

Procter, S. (2005) 'Parents, children and their therapists: a collaborative research project examining the therapist–parent interactions in a music therapy clinic.' *British Journal of Music Therapy 19,* 2, 45–58.

Ritchie, J. (2003) 'The Applications of Qualitative Methods to Social Research.' In J. Ritchie and J. Lewis (eds) *Qualitative Research Practice: A Guide for Social Science Students and Researchers.* London: Sage.

Ritchie, J. and Spencer, L. (1994) 'Qualitative Data Analysis for Applied Policy Research.' In A. Bymand and R.G. Burgess (eds) *Analysing Qualitative Data.* London: Routledge.

Robson, C. (2002) *Real World Research: A Resource for Social Science and Practitioner-Researchers* (2nd ed.). Oxford: Blackwell.

Saul, B. (2007) 'Looking In from the Outside: Communicating Effectively About Music Therapy Work.' In T. Watson (ed) *Music Therapy with Adults with Learning Disabilities.* Hove: Routledge.

Schmidt-Robyn, B. (2008) *Two's Company but Three's a Crowd? Assistants in Music Therapy Sessions*. Norderstedt: Books on Demand.

Snape, D. and Spencer, L. (2003) 'The Foundations of Qualitative Research.' In J. Ritchie and J. Lewis (eds) *Qualitative Research Practice: A Guide for Social Science Students and Researchers*. London: Sage.

Strange, J. (2014) 'Improvised Music to Support Interaction Between Profoundly Learning-Disabled Teenagers and Their Learning Support Assistants.' PhD thesis, Anglia Ruskin University, Cambridge. Available at http://hdl.handle.net/10540/314588, accessed on 30 April 2016.

Sutton, J. (2002) 'Preparing a Potential Space for a Group of Children with Special Needs.' In A. Davies and E. Richards (eds) *Music Therapy and Group Work: Sound Company*. London: Jessica Kingsley Publishers.

Tubre, T.C. and Collins, J.M. (2000) 'A meta-analysis of the relationships between role ambiguity, role conflict, and job performance.' *Journal of Management 26*, 155–169.

Twyford, K. and Watson, T. (2008) 'Introduction.' In K. Twyford and T. Watson (eds) *Integrated Team Working: Music Therapy as Part of Transdisciplinary and Collaborative Approaches*. London: Jessica Kingsley Publishers.

Watson, T. (2007) 'Working with People with Profound and Multiple Learning Disabilities in Music Therapy.' In T. Watson (ed) *Music Therapy with Adults with Learning Disabilities*. Hove: Routledge.

Wimpory, D.C., Chadwick, P. and Nash, S. (1995) 'Musical interaction therapy for children with autism: an evaluative case study with two-year follow-up.' *Journal of Autism and Developmental Disorders 25*, 5, 541–552.

Woodward, A. (2004) 'Music therapy for autistic children and their families: a creative spectrum.' *British Journal of Music Therapy 18*, 1, 8–14.

Chapter 3

Student Perspectives on Working with Assistants on Placement During Vocational Music Therapy Training

Catherine Warner

Introduction

As a trainer of music therapists and also a clinical supervisor for new and experienced practitioners, I have been struck by how often time in supervision is taken up with thinking about other people in the room – not the client but a teaching assistant (TA) or perhaps an assistant occupational therapist. Increasingly, it seems to me that trainees are required to work on placement with an extra support worker actually within the therapeutic space. This is perhaps to do with increasing emphasis on or anxiety around safeguarding in schools and for vulnerable adults. Whatever the reasons may be, it is clear that a trainee is quite likely to have their early work watched and sometimes mediated by someone, other than their placement supervisor, who is also in the therapy space.

I am interested in many questions that arise from this. How might the presence and the intervention of others affect the trainee's work? Could it have an effect on the confidence of the trainee and quite possibly the development of their identity as a therapist? How would it be helpful to learn from music therapists about their training experiences through their retrospective stories?

Practices vary considerably on different training courses and with different placement contexts. Some trainees do not need to work with assistants at all during training. Conversely, there are traditions of co-therapy as a standard practice, thereby reinforcing the student therapeutic presence and often removing the need for an assistant to offer 'hands-on' support for those clients who are severely physically disabled. The programme I have been involved with for several years at the University of the West of England offers a lifespan model training Master's students over 3 years, and as such, the first placement always involves working with a child or young person in environments where the presence of an assistant might be the policy of the setting. In many school placements, trainees are required to include a TA in the room during music therapy with an individual child as a result of the school safeguarding policy. From my perspective as a trainer and supervisor, 10 years ago this was more the experience of male trainees, bringing an associated implication of gender discrimination, as if only students that were men were likely to pose risks.

One common model of an early placement is that of the trainee working alongside the music therapist placement supervisor, first mainly observing, maybe working as a co-therapist in a small group or with a complex individual, and finally moving on to work with individual clients alone during the course of the first placement. One trainee recently used the apt description of 'apprenticeship'. This model allows the student to learn at a pace that suits his or her own needs, and for the supervisor to withdraw when both supervisor and trainee are confident that the trainee is ready to work alone. If assistants are also present in the room, for example in a group, the supervisor is on hand to model how the helper assistants are included and how the role might be managed between therapist and helper in a way that keeps the person engaging in the therapy central to the process.

However, there are circumstances where this is not possible, particularly in regions of Britain where there are too few supervising music therapists to go round. Here the training establishment may need to provide music therapy supervision externally or from a visiting music therapist who has not established ways of working from within the context. In some cases the designated supervisor on site is not a music therapist at all but someone else with some different professional status. With this comes the complexity of potentially different cultural values and practices which may have a strong influence on the formative experiences of the trainee and may also influence how the impact of assistants present in the therapy room might affect the therapeutic space and process.

This chapter presents perspectives from the stories of three practising music therapists. The extracts from these three narratives are taken from an ongoing narrative inquiry research study which involves 12 music therapists and music therapy trainees. This broader study has recruited women and men from eight UK music therapy training courses, past and present. The ethics of confidentiality and anonymity of this study are not straightforward: although all participants are adults who are able to understand the implications of involvement in the inquiry, I am conducting interviews with the interviewees as co-researchers and some are currently in training. My own position as a programme leader means that I bring complex agendas to the research process, and could hold influence, real or imagined, for some of the participants, particularly if they are still training. The three participants in this chapter have read and commented on transcripts of the extracts selected here, and there are aspects of both telling and retelling the stories as a consequence.

Here the trainee therapists seek to extend and develop their growing identities as therapists in the face of challenges posed by having an extra person in the room during therapy. In order to minimise the ethical complexities described above, the three music therapists chosen for this account have all qualified: one is in their first year of music therapy work at the time of writing, one has been practising as a music therapist for 4 years and the other for over 10 years. One music therapist, Kiki, had no experience of working with assistants throughout her music therapy training but in current practice has found the issues raised very troublesome. Another woman, Zoe, had no music therapist present on site for her first placement, and was working with a co-therapy trainee and a TA in the room, and the third, Susanna, worked with assistants on all three training placements in different contexts.

Why narrative inquiry?

Narrative inquiry involves a number of forms, practices and presentations, introduced and described notably by Riessman (1993) and more recently Clandinin and Connolly (2000), and can sometimes involve, for example, poetic re-presentation in order to balance the voice of interviewee and researcher. Daykin's (2005) narrative inquiry into how musicians constructed their own narratives about health and risk is a scholarly and rigorous example of music work. I also found Bateson's (1990) anthropological study of how women co-create their identities through creative processes of improvisation, dealing with discontinuity and divided energies, to be inspiring and of great interest, not only because of how she is able to look at musical processes, such as composition and improvisation, in the wider sphere of evolving identities for five working women, but also because I am inspired by her warm style of narrative. Psychotherapist and narrative researcher Jane Speedy (2008) writes that 'human identity is a social achievement, contingent on time, context, audience, culture, history, memory and personal agency' (p.xiv). This I hope to illustrate with the narratives of developing therapeutic identity presented in this chapter.

Narrative inquiry seems to be a helpful choice of methodology: although I am interested here in a process of research, narrative and story is often found too in the practice of clinical music therapy supervision. This may take many forms, and in particular the *aural* narrative of the music which is often recorded on placement and heard back during training supervision. In training supervision it is very helpful to have the time to hear the *oral* story of what happened on placement, allowing the training therapist to formulate and reformulate how they talk about and therefore understand their work. In group supervision the process of providing a narrative which is heard by others, and questioned, challenged, affirmed and reframed, is similar in some ways to processes of narrative inquiry where an interview, and then transcription of the work, can be examined and developed in discussion and review. In 1993 Riessman emphasised how the authentic voice of the speaker must be privileged in narrative inquiry, just as notions of authenticity in music therapy practice are also valued (John 2009).

Narrative inquiry may be especially relevant in investigating how training music therapists create their own identity, as it highlights and explores disruptions and how interviewees create new metaphors to preserve their moral status as therapists. Analysis of the narratives may be carried out in a number of ways, and the general focus is to explore how interviewees draw on cultural, linguistic and theoretical resources to create coherence within the narrative (Daykin 2005). I aim to do this in the text that weaves around the extracts from the interviews, bringing in my own perspective as a trainer and music therapist.

Narratives by three music therapists

The narratives below are from three music therapists (whom I thank) who wanted to share their stories about working with assistants in the therapy room on training placements, and their continuing thoughts as we explore the meanings and implications of what they have told. All their names and some other identifying features have been changed to preserve anonymity – quite a challenge in a small profession such as music therapy. Their pseudonyms bear not even a passing resemblance to their real names. There are no particular identifying features of either placement context or training establishment. The terms 'assistants', 'clients' and 'trainees' are all used here as they formed part of each participant's narrative; however, these terms themselves carry specific cultural meaning and emphases which need to be considered reflexively.

Susanna's narrative

Susanna started her first placement in a school where assistants were required to be present in therapy sessions as part of safeguarding policy. Consistency as to who attended was difficult to maintain and the person who acted as assistant changed from week to week. Susanna learned quickly what impact different assistants made. She said:

> Well, it was interesting that one TA was a musician herself, so I felt we had a bit of rapport immediately, that I didn't necessarily need to explain exactly what I was going to do and what the work was about…and I guess perhaps not to do with the fact that she was a musician, but she also sat back and allowed the child to explore the instruments more freely and more autonomously.

Here Susanna is talking about both her identity as musician and her therapeutic approach. John (2009), when writing about the developing identity of training therapists, emphasises the need for musical clinical skills and understanding of the therapeutic function to evolve together rather than the trainee retreating into an already established identity as musician, or taking on a therapeutic identity before it is fully understood. Susanna came to placement with some clear ideas about how she wanted to practise, formed from her reading and course lectures but most importantly from her lived experience of disability within her family. Although she does not reflect on this here, her confidence in her own therapeutic choices is evident even with very early work:

> I felt there was a real clash at times between ways I wanted to facilitate and the way the support assistant perceived that the session should be facilitated, or what their role in the sessions should be. So the support assistant would often want to offer lots of reinforcement, or lots of encouragement, or physically support the participant to play or discourage them from doing certain things...I think that was the part, what I found was most difficult...discouraging things.
>
> I think everybody wanted what was best for the child but had different understandings of how they would approach that, so some TAs would provide more active support and some would provide hand-on-hand support to access the instruments, others would really encourage the student quite vocally, quite often...whereas I was learning, and reading about working in more non-directive ways, so that kind of clashed quite a lot. But I guess as I progressed through the course I reflected a little bit, or maybe I managed that participation from support assistants in a different way. So by the third year I felt I was able to be a bit more assertive in managing that situation, whereas in the first year, it felt difficult to engage with that and change that then.

Susanna manages to preserve a good moral status for everyone: they want what is best for the child, therefore keeping a consistency with the idea, important to her, that the child is at the centre. So it is when the assistants 'discourage' a child from doing something, and this goes directly against her clearly theoretical non-directive position, that she experiences a conflict or 'clash'. This does not confuse Susanna but relates directly to her confidence, as later in her training she felt more able to have agency in that situation.

Susanna's narrative seems to have a continuous thread: using a notion of cultural difference to understand contrasts and conflicts of expectations and behaviour between herself and some assistants. It is interesting that the first example she gives is of an assistant by whom she felt supported, and who understood the therapeutic process, who shares musical knowledge. This signals to me that she is not hostile to the idea of having assistants within the room but is concerned when it is not helpful to the child.

In terms of the development of her therapeutic identity, Susanna does not necessarily relate to an idea of apprenticeship with her placement supervisor. This is exemplified by the decisions he has made in how he incorporates assistant support into his work. Susanna said:

> I learned so much from my placement supervisor. He was a brilliant therapist, but I learned how different I was from him, and how differently I wanted to practise. In no way as a criticism of how he practised; it just affirmed for me that I quite passionately wanted to work in a slightly different way. Perhaps...I felt like he was less... um...or his focus wasn't on this non-directive way of practising. There were times when it was more appropriate for the TAs to engage in his sessions, so he might be working on goals for physiotherapy, for example, where you would need hand-on-hand support...

Passion is a strong expression, yet 'quite passionately' linked with 'in a slightly different way' feels quite mediated. This raises questions about whether it felt risky for Susanna to have really strong feelings about wanting to do music therapy differently. Although she sees the place for a functional role for an assistant, it is apparently not for her. Is it alright to have a clear idea about what you want to do when you are supposed to be learning early on? She's quite polite and respectful about the therapist, yet she has the strong view that he is including people in the session when in fact it could have been just one-to-one work. As we discussed this, Susanna explained that her supervisor was extremely adept on the piano, in a way that she was unlikely to be able to emulate, but that her concern was more to do with her therapist function and the model she had already been developing, about which she feels 'quite passionately'. Noticing and articulating this difference seems to have been useful for her.

As a trainer I am interested in how stimulating it was for Susanna's therapeutic identity to be offered a placement where she could actively disagree with her supervisor. Susanna felt she was supported sufficiently to cope with the dynamic complexities of working with different people each week. However, because of the challenges she faced, I do also wonder whether her very clear theoretical line developed as a result of needing to survive the placement.

The focus on functional goals resurfaced in her subsequent placement. This was in an adult neurorehabilitation setting. She was paired with another trainee and they ran a group supported by assistants. Music therapy was new in this setting. Susanna said:

> In the second placement, the support assistants weren't quite sure what it was, or what they were supposed to do, and they had no blueprint, you know, they had no experience of doing it before. They were perhaps more open; when we gave some context or some guidance, they were more receptive to engaging with that, because they didn't have prior experience.

So lack of knowledge here was a distinct advantage in terms of influencing the therapy and feeling a developing sense of agency as therapist. Different knowing was a theme that Susanna returned to when considering her placement experience overall:

> …'cause of course in every context that I've worked in the support assistants have always known the clients better than I have…at the beginning *definitely*, and I couldn't begin to replace, I couldn't be without what they could offer and I couldn't do what they do, so it's not a lesser role, is it? It's a *different* but equally important role in the session.

Here the status of the assistant becomes more elevated because of their intimate knowledge of the people they are working with: again, it is through putting the client in the centre that the support assistants are valued. I feel that through showing respect for the different knowing, Susanna's narrative begins to move more towards a discourse of multiculturalism and tolerance which develops later in the interview. She begins this by exploring other aspects of difference between her and the assistants:

> [I] don't know if it's relevant but I often wondered about being younger than a lot of support assistants as well and what that gave to the dynamics, that they were potentially in a supporting role – an important role – but in the context of the session, if I was the therapist and they were supporting…I just reflected a bit on that in my observations as well sometimes what that brought to the dynamic.

Cathy, the interviewer, who has been listening to Susanna, asks, 'Would it have felt easier if you had been older than they were?' After hesitating, Susanna said:

> It's probably more my hang-up than it is theirs, and I'm very aware that that's something I've often wondered about, so it's more likely than not something that I bring to the dynamic as well, but I think it's valid to wonder about, though.

At this point I wondered if I had set the interview up in a way that viewed assistants as a distinct group that could easily be 'othered'. This challenged me to think about how I might tend to think in terms of professional groups rather than individuals. However, Susanna's exploration of perceived differences between her and assistants appeared to move her to a more reflexive position; she starts to think more about what perceptions of 'hang-ups' she might be bringing to the inquiry. This raises questions about which differences might be taboo or at least more difficult to think about. Age might feel easier to speak about than differences in social class, for example. Assistants are many different people, but they all have in common a low rate of pay and a tendency to be undervalued. I noted as one of the results of this interview a new desire to interview TAs and hear their stories.

The status of assistants was not an area that was directly addressed in any of these three interviews, but it was present. I wondered how the knowledge of the individuals in therapy enabled some assistants to legitimise their interventions in the music therapy sessions, even though the sessions were supposedly facilitated by the trainees. And what status does a trainee have in comparison with an experienced assistant? In some ways the trainee can be vulnerable to power dynamics between themselves and the assistant. It is helpful for placement supervisors to be sensitive to this on site.

The support assistant is likely to be with the client at other times during the week, so will the experience of being with the trainee influence and change how he or she perceives the client for the rest of the week? And if this is the case, how easy is it for trainees to get any sense of this impact?

Susanna questioned why some assistants might want to over-encourage clients to participate in music therapy sessions. She said:

> I don't know…I wonder…I've often wondered whether the support staff feel that it's a reflection on them, the levels of participation of the client. So I often think, I wonder whether…well, I don't know if they feel it's about them or about wanting the participant to succeed.

The narrative here is more one of a preoccupation about achievement, which is perhaps not surprising as the context is an educational establishment. Later in the interview, Susanna's narrative changes as she considers the coexistence of different cultures:

That's been an ongoing challenge…that a non-directive facilitating is so different from an educational approach, which is often more didactic and kind of behaviourist informed, and yeah, that's kind of been a thread throughout my training, in kind of coming to terms with that and *working out that those approaches have got to exist alongside each other* [my emphasis].

Susanna sees this now as a meeting of cultures, and with this comes her language of multiculturalism: respect for difference and acceptance that there are different models and values at play, and in fact there may be room for both. This language has resonances with Mahoney (2015) who writes about multicultural practice in music therapy.

On her final placement, Susanna did indeed consider taking on the values of the school philosophy to a greater extent:

I wondered whether the music therapy intervention could have been more aligned with the facilitation style of the setting generally. But then again, *I think there's a lot about being authentic as a therapist* [my emphasis], and that just didn't sit with me (smiles). But also, at the same time, I didn't believe that was the most constructive thing for the client. So I didn't feel that it would have been constructive for me to take that more behaviourist way of being in music.

This reminds me of John (2009) again: 'I feel strongly that a therapist's identity is quite a personal matter and that it can develop only if she has worked as a therapist in a way that has really made sense to her' (pp.84–85).

Zoe's narrative

Zoe's first placement experience involved working with a teenager who had been described as 'quite disturbed' and who also was not able to use language to express herself. She was on placement with a fellow student and they both worked with the young person referred to music therapy. For a number of practical reasons, there was no qualified music therapist on site. In early sessions a TA also sat in the room. Zoe said:

I think that was the biggest thing, that was really hard, because she (the TA) was asking, 'Why are you letting her behave like that?

Why are you letting her hold the drum over your head because of course she's going to drop it on your head…'

When we looked at the transcription of the interview, I asked Zoe to clarify how this had happened. She said:

I believe it was the head at the school who suggested having support in the room, but later following supervision at uni, it was felt this was having an impact on the therapeutic relationship, so it was suggested that the TA remain outside the room – available, if needed, to help manage behaviour.

In the interview Zoe took care to express just how difficult this was:

It was really hard to explain to her (the TA) why I was doing that…to have her understand that and then feeling that she was telling me how to be and that just went – what's the word – went against what I was being told at college. With all these different things coming at you… it was trying to understand that approach and sort of thinking you were getting there and wondering if you actually were, and if you'd understood it, and then somebody else tells you something different and you thought, 'Oh god, that's what I'm meant to be.'

At the time of interview, Zoe had been practising music therapy for over 10 years. However, the struggle of the experience, and the powerlessness she felt, did feel very fresh, as though it had happened recently. This seemed to be underlined by the way Zoe moved back and forth from first to second person, as if needing to distance herself at times from the immediacy and directness of the experience. It really did sound to me as though she felt things were being thrown at her both by the TA and by 'supervision at uni'.

Richards (2009) writes:

In a therapeutic relationship, the patient may legitimately hope for a non-judging response [from the music therapist]; in supervision, by contrast, the student supervisee is aware that part of her supervisor's role is to evaluate her and her work, and that to an extent her progress on the training will be subject to that evaluation. The supervisory setting is characterised by this central conflict. (p.31)

Zoe was only too aware of this:

I think that as a student as well it's really hard because you feel you're being appraised. I think that's what you feel as a student anyway:

you're constantly being appraised and you're doing your best, and of course having someone actually sitting in the room when you're not that confident yourself with what you're doing…and to be honest, I still feel that now, if I'm honest, I still feel a little bit…like someone's watching you and (said very quietly) judging.

Zoe's account struck me as a powerful formative experience which still has an impact on how she experiences work as a music therapist. Given Zoe's powerful recall of the experience, it occurred to me how significant the first placement could be in terms of compromising the growth of confidence or even identity development as a therapist if there is insufficient support to manage the cultural differences presented by an assistant.

John (2009) asks of trainee placement experiences, 'What creates discovery, growth and a sense of change? What creates blocks, impasse or false understanding and a sense of what may be termed "stuck knowing"?' (p.87), and later states that 'some experiences in and out of the consulting room activate and contribute to the therapist inside us, whereas others interfere with and disrupt the working of the therapist inside' (p.91).

Zoe's account is an example of a disruption occurring early in her development as a therapist, perhaps crucially. Zoe's narrative emphasises how hard this is, so that keeping the assistants out of the room still feels like the best option in order for the space to feel safe enough to work as a therapist. With further reflection and time in the interview Zoe and I might have explored more of her thoughts about her supervision and perhaps even whether this training experience linked to previous experiences of feeling judged in her personal history.

I found myself wondering about the impact these experiences might have had on the other players involved, such as what the TA might have made of the requirement via 'uni' supervision to stand outside the room the following session. What might that have been like to communicate to this unnamed TA for Zoe and her fellow trainee? And what might the young woman in therapy have made of the changes with three people in the room one week and two people the next?

However, I note that Zoe is still practising as a busy music therapist 10 years later. I agree with John (2009) when he says that therapists need to create a clear therapeutic stance but must also have 'faith in the process and possess the courage of their convictions' (p.87). Despite Zoe's formative training experiences, it seems she has found a way to believe in music therapy processes that make sense to her and sustain them over time.

Kiki's narrative

Kiki's narrative throughout her interview focuses on the great difficulty and complexity of working with assistants when the clients themselves have complex needs. For Kiki, working with assistants is what happened for *other* trainees but not for her on any of her three training placements. Kiki described first in interview how disruptive she had found working with care assistants in music therapy sessions at a home for adults with complex needs. She was clear, however, that they did need to be in the room because of risks to do with epileptic seizures and other medical needs. She was keen to explore how she had been prepared for this kind of work during training.

> Cathy: Looking back on it now, what are your feelings now about what experiences you had on placement and how they helped you prepare for work with assistants afterwards?

> Kiki: I think that the sharing of work in the college workshops, you know the sessions we had around presenting the work to each other and also the role-play exercises we did in clinical improvisation class, were helpful; so we would try and be those people ourselves, we took on those roles, and some of the video people shared, though I was really aware of the issue already – because of their kind of struggles and the complexity of what they had to deal with in classrooms and college groups.

> Cathy: So there were trainees who were working with assistants?

> Kiki: Yes, there were, and I did realise that it was…quite a hard thing to do. Some of the issues around what's in the transference and whose it is; you know, projection – *Why do I feel like this?* It's just massive, isn't it? It's a spiderweb.

I found it interesting to hear how Kiki made use of the idea of emotional transactions between people, using psychodynamic theoretical notions such as projection and transference, to illustrate and explain the complexity of working with more people in the session. She was aware of the feelings of others in the room; when they come in they also need to be considered.

In her recent care-home work Kiki had set up a group for several of the residents, supported by care assistants.

> Cathy: In your more recent work are there themes that still continue?

> Kiki: I think that's why it's hard to have someone in there (the therapy room) because…are they there to just…facilitate and keep an eye on someone's medical needs, manually help them with instruments in a sensitive way, or are they part of the group? Are they in the group? I think that our understanding of therapy in this society is…at not a very good level really… thinking about someone's emotional world and how important that is…how much space people need in order to do anything with their feelings, you know, they need to be given that space and not cheered up and geed along.

Whereas Susanna was concerned about assistants in a school actively discouraging initiatives that the clients might take in the music therapy room, Kiki is concerned about clients being actively encouraged by care assistants to participate when they might not want that, or at a pace that is too fast. Susanna focuses on the primacy of a client-led approach, and Kiki talks about the need for space for her clients to respond, react and feel authentically, rather than being 'geed along'. There seem to be common factors between Kiki's and Susanna's accounts; they are talking about the same kind of client needs and therapeutic processes although using somewhat different theoretical narratives.

I also find it interesting that Kiki considers how assistants' attitudes within a therapy session may be reflections of the attitudes and perceptions of society in microcosm. This is something with which she is dissatisfied and frustrated.

Of what could assistants be doing more? Kiki relates the need to sit back as something which she, as well as the people who assist her in a group, needs to work on. In this way, despite her frustrations and concern for the vulnerable people who are having things done for them, she is able to think about herself and the assistants as having a similar task. Her implication is that with the benefit of her training she may be further on in thinking about this:

> Something like the codependency of care…you know, it's so hard for support workers or carers to sit back and see the client or relative sitting on their own, and to resist their own need to be constantly doing things for them. All of those things…I think they're an uphill struggle. I can see myself in therapy – you know, *Do I need just to sit back a bit?* It's quite a huge part of the work, I think, to just not do anything. So I'm aware of that in myself and I can see it all around.

In contrast to Susanna's question about whether TAs needed clients to achieve as a reflection of the assistant's own competence, Kiki sees the issue as one of the need for emotional separation rather than the assistants being dependent on the resident they are supporting, perhaps as an extension of their own identity.

Enhancing the trainee experience

In a chapter about supervising trainees on placement with people with learning disabilities, Richards (2009, pp.23–44) considers the strategies trainee music therapists might employ to defend against the helplessness or dependency they might feel when working with people with profound learning disabilities or complex needs. These strategies might involve focusing on theoretical notions or information about disability rather than on feelings, or arriving in supervision armed with precise and detailed notes and a clear plan about how to spend the time. I think it would be well worth trainees and their supervisors thinking about why assistants in their sessions might also need to focus on 'doing' and how they might be supported to stay with uncertainty or allow themselves to see the residents differently through music.

Zoe, Kiki and Susanna are not speaking on behalf of their trainings or placement experiences; rather, they are individuals reflecting on their own unique set of experiences. Their stories nevertheless raise many questions for supervisors, trainees, placement coordinators and placement supervisors. Susanna and Zoe have moved beyond challenging first-placement experiences to form working identities. Kiki is using her training experiences at college to help her identify and think about what work she needs to do to support residents and their carers within a residential home.

Conclusion

There are risks attendant on assistant presence. Within the narratives are examples of the potential for assistants in a therapy session to create considerable disruption which can impact on the trainee's important professional identity formation and reframing during training. The assistants may have needs and agendas that can interfere with the client's need for space and the capacity to respond in a way they can best manage. Trainees struggling to think about the role of the assistant within a therapeutic space, where this has been imposed, may result in 'othering' the assistants, which can cause continuing problems.

However, there are useful ways of beginning to think about how assistants contribute to the therapy space. First, an acknowledgement of the value of their knowledge of clients seems important. A critical reflection on the issues of difference that might be present between trainee and assistant would also seem to be a helpful practice. A supervisor's sensitivity to the unspoken differences which may be difficult to voice in relation to age, class or status may help the trainee to feel more confident to address this on placement.

One latent theme from the narratives is that of multiculturalism. Contemporary multicultural working practices, such as tolerance and respect of difference, the recognition of dominant or privileged narratives and the capacity to allow different cultures to sit alongside one another, offer new and expanded ways of thinking about the practice of assistance within music therapy. Models of co-therapy, where resources allow, could also ameliorate some of the difficulties described in the stories.

Finally, I feel I have learned most from the recognition of the narrators that assistants are *people* first and foremost, with their own histories, abilities, hopes and needs. If this is considered within placement work (but not necessarily foregrounded), then there will be ways for potential conflicts and disruptions to be avoided or worked through for the well-being of all concerned.

References

Bateson, M.C. (1990) *Composing a Life: Life as Work in Progress – The Improvisations of Five Extraordinary Women*. New York, NY: Penguin.

Clandinin, D.J. and Connolly, F.M. (2000) *Narrative Inquiry: Experience and Story in Qualitative Research.* San Francisco, CA: Jossey-Bass.

Daykin, N. (2005) 'Disruption, dissonance and embodiment: creativity, health and risk in music narratives.' *Health 9*, 1, 67–87.

John, D. (2009) 'Getting Better: Some Thoughts on the Growth of the Therapist.' In H. Odell-Miller and E. Richards (eds) *Supervision of Music Therapy: A Theoretical and Practical Handbook.* Hove: Routledge.

Mahoney, E. (2015) 'Multicultural music therapy: an exploration.' *Voices: A World Forum for Music Therapy 15*, 2. Available at https://www.voices.no.index.php/voices/article/view/844/693, accessed on 28 September 2016.

Richards, E. (2009) 'Whose Handicap? Issues Arising in the Supervision of Trainee Music Therapists in Their First Experience of Working with Adults with Learning Disabilities.' In H. Odell-Miller and E. Richards (eds) *Supervision of Music Therapy: A Theoretical and Practical Handbook.* Hove: Routledge.

Riessman, C.K. (1993) *Narrative Analysis.* London: Sage Publications.

Speedy, J. (2008) *Narrative Inquiry and Psychotherapy.* London: Palgrave Macmillan.

Chapter 4

Involving Family Members Who Are Primary Carers in Music Therapy Sessions with Children with Special Needs

Pornpan Kaenampornpan

Introduction

This chapter describes the music therapy work at a special education centre in Thailand, where my PhD research investigation (Kaenampornpan 2015) took place. The investigation aimed to explore family members' experiences of participating in the music therapy sessions with their children with special needs. First, I explain the context, and then I describe how music therapy sessions were conducted in this setting. I then explore how the music therapist involved family members who are primary carers in the therapeutic process and examine how the family members' involvement strengthened the relationship between the children and their families. Finally, some findings relating to the family members' experiences of participating in music therapy sessions with their children with special needs are reviewed.

Context

In Thailand special education centres are sponsored by government and aim to provide free services to children with different needs from when they are first diagnosed. According to the latest national legislation on special education, the term 'special education centre' refers to an educational institute which has a responsibility to provide early intervention. It also conducts education for people with special needs and educates the families, carers, teachers and anyone who is involved in the life of a person with special needs (Ministry of Education of Thailand 2008). Moreover, the centre provides help to children with special needs at home and also children with chronic illness in hospital. Region 9 of the Special Education Centre, where the clinical work which was the subject of my research took place, receives referrals mostly from hospitals and schools, but also directly from family members who learn about the centre from the families of other children. Physiotherapy, speech training and life skills are provided. There are seven classrooms: two for children with autism spectrum disorder (ASD), two for children with learning difficulties and three for early intervention, children with hearing impairment and children with physical difficulties.

Every new child, regardless of the nature of their needs, receives a preliminary assessment by a classroom teacher, an art teacher, a teacher specialising in speech and a physiotherapist. Assessment results are discussed among the teachers and also with the family members in order to set goals and design an individual education plan. Then the children are allocated to a suitable classroom. After the children are ready to go to the next academic level, the centre normally refers them to either a mainstream school which provides an inclusive classroom or to schools which provide education specifically for children with hearing difficulty, physical difficulty and visual difficulty.

I first came to this centre as a volunteer about 6 years before I started my PhD because I wanted to learn about, and experience working with, children with special needs. Therefore, I was relatively familiar with the centre before I conducted this study. I found that in the setting the family members were expected to attend with their children every day to work collaboratively with the teacher to support their children, and to learn from the teachers how to educate their children. The centre encourages the family members to participate in organised activities alongside their children; therefore, it was a very good opportunity for a music therapy investigation to promote and support the centre's idea of involving the family members in the sessions.

Researching music therapy for children and family members

Subjects

The eight children whose music therapy I investigated presented with ASD, physical difficulties and learning disabilities. The teachers had many aims for music therapy including improving concentration, developing social skills or encouraging the use of verbal communication.

Eight children and the family members who were their primary carers were invited to participate in the research project. At the end of the project, only six children and their family members had attended sessions regularly. They all received 24 music therapy sessions, twice a week. Initially, I had intended to work with the children's parents; however, all the children who were referred to me were accompanied to the centre by other family members such as their grandparents or aunts. Parents of the children could not afford to come to the centre with their children every day; therefore, the grandparents or aunts accompanied the children to the centre instead.

In Thai society, family members, including those in extended families, tend to develop strong connections and support each other, including helping parents and children with disabilities in the home environment (Vorapanya 2008). Thai people put a very high value on being able to take care of family members with illness or disabilities. Influenced by Buddhist teaching, Thai people believe that each family member has an obligation not only to take care of himself or herself, but also to take care of others and share responsibilities with other family members (Payutto 2003; Pongsaksri 2004).

Characteristics of my music therapy approach

Children with special needs are very different from one another. They also may have unpredictable behaviour which changes from session to session. Therefore, it is necessary for a music therapist 'to be flexible and not get frustrated by any unexpected events' (Oldfield 2006b, p.23). Musical improvisation is useful because it provides enough flexibility for the therapist to be able to follow the children's leads and to respond appropriately, and also for the therapist to musically reflect and express their thoughts and attitudes to the child in the moment. Improvisation not only helps me to engage with the children;

it also enables me to extend the children's cues to make them more meaningful and to provide a starting point for our music-making (Nordoff and Robbins 1977; Sorel 2010).

I work towards many different goals which help to give a clear focus and direction to my work, and this also allows me to fit in with the goals set by the class teachers. Each goal is achieved through musical games, musical conversations and musical instrument explorations. In my musical games, I normally have a very simple rule, such as whose turn it is to play, playing music in different positions, moving along with different tempos of music, or musical imitation games. As the work for this study was progressing, the children became willing to participate in more challenging tasks with me. This led to the interactive phase, where turn-taking, sharing and listening to each other can start to emerge. In this approach, we take it in turns to be a leader and follower. Sometimes I follow the child's rules in order to make them feel more at ease, and then I set simple rules for both of us to follow. Occasionally, the children found it difficult to follow my suggestions as some had ASD and might not have wanted to engage with others; therefore, I would return to following and copying them again until they showed interest in me, and then I could incorporate their ideas to create a moment where we could play together. This is similar to Thompson's (2012) way of working with children with ASD which she describes as responding to the child's initiations and then introducing new ideas to the child in order to extend the child's initiations into a new experience.

Maslow's (1970) and Erikson's (1959) psychological theories inform the goals and my understanding of each child. Sometimes when working with people with special needs, my perception of them as people is hindered by their difficulties. So Maslow's hierarchy of basic needs reminds me that no matter what difficulties people might have, they still have the same basic needs as others. Erikson's development theory is helpful because children with special needs often have difficulties in reaching the 'usual' milestones, and this theory helps me to understand the children at different stages of development.

In the sessions I researched, I found myself becoming active and playful because most of the children I worked with appeared to be in their own world and did not show much interest in engaging with me. Therefore, it was important to be enthusiastic and active in order to gain the children's interest and engage them in what we were doing.

However, I was not constantly active because it is important to leave some space for the child to respond, and also because some children enjoyed soft and gentle music. Most children are full of playfulness and they experience the world and learn new things through play; therefore, being playful allows the adult (the family members and myself) to enter into the child's world in order to foster closeness, confidence and connection (Cohen 2002). There were many occasions when I saw the children resisting engagement with me and becoming upset if they were encouraged too strongly to do so, thus causing frustration for the family members. Instead of forcing children to participate in the session, playfully turning the children's interest into a game could turn these situations into fun and enjoyable moments.

When working with children who are mostly non-verbal, it is particularly important to first build a relationship. In order to do that, my first aim is to make the children comfortable and relaxed enough to extend their interaction with me. This is similar to the client-centred humanistic approach which was developed by Rogers (1979). Client-centred therapists regard highly the quality of their relationships with their clients. Rogers believed that the therapeutic relationship enables the therapist to gain the insight into the client's challenges and maintain the positive changes in the client. Through this relationship, the client can feel accepted and safe from judgement. This enables him to have a healthy attitude towards himself and towards the world. The client-centred therapist considers the client and the therapist as equals rather than the therapist being an expert treating the patient. Rogers also stressed the power of the client to overcome his difficulties and to control his own life.

Working with family members

One of the important characteristics in my work is involving in the sessions family members who are the children's primary carers. There were many reasons why I asked the family members to be involved in the sessions. First, I like to see family members and their children together, as I believe family members have such a big influence on their children. From my previous experience of being a piano teacher to children, I had found that family members have a big influence on the effectiveness of children's learning. They spend much of the day with their children and often know most about their child.

Having the family members involved in the learning process helps both them and me, as the piano teacher, to have the same expectations of the child so that we can appreciate every progression the child makes. The family members help me to understand more about their child and they motivate the child to practise and are the most important source of support. Similarly, the way in which the family members reacted and responded to the children in the music therapy sessions helped me to understand the children.

During the course of the project, the children and their families appeared to engage in a more positive way owing to being together. These experiences provided a good memory for them both, which was very helpful for them to think about at more difficult times. Also, the family members could see their children in a different way, and they could see the way I engaged with their children through music. By the end of the process, I hoped the family members would be able to use some techniques from the music therapy sessions with their child at home. I expected to work collaboratively with the family members.

Some of the family members initially found attending the sessions strange and unfamiliar, and thought that they might be barriers preventing the children from engaging with a new person. For example, one of the family members, Jan, initially wanted her nephew, Aden, to attend the sessions by himself because she was afraid that, if she accompanied him, he would feel forced to engage in the sessions. Also she wanted Aden to be independent from her, as he was always shy with new people. The family members were asked to attend every session, but they were free to decide when and how much they wanted to participate in the musical interactions. Nevertheless, it was my aim to enable them to become interested in participating, and to create sessions that were suitable for both the children and the family members. From my experiences of working with the family members during this project, I believe that the work with the family members may have been challenging during the first period. Then the family members and the children found ways to interact through music, and the family members became a bridge between the children and the music therapist. Returning to the earlier example, when the family member and I took turns being a music partner with Aden, this enabled him to gradually increase interactions and communications with me and become less clingy with Jan. This then allowed Aden to form a relationship with a new person (Woodward 2008).

Contraindications for the inclusion of family members

Including family members in music therapy with their children is not always appropriate. At the Croft Child and Family Unit in Cambridge, for example (Holmes, Oldfield and Polichroniadis 2011), children with severe emotional and behavioural difficulties and their families are provided with day and inpatient mental health care. The general aim of the unit is to assess the child holistically in his or her family context; therefore, the adults' opinions or pressing problems and needs must not be allowed to stand in the way of a full consideration of the needs of the child. It is therefore sometimes necessary to see the child on their own in order for the therapist to gain a true picture of the child's needs and, if appropriate, to set up one-to-one therapy. That way, the child can be held in a safe environment, and have a much-needed space for their own expression and development, allowing for freedom of psychological and musical development. In these cases, particularly with a very disturbed child, it can be more effective to work following an approach which would not be possible with a family member present. However, the children I worked with at the centre did not present severe emotional or behavioural difficulties, and none of the family members accompanying these children presented with overwhelming needs of their own. It was therefore entirely appropriate for the children to be seen with their family members.

Three phases in the developing relationship with family members

Throughout the research process, I learned that the relationship between each carer and myself was developed in similar ways. However, I am aware that each music therapist has different ways of working. Nevertheless, a pattern emerged of three clear phases in the development of my relationship with family members which is now explained, and which might be useful to other music therapists working in this context.

Phase 1: Introducing the music therapy work and myself to the family members

During the first phase, I mainly aimed to establish relationships with the children and hoped that the family members could see the benefit from their children participating in the sessions. Some family members may find music-making uncomfortable; therefore, giving them some settling-in time is important (Molyneux 2008). It was important to emphasise to the family members that the main aim of having them in the sessions was to allow them to witness their children's joyful moments. They could decide later when and how they wanted to engage in the musical interactions; therefore, in this first period, I mainly worked with the children and did not ask the family members to participate in the activities directly (Figure 4.1).

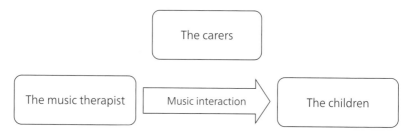

Figure 4.1 Phase 1: I introduce music therapy and myself to the family members

Although my aim was to encourage the children to engage with me in these early sessions, building a rapport with the family members was also very important. It was crucial to show that through this process I was open to hearing their thoughts and that they were very highly valued and fully listened to (Hornby 1995; Walworth 2012). Some family members appeared to be very anxious if their children were not engaged with me, so they tended to push their child by holding their hand to play the musical instrument, or they did not give the child enough time to respond spontaneously. This could prevent the children from engaging or give them a negative impression of the music therapy sessions. As for the children who struggled to engage with other people or to share attention, it was crucial to provide chances to respond and to wait long enough for the children to respond (Rainey Perry 2003). Therefore, it was very important for me to remind the family members that the children were not expected to 'learn or to be able to follow directions all the time'; instead, I aimed to explore different ways to use music to engage with them so that the children could engage with me at their own pace and in their own ways. Moreover, providing chances for the family members to see me waiting and listening to the children's responses, and trying to match their responses in order to extend them into a more meaningful interaction, enabled them to appreciate this as the way the children engaged, rather than believing that they were being naughty (Loth 2008).

Phase 2: Letting the family members join in and provide input

In the second phase, I felt that the family members and the children started to be familiar with the activities and that they came to the session with the expectation that they would participate in some way. I noticed that the family members began to recognise my signals such that they could join in more naturally. They started to wait for the children to respond longer before playing for the children. I saw that the family members started to be more playful with their children. They extended their roles from passive participants who observed the sessions from one corner of the room, to being active participants who engaged in the musical games with their children. I expected to work collaboratively with the family members; therefore, in this phase I felt that I stepped down from my leading role a little in order to provide some space for the family members to join in and sometimes take the lead.

I encouraged the family members to share their thoughts and take part increasingly in the therapeutic process, rather than taking the lead myself all the time. I wanted to share control with the family members. They tended to believe that I was the expert and would know more than they did, and this was a challenge to getting their input. Also, being shy or reluctant to ask for favours, being humble and not responding too quickly in interactions is considered polite and a way to gain social respect and recognition in Thai society (Chaidaroon 2003). Thai people are taught not to reveal their emotions and to avoid open expression of their feelings and thoughts to others to prevent trouble, and to avoid challenge or confrontation (Pratomthong and Baker 1983). These thoughts might not exist so strongly in the younger generation since Western culture is becoming more influential in Thailand, but it was still important to be aware of this characteristic and give the family members time to feel comfortable and safe enough to make a suggestion regarding their children's therapeutic process. It is important to be open and give due weight to the family members' ideas; even a small idea had to be acknowledged. Such acceptance and support from others could enable the family members to feel empowered and gradually play an important role in the therapeutic process and the development of their child's skills later (Walworth 2012).

During this phase, the family members shared their concerns with me regarding their children's development and behaviour, and also their own personal concerns. They were eager to make suggestions about what the children might like, and we were developing a partnership. Sharing with the therapist information and insight into their relationship with the children enabled the family members to gain confidence and to enjoy the positive abilities of their child (Twyford and Watson 2008). This phase allowed me to learn more about both the children and the family members, and therefore, I could adjust the sessions and my expectations to take account of those of the family members (see Figure 4.2).

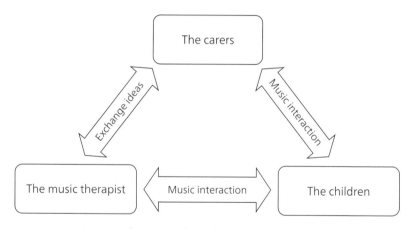

Figure 4.2 Phase 2: Family members join in and provide input

Phase 3: Letting the family members lead as we work together

In the final phase, the relationship between the family members and myself was firmly established. I saw them as part of the team, a partnership. We exchanged ideas more often, both on the spot and after each session. I felt that we supported each other. Some of the family members not only shared their concern regarding the children during the sessions, but also, during the video-review process, they started to share concerns about the children's behaviour at home. When their comments were incorporated into the sessions, they seemed to recognise their input. This enabled them to see themselves as experts on their children within the therapeutic process. When they and I reached this phase, I felt it was easier to work together, as we supported each other and we were able to focus on nurturing the children's development.

I now felt that the family members were willing to take more risks and try different things. They could respond to the musical games or activities in the sessions naturally and appeared to be more playful and childlike with their children. Sometimes they spontaneously took turns in leading both the children and me in musical games, resulting in more frequent laughter together. They appeared to have fun in the sessions with their children. They seemed to be more tolerant of the children being 'silly' and noisy. I felt that I was a facilitator in the sessions to keep the interaction between all of us going. The family members might need to be reminded that their children were allowed to be a leader in the sessions too. At this point, the family members only needed some space to explore their own creativity and encouragement to bring out their childlikeness and playfulness. They were able to take more control of the sessions, for example, by choosing what they wanted their children to participate in and contributing to session planning. Their feedback helped extend the activities and to better meet the children's needs and interests. The family members devote their time and lives to taking care of their children, and the more the children developed, I felt that the family members could have more hope.

Figure 4.3 shows that in the third phase I positioned myself outside the cycle of the children and their family members' interaction, not only because I wanted to share control with the family members so we could work as a partnership, but also because I realised that the level of the children's engagement depended very much on the family members' involvement, and vice versa. I was aware that my practice was influenced greatly by the interactions between the family members and the children – not just the children alone or the family members alone. Although the children's interests and their needs were my first priority when I decided what intervention I should provide, I also expected that interventions would affect the family members.

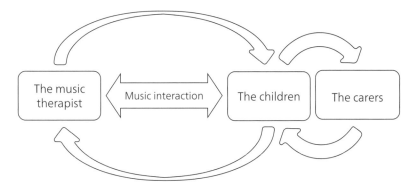

Figure 4.3 Phase 3: I let the family members lead and we work together

I had three main aims for the family members: to have a positive time together with their children, to witness the children's achievement so they could be more hopeful, and to explore a new way of engaging with the children; other aims would come later. Therefore, when I provided any intervention for the children, I always made sure that the family members could achieve these aims too.

This progression in three phases is a cyclical process. The family members and I sometimes returned to the previous phase. For example, in the third phase, the children appeared to respond well to the games and they were ready to move to a new level, so I introduced a new activity or added a new rule into the game, either to challenge the children to take a step further, or when the family members appeared to be tired and not so keen to join in. I was then more of a leader while the family members observed and waited until they were familiar with the new games and ready to participate. It is interesting that, although the context of the study is different, the way I worked with the family members is similar to Oldfield's (2006a) approach in many ways, for example the focus on what the children can do and are interested in doing, the empowerment given to the family members in having fun and the hope that they would pick up from the music therapy sessions some ways of communicating with their children in other contexts.

Researching the family members' experiences of seeing themselves in the music therapy sessions

Each music therapy session was videoed and the video recordings were discussed every 2 weeks with the family members. In order to investigate family members' experiences of participating in the music therapy sessions and in order to understand their experiences, all six family members who participated in this study were interviewed. There were three interviews focusing on their experiences of using music with their children during the research process. The first interview was conducted after the assessment sessions and before the music therapy sessions with the family members started. Then they were interviewed again after the twenty-fourth session was finished. The last interview was held two months after the twenty-fourth and final session. All the interviews were analysed using interpretative phenomenological analysis (IPA).

From the analysis, 28 themes under five categories emerged (see Table 4.1). Themes under the category of family members' experiences of seeing themselves in the music therapy sessions with their children show that they were positively influenced by participating in the music therapy sessions with their children. They all reported that being in the sessions with their children allowed them to have a good time and good experiences together. They said that witnessing their children's enjoyment could lessen their concerns about the children.

In addition, family members' involvement in the sessions encouraged the children to engage in the sessions more. Family members described different ways in which they encouraged their children to engage. Some family members reported that when they gave praise or sang along with the children, the children appeared to be more enthusiastic, and this enabled them to be more confident to engage in the sessions. Some said that their engagements in the music-making encouraged the children to join in the sessions because sometimes the children were shy of a new person. So having the family members engaging in the sessions allowed the children to play with them first until they were more familiar and ready to engage with another person. One family member stated that she knew the child very well so that she could help the music therapist manage the child's challenging behaviours.

Some family members reported that they found themselves motivated to engage more with their children. They stated that seeing the music therapist successfully engaged with the children encouraged them to experiment with different ways to engage with their children. Furthermore, they felt that they could work in a partnership with the music therapist towards the same goals. Some family members reported that the music therapist was open and accepted their opinions. They felt that they could learn what the music therapist thought about their children, and this enabled them to share their thoughts.

Some family members reported that being involved in the music therapy sessions enabled them to see the children in a different light and to give them more hope. The music therapy sessions provided many chances for the children to show their abilities rather than focusing on their disabilities (Loth 2008). When the family members could recognise more of the children's strengths, they were able to move on from dysfunctional patterns of relating to the children which prevented their healthy growth (Elman 1991, pp.369–406).

All the categories and themes found are set out in Table 4.1.

Table 4.1 Overall categories and themes from the interviews

Category	Theme
The carers' expectations of the music therapy	Increasing long concentration
	Understanding signals and accepting others' requests
	Having more interest in engaging with others
	Improving motor skills
	Becoming less shy and expressing themselves more
	Vocalising more and using more verbal communication
	Learning to regulate moods
The carers' experience of seeing their children in the music therapy sessions	Understanding signals and accepting others' requests
	Vocalising more and using more verbal communication
	Increasing their concentration
	Having more interest in engaging with others
	Relaxing
	Improving their motor skills
	Becoming less shy and expressing themselves more

The carers' experience of seeing themselves in the music therapy sessions with their children	Involving the carers in the music therapy sessions enabled them to have a good time and a good experience together
	Involving the carers in the music therapy sessions encouraged their children to engage more
	Involving the carers in the music therapy sessions encouraged them to engage with their children more
	Involving the carers in the music therapy sessions enabled the carers to work in partnership with the music therapist
	Involving the carers in the music therapy sessions gave them hope and allowed them to see the children in a different light
The carers' experiences of reviewing the video recordings from the music therapy sessions	Providing good memories
	Changing their opinions towards their children and themselves
	Seeing the children's responses and their interactions in more detail
The carers' experiences of using music at home	The changes in using music at home after participating in the music therapy sessions
	The use of music at home creating a good atmosphere in the family
	The differences between having music therapy sessions and using music at home
	The children's perception of the music therapist making visits
	Home visits helping the music therapist to gain more understanding of the children
	Home visits encouraging the carer to use music

Conclusion

This chapter shows that the family involvement and partnerships positively influenced the children, the families and the music therapy process. The family members played a central role in this work. They not only encouraged their children to engage in the sessions more; they also helped the music therapist to understand the children's needs.

Including family members in music therapy can sometimes be challenging and not always appropriate.

I hope that the patterns in the way the relationship with the family members developed presented here could lessen some of the challenges and might encourage music therapists who work in similar contexts to include family members in the treatment process.

References

Chaidaroon, S. (2003) 'When shyness is not incompetence: a case of Thai communication competence.' *Intercultural Communication Studies 12*, 4, 195–208.

Cohen, L.J. (2002) *Playful Parenting*. Toronto: Random House of Canada.

Elman, N. (1991) 'Family Therapy.' In M. Seligman (ed) *The Family With a Handicapped Child* (2nd ed.). Boston, MA: Allyn and Bacon.

Erikson, E.H. (1959) *Identity and the Life Cycle: Selected Papers*. New York, NY: International Universities Press.

Holmes, J., Oldfield, A. and Polichroniadis, M. (2011) *Creating Change for Complex Children and Their Families: A Multi-Disciplinary Approach to Multi-Family Work*. London: Jessica Kingsley Publishers.

Hornby, G. (1995) *Working with Parents of Children with Special Educational Needs*. London: Cassell.

Kaenampornpan, P. (2015) 'The Inclusion of the Family Members as Primary Carers in Music Therapy Sessions with Children in a Special Education Centre: How Does This Help the Child and the Carer?' PhD thesis, Anglia Ruskin University, Cambridge. Available at http://hdl.handle.net/10540/550334, accessed on 1 March 2016.

Loth, H. (2008) 'Music Therapy Groups for Families with a Learning-Disabled Toddler: Bridging Some Gaps.' In A. Oldfield and C. Flower (eds) *Music Therapy with Children and Their Families*. London: Jessica Kingsley Publishers.

Maslow, A. (1970) *Motivation and Personality* (2nd ed.). New York, NY: Harper and Row.

Ministry of Education of Thailand (2008) *The Act of Legislation of Education for People with Special Needs of Thailand*. Available at www.mua.go.th/data_main/law/25_03_51.pdf (in Thai), accessed on 1 June 2015.

Molyneux, C. (2008) 'Music Therapy as Part of a Multidisciplinary Family Assessment Process.' In K. Twyford and T. Watson (eds) *Integrated Team Working: Music Therapy as Part of Transdisciplinary and Collaborative Approaches*. London: Jessica Kingsley Publishers.

Nordoff, P. and Robbins, C. (1977) *Creative Music Therapy: Individualized Treatment for the Handicapped Child*. New York, NY: John Day.

Oldfield, A. (2006a) *Interactive Music Therapy: A Positive Approach. Music Therapy at a Child Development Centre*. London: Jessica Kingsley Publishers.

Oldfield, A. (2006b) *Interactive Music Therapy in Child and Family Psychiatry: Clinical Practice, Research and Teaching*. London: Jessica Kingsley Publishers.

Payutto, P.A. (2003) *A Constitution for Living*. Bangkok: Sahadhammika.

Pongsaksri, A. (2004) 'A Trans-Cultural Study of the Practice of Occupational Therapists in Thailand and Australia: Reframing Theories of Practice.' PhD thesis, Curtin University of Technology, Perth, Western Australia.

Pratomthong, S.J. and Baker, S.B. (1983) 'Overcoming obstacles to the growth and development of guidance and counseling in Thailand.' *The Personnel and Guidance Journal 61*, 8, 466–469.

Rainey Perry, M.M. (2003) 'Relating improvisational music therapy with severely and multiply disabled children to communication development.' *Journal of Music Therapy 40*, 3, 227–246.

Rogers, C.R. (1979) 'The foundations of the person-centred approach.' *Education 100*, 2, 98–107.

Sorel, S.N. (2010) 'Presenting Carly and Elliot: Exploring roles and relationships in a mother–son dyad in Nordoff–Robbins Music Therapy.' in S. Hadley (ed) *Qualitative Inquiries in Music Therapy* 5, 173–238.

Thompson, G. (2012) 'Making a Connection: Randomised Controlled Trial of Family Centred Music Therapy for Young Children with Autism Spectrum Disorder.' PhD thesis, Melbourne Conservatorium of Music. Available at http://hdl.handle.net/11343/37719, accessed on 1 June 2015.

Twyford, K. and Watson, T. (2008) *Integrated Team Working: Music Therapy as Part of Transdisciplinary and Collaborative Approaches*. London: Jessica Kingsley Publishers.

Vorapanya, S. (2008) 'A Model for Inclusive Schools in Thailand.' PhD thesis, University of Oregon. Available at http://proquest.umi.com/pqdweb?did =1690952231&Fmt=7&clientId=47904&RQT=309&VName= PQD, accessed on 1 June 2015.

Walworth, D. (2012) 'Family-Centred Practice: Integrating Music into Home Routines.' In P. Kern and M. Humpal (eds) *Early Childhood Music Therapy and Autism Spectrum Disorders*. London: Jessica Kingsley Publishers.

Woodward, A. (2008) 'Martha and Rio.' In K. Twyford and T. Watson (eds) *Integrated Team Working: Music Therapy as Part of Transdisciplinary and Collaborative Approaches*. London: Jessica Kingsley Publishers.

Chapter 5

Exploring the Significance of the Role of Assistants in Music Therapy Groups in Adult and Older People's Mental Health Settings

Helen Odell-Miller

The clinical context

This chapter describes the integral role of attendants who are not music therapists in music therapy groups in the adult mental health field and dementia care, and considers the dynamics arising from their inclusion. Sociological and psychological phenomena, including the therapeutic community movement and theories of family dynamics replayed or represented within therapy groups, are considered in relation to the attendant role in music therapy. The main settings considered are (a) inpatient music therapy groups for people with dementia and (b) acute-admission-ward music therapy groups for adults with mental illness.

I was lucky enough, early in my career as a music therapist, to work in quasi-therapeutic-community adult mental health settings within the UK National Health Service, where nursing staff, occupational therapists, psychologists, psychiatrists and others regularly acted as accompanying assistants in music therapy sessions. In fact, it was the norm to run groups with significant others present, and it was these attendees which made the groups what they were. The atmosphere was one of collaboration; we looked forward to working together, our different roles and perspectives bouncing off each other, while helping the group therapy process, the preparation for people attending the group and the containment and processing afterwards. The purpose of this collaboration was not only to create a link with the daily life of the residents outside the music therapy group, but also to enhance residents' special relationships with the staff who attended the group with them. In adult mental health services today these staff are termed 'key worker' or 'case manager', or sometimes 'peer worker'. Thinking about these relationships and their integral part in the music therapy group process was central to group members' engagement and participation. Very often the attendance of the significant staff member would be the key to enabling music therapy group members to participate and make the most of the complex dynamics of the groups.

Music therapy groups are multilayered. Added to the ordinary conscious and unconscious processes and the dynamics of relating, seen in all groups, is the phenomenon of making music, which requires physical, intellectual and psychological engagement. The attendant can help on all or some of these levels, and it is these levels that this chapter explores. Little emphasis in the music therapy literature to date has been placed upon the integral function of an accompanying assistant or co-worker in group work, acting as a dynamic force to enable trust and interaction to develop in musical and other ways, which might not, without that assisting relationship, be possible.

I focus upon that dynamic in an adult mental health setting where the 'extended family' of key nurse, occupational therapist or assistant always attended activities and a participant's depth and level of functioning and participation were regulated and enabled by their presence. However, as with parents of young children, attachment figures and 'significant others' can be a distraction from therapy, instead of facilitating participation; this possibility always needs to be considered.

Parallels with family work

Assistants who work with music therapists in mental health settings may have a function similar to that of a family member. Oldfield (2011) provides strong evidence that for parents with young children attending music therapy, their involvement in a music therapy dyad or group can have a significant effect upon the quality of their relationship with their child. Kaenampornpan (see Chapter 4 of this volume) indicates that in culturally specific environments the involvement of parents and other family members assisting a young child in music therapy individual sessions is beneficial and enhances family social and developmental relationships with these children. Jacobsen, McKinney and Holck (2014) provide strong empirical evidence that the dyadic music therapy intervention examined in their study improved emotional communication and interaction between parent and child after 6 to 10 sessions. Grant (2016) explores in depth the intense impact of the involvement of a member of the client's community upon the complex relations within group and individual music therapy, involving relationships between client and therapist, client and attendant, therapist and attendant, and the triangular relationship. From a synthesis of case studies and thematic analysis of interviews with music therapists and trainees, she concludes that the effect upon transference and countertransference processes is likely to be heightened by the presence of what she terms the 'auxiliary attendant'. The impact and intensity of the relationships involved are considered something to examine and work with, rather than ignore or treat as separate from the direct therapist–client relationship. These ever-changing and complex dynamics enhance the therapy process if handled well and if the attendant is well prepared and included in discussions with the therapist.

Within a family, parents and siblings may play an important role in assisting other family members to relate, to 'do' things and to develop external relationships outside the family. Siblings may also be inclined to feelings of rivalry and ambivalence, and this dynamic is sometimes played out by assistants who may find it hard to encourage their participants and who may be hostile, resistant or passive and unhelpful within the group setting as a result of unconscious (or even conscious) envy or rivalry towards a colleague who appears to have a special relationship with a group, or who has skills they do not possess.

The historical prevalence and nature of group music therapy in hospital settings

While assistants have always been used regularly in music therapy sessions, there has been little emphasis on their inclusion and a lack of in-depth study and investigation in the literature. In the 1970s, group work in hospital settings for people with severe learning difficulties and mental health problems was more prevalent than individual work. Assisting people to be able to make use of a larger group relationship seemed integral to this relationship between the attendee and their significant other or assistant. Here, the model of the family is an important theoretical consideration. It is important to note that there may be layers of transference and countertransference relationships and meaning behind the ordinary dynamics between colleagues at work which, when working with disturbed participants, it is important to understand through discussion in supervision. At best, these dynamics also make possible a better understanding of participants and of the group music therapy process. Although it may not always be important or appropriate to analyse them, they should always be held in mind as possible factors in the working music therapy group alliance. In this context, group members are often reliant upon a helpful bond with an assistant, physically or emotionally, in order to participate and find meaning in the music therapy relationship.

In a family, especially where young children are not able to travel independently or unassisted, accompaniment by parents or older siblings to assist them safely on their journey is routine. In the same way, in order for participants to access music therapy groups, many populations need to be assisted. Those accompanying may stay and join in the activity in order to facilitate enjoyment and participation. They know the person intimately and are an extension of their inner and outer world, and sometimes their physical world when physical assistance is needed.

The intimate nature of the assistant–patient relationship

One of my earliest experiences as a music therapist was working as an assistant in a 'Music and Movement' group (see Chapter 12), run by a music therapist, where my role was to physically assist learning-disabled participants' movements as advised by physiotherapists, in relation to the moment-by-moment improvised music. In that quite intimate relationship I witnessed the dynamic of musical interaction enabling a close, more relaxing bond to develop week by week. Variation and sensitivity to musical pace and metre appeared to increase trust and synchrony within the working relationship. I considered reflecting upon countertransference as important in this context, and at times I felt that I was functioning in a parent or sibling 'role' within this intimate process for people who lacked a significant other in their lives and were extremely disabled.

This weekly experience over some months also made me wonder how people cared for residents who were severely learning impaired and physically disabled without the use of music. Music provided an accessible way of relating to these multiply physically and learning-disabled participants, through musical synchronising, meeting and matching mood, containing emotional states and enabling relaxation. Such experiences can have a profound effect in later work, enabling the music therapist to understand more deeply the potential and nature of the role of those supporting and assisting professional music therapists. In the Master of Arts training course in my role as lecturer, I find that trainees who have had previous experiences of assisting music therapists, or who have previously been in a caring role, are more aware of how to include therapeutically significant others positively in the music therapy setting.

Assistants in groups for people with dementia

Previously I have discussed a group approach in music therapy and dementia (Odell-Miller 1995) including research outcomes indicating that group music therapy may help develop levels of engagement within groups with assistants attending as relational partners of the persons with dementia. Well-known material such as songs, or original improvised material, is enacted musically between different members in pairs, threes, small groupings or as a whole group. Working in, and being aware of, a whole group may be hard for a person in the final stages of dementia, and their immediate relational non music therapist partner may be crucial to gaining a feeling of music therapy groupness.

A group for people with dementia might include six to eight people, each with an assistant sitting next to them so that they can get the most from the group while the music therapist works to keep the musical flow and dynamic consistent and grounded. The music therapist can focus upon the musical and group dynamics in terms of the overall musical structure, responding in the moment to what is needed. It is also possible to reflect the group dynamics musically, and listening to the whole is important for this and is facilitated by the assistants' close contact with members around the group.

An excerpt from early clinical research (Odell-Miller 1995) describes the role of the assistants (termed 'helpers') as intuitively encouraging participants by musically interacting or holding back:

For example if a member began humming or beating in a particular way, the therapist would interact using the same instrument or a different one to build on this. This could lead to helpers encouraging others to join in, or remain as a dialogue between the therapist and one member. (p.99)

Decisions about level of interaction and contact, and also type of musical approach or technique, depended upon what seemed necessary to the helpers and therapist in their direct relationship with the participants in the moment. For example, providing support in an improvised duet with the assistant, where the therapist is facilitating their musical relationship, was a regular occurrence (compare with Chapters 1 and 13 of this volume). The assistants, occupational therapists or nurses, who spent a large part of their working day enabling the person with dementia to access daily activities, took part in other therapies and arts-based or occupational activities, or actively accompanied them in undertaking practical activities of daily life. The musical facilitation could thus add an extra layer of relating which could perhaps extend to a different way of emotional or social engagement, inside and outside the group, sometimes by becoming more playful for example, or changing the emotional and social quality and understanding of 'being with' the person with dementia.

Other musical approaches would enable the creation of a feeling of the participant musically leading the whole group in a duet with the assistant, for example, or encourage freedom of expression between the pair, with the therapist taking a musically 'containing' role. This could mean the therapist playing firm harmonic rhythmic notes in the bass register while the member and assistant improvise in a free way, higher up the keyboard, or sharing a large drum or bass metallophone.

A participant and helper may share a drumming dialogue where the aggressive drumming in irregular rhythms is contained and supported by the therapist harmonically. The dynamic of the relationship between the group, subgroups (trio and pairs) and between different members or assistants and therapist can be likened to the family, with a parental role taken by the therapist – perhaps with two rival siblings expressing their feelings of aggression, or even of envy or conflict, openly and in a way which can bring relief.

Although the therapist has countertransference reflections to draw upon, considering their possible meaning in each instance, it is not always appropriate to share these thoughts with participants who may be severely cognitively impaired. For this population, exploring and analysing relationships verbally may not have explicit meaning. But the authentic musical and non-musical relating among the therapist assistants and participants can be implicitly experienced, and the meaning discussed and reflected upon by assistants and therapists in group meetings. Discussions can also take place between therapist and assistants in a group during the moment-to-moment unfolding of the events and process, wondering aloud with the participants about what might be happening; although not all members will gain clarity of meaning, this may act as clarification for the therapist and assistant in order to move forwards in a particular way, without appearing to be talking 'over' the group members or interrupting the group process.

The types of musical structures set up in such groups will vary depending upon the needs and moods of the members at the time, but they include sharing instruments in pairs, or using instruments in the centre of the circle for members to be helped towards by assistants, while the music therapist maintains musical flow through structured and free musical improvisations. There would also be 'solos', sometimes accompanied in 'concerto' style by the therapist, assistants or other group members.

Acute adult mental health settings

The other setting to be considered is the acute admission ward, where recent research has shown that music therapy group members benefit from seeing other members making music and succeeding, and also welcome active involvement from the music therapist, especially through the use of pre-composed songs and also songwriting (Carr, Odell-Miller and Priebe 2013; Carr 2014).

Music therapists often work as specialists, arriving at a home, ward or unit as 'outsiders', external to the core team or establishment. In an acute-admission-ward setting where I worked in the 1970s, a member of the 'in house' team would ideally attend the music therapy group alongside patients, acting to 'carry the culture' and as a 'family member' linking with the whole community. The patient population changed each week, so attendees who were not music therapists provided stability and enabled a core group process to exist. I was usually able to attend regularly, thus building up a rapport with the changing group of members and therapist. The music therapist should also be a member of the community and attend appropriate community meetings or meet with staff prior to the group, in order to better understand the dynamics on the ward that day and gain a perspective on likely participants.

A helpful model on an acute admission ward can be for the assistant in the music therapy group to be a permanent member of the nursing, junior medical or occupational therapy staff on the ward. There may also be students attending, but their roles may be more transitory. The role of the assistant or co-therapist in the group is one of representing the ward 'family' as a culture carrier and also to provide a grounding presence, when members may be new to each other in a fast-changing population. These assistants, or sometimes co-therapists, may be able to act as collaborator, or advocate, and provide a secure base as the music therapist necessarily only visits the community or ward once a week.

In a therapeutic community or similar setting, where roles are sometimes overlapping and 'blurred', assistants to the 'external' or 'outsider' music therapist may act as an advocate in accompanying the participants to different sessions, and facilitating transfer of information and cultural dynamics from one therapy setting to another. In an acute setting with an emphasis upon group work and community participation, such groups often offer ways of understanding the living dynamics on the ward and unit as well as fulfilling therapeutic objectives for each individual participant. Historically it has been normal practice for music therapists to work with assistants who made connections between the dynamics within the group therapy session and events on the ward, such as: '…that rather cacophonous music reminds me of the noisy disturbed events in the night on the ward last night', or '…it sounds as if we are celebrating, as the music sounded like the party we had yesterday for Mary's birthday'. I am talking here of a more confident assistant role where trained members of staff regularly attended as co-workers or assistants, as distinct from some assistant roles discussed elsewhere in this volume.

The assistant can act as 'moderator' and facilitator encouraging people to participate by modelling, as they know people well, whereas the music therapist may only meet them once. The music therapist can gauge how much to focus upon a particular participant, by observing the reactions of the assistant known to the participants on a daily basis.

Their reactions can be both musical and non-musical, and some regular training for such assistants is desirable, such as regular meetings with the music therapist and workshops run on the ward for staff. The scenario below, which illustrates the facilitating role of attendees in an acute-ward music therapy group, is a composite based upon real events but in itself not an actual case. (The music therapist had been working with the same multidisciplinary team for 5 years, and during that time had always had at least one regular assistant from the trained staff team regularly attending the music therapy group. In addition, students were involved as assistants for 12- to 20-week periods during placements, and also worked closely and regularly with the groups.)

CASE STUDY[1]: A TYPICAL SCENARIO

Fostering secure attachment to facilitate play

Ann is suffering from symptoms of paranoid schizophrenia, Hazel has severe depression and Roy is feeling quite elated and manic; he has a diagnosis of bipolar disorder. Group members are accompanied to the music therapy group by a psychiatric nurse named Polly. She is a member of the ward team and is also the case manager for Ann. The music therapist, Colleen, welcomes everyone and encourages them to introduce themselves using a musical instrument and then choosing the next person to play. Ann shouts out that she knows everyone is looking at her, and there is an outburst from other members who try to tell her to be quiet and stop interrupting. At this point the music therapist starts to play the piano gently, and Polly joins in, on the metallophone, introducing herself and also looking at Ann, while improvising a song in triple time about how pleased she is to be there. It turns into a waltz, and Polly looks warmly at Ann, who then picks up her beaters and joins Polly next to her, sharing the metallophone also in waltz style. The close link between Polly and Ann enables Ann to become involved and move away from her paranoid fears for the rest of the session.

In this scenario Polly was able to use her knowledge of Ann and it was as if Polly could act as a family member – a comforting link and quasi-attachment figure in those moments, which allowed Ann to become absorbed and playfully trusting of the others for the rest of the therapy group.

In my experience, anyone present in the acute-ward music therapy group is treated as part of it, and not as an observer or visitor. The music therapist's attitude and manner towards any attending member, including other staff or those accompanying participants, should be inclusive. This may mean enlisting the attendee as a co-worker or helper to the whole group, or even developing a relationship as co-therapist

1   This case study is fictional.

over time; or as in the above example, in the moment, thinking about the attendee as related to a specific member with whom they are acting as an advocate or fellow participant or quasi-family member, facilitating the member to gain the most from the therapy. As such, it is extremely helpful and important for communication to take place between the therapist and attendee after the session, or in between sessions when appropriate. This can be in the form of a review of the group or as part of training, or purely a short conversation exchanging any feedback and information, which will help in the future.

Boundaries in this model are necessarily different from those in the closed therapy group. Attendees will need some training in how and when to keep a boundary between what happens inside and outside the group, depending upon the open, closed or semi-closed nature of the group, and the exact relationships and roles of non-music therapist attendees, but this is something the music therapist and attendees can think about in discussions between sessions. The symbolic role of the non-music therapist staff attendee may be important, and there should be some reflection upon whether they are taking on a role similar to a family member or (in the case of the acute admission ward when people are detained under the Mental Health Act) more one of custodian.

Conclusion

This area of non-music therapy assistant practice, neglected in the literature thus far, is crucial and integral to the music therapy group process and must be considered differently from the role of co-therapist. A co-therapist is not necessarily linked to a particular participant or group of participants in a special way outside the group, and their role is to facilitate the whole group. The role of an assistant providing a link between the inner and outer lives of the therapy group needs to be considered by the music therapist dynamically and inclusively as discussed above. The thought given to role, representation, symbolic meaning and dynamic musical interaction between the patient participants, music therapist and assistants is crucial and should include consideration of conscious and unconscious processes. Furthermore, training for both music therapists and others who may assist music therapists is important. Hopefully the work described in this chapter and this book as a whole will contribute to the training process and to putting a greater emphasis upon this phenomenon during music therapy training in particular.

References

Carr, C. (2014) 'Modelling of Intensive Group Music Therapy for Acute Adult Psychiatric Inpatients.' PhD thesis, Barts and the London School of Medicine and Dentistry, Queen Mary University of London.

Carr, C., Odell-Miller, H. and Priebe, S. (2013) 'A systematic review of music therapy practice and outcomes with acute adult psychiatric in-patients.' *PLoS ONE 8*, 8, e70252.

Grant, E. (2016) 'An Exploration of the Impact of Involving an Auxiliary Attendant from a Client's Immediate Community in Music Therapy.' Unpublished master's thesis, Anglia Ruskin University, Cambridge.

Jacobsen, S.L., McKinney, C.H. and Holck, U. (2014) 'Effects of a dyadic music therapy intervention on parent–child interaction, parent stress, and parent–child relationship in families with emotionally neglected children: a randomized controlled trial.' *Journal of Music Therapy 51*, 4, 310–332.

Odell-Miller, H. (1995) 'Approaches to Music Therapy in Psychiatry with Specific Emphasis upon a Research Project with the Elderly Mentally Ill.' In T. Wigram, B. Saperston and R. West (eds) *The Art and Science of Music Therapy: A Handbook*. Chur: Harwood Academic Press.

Oldfield, A. (2011) 'Parents' Perceptions of Being in Music Therapy with Their Children.' In J. Edwards (ed) *Music Therapy and Parent–Infant Bonding*. Oxford: Oxford University Press.

Chapter 6

'Let Them Bring Their Own Song'

A Qualitative Study of Developing Relationships Between Care Staff and Nursing Home Residents with Dementia Through Music Therapy and Dance Movement Therapy Groups

Ruth Melhuish

Background

The publication of the National Dementia Strategy in the UK (Department of Health 2009) endorsed significant developments in dementia care over the previous two decades which were led by the pioneering work of Tom Kitwood. Kitwood (1997) advocated a 'person-centred' approach to dementia care that addresses the emotional, relational, sensory and spiritual needs of the individual with dementia, and also places emphasis on the impact of the living environment and day-to-day relationships. This approach has stimulated the development of a wide range of psychosocial interventions in dementia care and led to increased recognition of their value as a serious alternative to the standard pharmacological treatments (Douglas, James and Ballard 2004; Kverno *et al.* 2009; Cooper *et al.* 2012). National Dementia Strategy guidelines promote quality treatment for people with dementia and stress the need to support and enhance the input of care staff; it is in this context that music therapy and dance movement therapy are continuing to develop evidence of their effectiveness.

The potential to use music therapy (MT) and dance movement therapy (DMT) to support those with a cognitive impairment, even at an advanced stage, has long been recognised (Clair 1996; Aldridge 2000; Coaten 2001; Nyström and Lauritzen 2005; Ridder and Aldridge 2005; Ridder, Wigram and Ottesen 2009; Newman-Bluestein and Hill 2010). The emotional, psychological and social benefits of MT groups for people with dementia were identified by researchers in UK National Health Service settings (Odell-Miller 1995; Moss 2003; Powell 2006). A randomised controlled trial carried out by Hsu *et al.* (2015) in care home settings showed significant improvements in the well-being of people with dementia who received regular individual MT, as well as a reduction in behavioural and psychological symptoms of dementia (BPSD). In contrast, the control group which did not receive MT showed a decline in well-being and increased BPSD.

Recent systematic reviews of MT in dementia found several studies which identify a range of positive effects. These effects include a reduction in the cognitive, behavioural and psychological symptoms of dementia as well as improved social, emotional and physiological functioning (McDermott *et al.* 2013; Vink, Bruinsma and Scholten 2013). MT has also been shown to have a positive impact on the environment in both community and care home settings, helping to improve staff morale and foster closer relationships between staff and residents (Powell 2006, 2010; Pavlicevic *et al.* 2013; Hsu *et al.* 2015). A few studies have found benefits of MT for both paid and unpaid carers, who report greater satisfaction in their caring role and more engagement with the person receiving care (Bright 1992; Clair and Ebberts 1997; Brotons and Marti 2003).

Research into DMT is increasing, led by Karkou and Meekums (2014), who are currently conducting a Cochrane Review to assess the effect of different forms of DMT on behavioural, social, cognitive and emotional problems of people with dementia. A systematic literature review of various dance-based interventions, including psychomotor dance therapy, social dancing and dance improvisation therapy, in care homes (Guzmán-García, Hughes, James *et al.* 2012) found seven qualitative and three quantitative studies which showed a decrease in behavioural and psychological symptoms of dementia as well as improvements in the quality of interaction between staff and residents. Kowarzik (2006) evaluated a staff training programme developed by the late Marion Violets Gibson, who drew elements from her DMT practice to enable residential care workers to support people with dementia. Through observational assessment of clients, video analysis of sessions and interviews with trainees, Kowarzik showed how Gibson's programme opened up new avenues of communication for both residents and care workers.

The study described in this chapter explored a collaborative approach between a music therapist, a dance movement therapist and care staff working alongside residents in a nursing home. The study began in 2007, but the relevance of our findings is highlighted by recent research, especially in the field of MT and dementia. There continues to be a lack of consistency in the provision of MT and DMT in care homes; consequently, there are few opportunities to explore such collaborations and there is scope for further investigation of the potential benefits for staff and residents. The study examined the experience and perceptions of nurses and health care assistants who took part in either MT or DMT groups for residents, with the aim of understanding how direct involvement in these therapies might have an influence on staff attitudes and approaches to practice.

Participants

The study took place in a nursing home in inner London housing 30 residents with an average age of 76 years. Fifteen residents had a diagnosis of moderate dementia and 12 were at an advanced stage. At that time there was a staff-to-resident ratio of 1 to 3. MT and DMT services had been in place for several years. Ruth Melhuish (RM), the music therapist, and Catherine Beuzeboc (CB), the dance movement therapist, visited weekly on separate days to run their respective groups. The therapists had regular contact with the staff team, but this was limited by time constraints as each therapist was contracted to be on site only for 3 hours.

The study was initiated by RM and CB in response to an arts therapies service review, which identified a need to develop and evaluate ongoing provision in the home. RM's post was extended by 3 hours a week so that she could lead the study. RM and CB chose to focus on working more closely with staff through giving them the opportunity to participate regularly in the MT and DMT groups. This had the advantage of allowing the therapists to maintain the ongoing groups for residents while also developing closer links with staff.

RM and CB ran an initial workshop session for staff which provided information about the study and a brief practical introduction to MT and DMT. Fifteen of 34 staff members attended and 8 volunteers were recruited to participate in the project. One staff member did not complete the study due to illness. Table 6.1 shows staff demographic information using pseudonyms to preserve anonymity.

Table 6.1 Staff demographics

Staff	Qualifications	Dementia care experience (years)	Gender	Age (years)	Ethnicity
Alicia	Registered Mental Nurse	20+	F	50+	Southeast Asian
Naomi	Diploma in Mental Health Nursing	10–15	F	35–45	Black African
Jane	NVQ3	12	F	25–35	Black African
Chantal	NVQ3	10–15	F	25–35	Southeast Asian
Ruby	NVQ3	20+	F	50+	Black Caribbean
Alex	NVQ3	7	M	25–35	White British
Chris	NVQ3	6	M	25–35	Black African

Intervention

MT and DMT group sessions were carried out according to established practice (described in more detail below). Groups were open to all residents, with weekly attendance ranging from 8 to 12 people. In total, 24 residents attended at least one session during the period of the study. MT groups were held on a different floor each week in the sitting room, while DMT groups were held in a separate activities room. About 60% of residents attending the groups were independently mobile and the others were in wheelchairs. Groups lasted 50 to 60 minutes.

RM and CB shared a similar working model in their approach to running groups. The central aim was to recognise and facilitate spontaneous self-expression and to develop interaction through live or recorded music, movement and verbal responses. The work followed the pace of the participants, allowing time and space for musical, physical, verbal and emotional responses to be developed, choices to be made and individual wishes to be respected.

The MT group typically began with a familiar song played by RM on a keyboard to stimulate recognition. Subsequently, RM played and sang from a wide musical repertoire including popular music from the 1920s to the 1960s, folk tunes from different cultures to reflect the diversity of the group members (e.g. British Isles, Italian, Greek, Jamaican, African) and well-known classical themes such as Beethoven's *Ode to Joy*. Group members were encouraged to make requests and suggestions, to join in singing and to play a variety of percussion instruments which were provided. RM facilitated the participation of all group members in whole-group improvisations, as well as developing closer interactions in dyads with herself or another member of staff.

In the DMT group, CB invited residents to sit in a circle and began the session with a ball game or a movement of their choice, facilitating the development of eye contact and awareness of others. Residents could then choose from a selection of recorded music, for instance familiar songs and dance tunes from the 1920s to the 1960s, and music from different cultures, such as Ireland, the US and the Caribbean. CB mirrored people's body movements and encouraged them to share each other's movement, in order to develop interaction between group members. Sometimes residents would stand up to dance, supported by staff if necessary.

Procedure

The design was an exploratory qualitative study. MT and DMT groups were separately conducted once a week by RM and CB, respectively. Two staff members were assigned to each therapist, to assist in running the groups for 6 weeks. Prior to the study, staff participants completed a short questionnaire about their understanding and expectations of the project. At the end of the 6-week intervention, each of the four staff members took part in an in-depth individual interview based on a semi-structured interview schedule. Interviews lasted between 45 and 60 minutes. Questions were developed by RM and CB; they were constructed in order to prompt narration, reflection and evaluation of staff experience of taking part in the sessions. The above procedure was repeated with a second cohort of three staff. To minimise bias, the music therapist conducted interviews with the staff members who attended DMT groups, and the dance movement therapist conducted interviews with those staff who attended MT groups. The project was registered by North Central London Research Consortium as a service development project focusing on staff development.

The pre-intervention questions were as follows:

1. Why are you interested in taking part in the project?

2. What is your understanding of the aims and approach of MT and DMT?

3. What do you find most rewarding in your work with the residents?

The post-intervention questions were as follows:

1. Describe in your own words what happens in a typical MT/DMT session. (Prompt: If I was present in the session, what would I actually see happening?)

2. Tell me about one incident or event in the sessions that is especially memorable to you. What was important to you about it?

3. How has it affected your own work with the residents?

4. What do you think the residents gain from the sessions?

5. Were your expectations fulfilled?

6. Has your understanding of MT/DMT changed in any way? If so, how?

7. One of the main aims of this project is to enable staff to learn more about MT and DMT. What changes or improvements would you suggest to make it more effective?

Data analysis

Data were analysed using interpretative phenomenological analysis (IPA) (Smith 1996; Smith, Jarman and Osborn 1999). Interviews were audio recorded and transcribed in full by RM, who then undertook the initial analysis as described below.

A list of themes was compiled from readings of the first interview, and codes were assigned to each identified theme. For subsequent interviews, themes were matched to existing codes. If new themes appeared, new codes were created. The initial analysis comprised nine thematic clusters, which through a process of re-reading and re-organisation were reduced to four principal themes, each with subthemes. RM and CB then reviewed the analysis together. Drawing on their professional understanding and experience to interpret the data, they finalised the themes and linked them into an overall structure or matrix. In order to validate the main themes and subthemes of the study, the theme matrix was further reviewed and categorised by an external researcher with expertise in psychosocial interventions in dementia, Dr Azucena Guzman. Her findings were discussed and agreed with RM and CB and a matrix of three principal themes (one with three subthemes) was finalised. These are described below.

Results

Theme 1: Discovering residents' skills and feelings

Staff commented on the impact of the therapy sessions on the residents. They observed how the groups engaged the residents and stimulated different forms of participation. This enabled staff to gain a greater understanding of residents' individual skills and abilities, as well as their capacity to respond on an emotional level. The sessions were seen to provide important mental, physical and sensory stimulation:

> Jane: It stimulates their brain. When they listen to music or when they are singing it makes them remember olden days, they come back to their past.

> Chantal: It's like an exercise for them…the music will make [them] move…she sits on her wheelchair and dances…she lifts up her legs like this and like that.

Chris: …to give them the opportunity to touch what they haven't touched before.

What appeared to be of greater importance, however, was the sense of fun and enjoyment that often characterised the sessions:

Ruby: Everybody enjoyed that, such great fun, it went down a storm, actually.

Alicia: They were really enjoying the sessions; participation is good.

Chris: …let people be happy…bring joy back to them.

The opportunity to take part and join in with the group was seen to reduce residents' isolation, allowing for the development of communication, social interaction and self-expression, which had a profound impact on their mental well-being:

Ruby: They communicate with other residents and staff as well. R (a resident) at one time never used to talk to anyone on the floor; she sulks a lot, but in the groups I find she does very well, like a flower, you know, she just opens up, gets involved.

Naomi: They start to explain their feelings, relating their ideas and views…some service users will come in very low in mood, very subdued, but by the time they are leaving here, they're fine.

The groups were not only seen to be enjoyable and stimulating, however. Staff reported how they could also support residents in expressing and sharing difficult feelings such as anger, frustration and loss:

Naomi: This one's saying, if I ever had a wish, I would always wish for my wife to come back, and you could tell from the facial expression of all the other service users, they really felt it was really a bad feeling, because apparently the wife died, so he couldn't care with all these earthly things, but that was only his one wish that can be fulfilled.

The ability and motivation of residents to take part in the groups was often unexpected by the staff, and in several cases they witnessed an almost transformative effect. In a MT session, a woman who was usually seen to be quiet and withdrawn became very alert and responsive, much to the surprise of the staff member present:

> Jane: That day, she gave us at least two or three songs…she was very alert and I was so surprised. *Oh, so she can talk, she can participate in music therapy.* That really surprised me.

Even greater changes were observed in one resident who was reported to be frail and highly dependent on staff for her personal needs:

> Naomi: She used to say she can't dry her body, she used to say she can't hold onto anything, she used to say she couldn't walk, but when we got here she was the most forward lady, she would get on with it, even you could see the strength in her hand with throwing and kicking the ball. After that, I have seen a lot of changes in her…she is not using a wheelchair on the floor, she can talk when she is ready, she can dry herself… it was funny…when she's on the floor she doesn't say much, but when she comes to the group, she just outshines everybody.

It is notable that these reported changes were also sustained outside the session. These accounts illustrate how participation in the sessions with the residents enabled staff to learn more about the skills and capabilities of each resident and, as a result, to appreciate their individual personalities more fully.

Theme 2: Learning from therapists' skills to change care practice

Staff described some positive outcomes of the project which were a useful learning experience and contributed to changes in their own approach to the residents. They identified key elements of the therapeutic approach, and these elements were categorised into the following three subthemes:

Time, space, pace

Staff observed how the therapists paced themselves carefully in their interactions with residents, allowing ample time and space to explore and respond during group activities:

> Ruby: She hold [it], look at it. Although she's seen it several times, she'll be reading it…we go with them, at their pace.

Staff described greater attention to body language and other techniques to support good communication, including the importance of a sensory approach when language may not be adequate:

> Alex: A lower tone of voice, being calm, approach the client one to one, maybe eye contact…getting down with them at their level.

> Naomi: You need to give them time, you don't need to rush them… they want to know who you are, they want to read your body language, they want to appreciate what you are talking about. Some of them…touching makes them happy, and by reading them you will understand exactly what their needs are and their understanding.

In the busy nursing home environment there was a clear contrast between the therapists' pace and that of the staff, who responded to this in different ways:

> Alicia: We do give them a chance, but we don't give as much chance as Catherine taught us to give.

> Chantal: I don't think I could do her job as she have patience, isn't it!

Choice

The element of choice was seen to be central to the therapists' approach to the residents. Staff reported that residents were not compelled to attend the sessions each week, and there was no obligation to stay for the entire session:

> Naomi: Catherine will always introduce herself so that they can warm to her and either accept to join or decline to join the group.

> Alex: The group may run for one hour, but there's nothing to say that the client has to participate for that period of time. Even though people only participate for 5 or 10 minutes, that's equally important as, say, them participating for the whole session.

The therapists were seen to encourage and support individuals in making their own decisions and choices within the groups as well:

> Chris: Ruth she make them to have a choice of what to play with the instrument.

> Jane: She ask them do you have any song you'd like to sing?

This appears to have had an impact on how staff approached residents in their own work, enabling them to understand and experience the potential benefits of offering more choice and freedom to residents during everyday routines:

> Alicia: So though I have been nursing for many years, I just didn't know the importance of allowing them to make a choice. We need to have an idea built in our mind that it's important to give them a chance, allow them to make the choice to a degree like, say, meals and things, you know. There's a lot of difference from like asking them to come or telling them to do things…better to allow them to.

Following the residents' lead

The staff noted how the therapists supported the residents in taking the lead as much as possible, facilitating a considerable degree of autonomy through an open, flexible approach. They reported that sessions developed in a spontaneous, unplanned way:

> Ruby: It can also go in different directions, depends on what one of the residents decides to do…it leads off a little bit sometimes, depending on what they want to do.

Residents could take the opportunity to be assertive:

> Alicia: One of our residents, she say, 'I would like to tell you that we don't want to do what you want us to do, we want you to do what *we* want', and we respected her request…so the whole session had to be Irish, according to her request, and she was so pleased…and said she had a fulfilling day.

The flexibility of the therapists' approach, their ability to respond to the unexpected and to support self-determination for individuals brought about a change in staff attitudes and expectations in their interactions with the residents:

> Ruby: My expectations have changed as well. You get to learn that you can also be more flexible yourself…more choice…more space, more time…

Staff highlighted the value of being released from their normal activities in order to concentrate on observing another professional at work:

Alicia: When we were working, we didn't pay much attention because we do hundreds of things, because [we are] always busy, but when we got a chance, a full-time opportunity to observe what and how Catherine deal with the session...that was really, really a big lesson and good...uh...therapeutic value.

As a result, it appears that their communication skills improved, for example finding greater meaning and purpose in conversations with the residents:

Ruby: Sometimes when they say something, we just take it at face value, what they mean, but you know if you sort of probe it and talk a little bit more into it, you actually know what they mean or what they're talking about. I talk to them more about, like, families...their life they had before...work and all that, you know.

Ruth: You do that more now than you did before?

Ruby: Yes, I do that more than I used to.

Staff also reported more confidence in organising groups and activities themselves:

Alex: It's given me a bit of an idea of how to run an open group. I've got ideas on other groups that I'd like to run myself. I've put some planning down on paper.

Chris: [If] the music therapist is not around, I can handle it. I can arrange it myself.

Theme 3: Connection between staff and residents

The project provided an opportunity for staff to observe the therapists at work, to participate in MT and DMT sessions with the residents and to reflect on these experiences. Staff demonstrated increased insight and self-awareness, a more reflective, empathic approach and a greater sense of connection with the residents. This is illustrated in the following accounts.

The first account describes an understanding through personal experience of the emotional release that singing can provide:

Jane: When they are singing, I sing along with them, so I learned from there. Sometimes when I'm doing something, I still remember and I sing. Maybe you have something bothering you in your mind and you are singing – like you are bringing it out, that's how I feel it.

The second account conveys empathy and emotional resonance with a resident who in one session requested music from her own culture (Irish) to the exclusion of any other:

Alicia: And it was really heartbreaking and it was good. Though she was living in England for 45 years, she still had patriotism for her country, so that was a very valuable point – how their heart belongs to their native country.

Staff described a deeper understanding of the role and purpose of the therapy groups:

Naomi: I realise it's more than what I thought. The group formation, the empowerment, their participation, and knowing one another, the relationship [between] each other, and their approach, their different feelings, their different values, how they value their own issues. I thought it was really more to do with that.

Naomi's account emphasises the role of the therapy groups as a place where people can make themselves heard, explore relationships and come to know each other better as individuals. This understanding contributed to changing staff attitudes to the residents:

Chris: Before, maybe I'm trying to dominate, but now I see that it changed my way to let them have their own say. Normally I have my own say, I bring my own song any time I like. Let them bring their own song as well.

This theme highlights the staff experience of a sense of closer connection with the residents, a greater appreciation of their individuality and a commitment to supporting their right to autonomy and self-expression. The events and processes described in themes 1 and 2 appear to have supported the development of the new attitudes and insights expressed in theme 3, contributing to greater confidence and morale among the staff.

Discussion

The study identified three themes related to the impact on staff who worked closely alongside therapists in MT and DMT sessions for 6 weeks, as follows:

- They discovered more about the skills, capacities and emotional responses of residents.

- They identified specific features of the therapeutic approach that could be utilised in their own practice.

- They felt a sense of closer connection with the residents.

These findings indicate that closer collaboration between music therapists, dance movement therapists and care staff may be an effective means of improving interactions and supporting relationships between staff and residents in dementia care settings.

Previous research findings have similarly shown increased carer engagement following involvement in MT sessions (Clair and Ebberts 1997; Brotons and Marti 2003) and have described how the positive impact of MT can extend throughout the care setting (Powell 2010; Pavlecevic *et al.* 2013). All three themes support recent qualitative findings that link dancing to improvements in staff caring practice (Guzmán-García, Mukaetova-Ladinska and James 2012) and suggest that MT interventions can enable those with dementia to maintain their sense of identity and can help staff and residents to experience a sense of connection and relationship (McDermott, Orrell and Ridder 2014). Developing and maintaining positive relationships is an important goal in long-term care, as they are paramount in maintaining quality of life for people with dementia (Clare, Rowlands and Bruce 2008; Brown-Wilson and Davies 2009; Bradshaw, Playford and Riazi 2012; Daley, Newton and Slade 2013).

This study highlights the potential for music therapists, dance movement therapists and care staff to share skills and work together more effectively. Coaten (2001) has previously suggested that working alongside arts therapists helps to improve existing communication skills for staff, rather than supporting the acquisition of new skills in music and dance. Similarly, this study found that the main benefits described by staff were improved communication skills, increased empathy and greater ability to develop connections and relationships with residents.

Strengths and limitations

The number of participants interviewed was small and the findings of this study are limited to this one setting, and thus may not be applicable on a wider scale. Nevertheless, the study demonstrates the positive effects of MT and DMT in a long-term dementia care setting, both for the residents and for the staff, who appear to have benefited regardless of their varying levels of experience, skill and qualification. Staff were committed to the project, with over 80% attendance overall. In the interviews they supplied rich data, which were independently validated by an external researcher with expertise in psychosocial interventions in dementia care.

It is clear that greater objectivity in gathering the data might have been achieved if it had been possible to involve the external researcher at an earlier stage, for example to monitor staff–resident interactions during the sessions and to conduct separate interviews. There was little evidence of any negative aspects of participation, but this may have been because the interviews were conducted by the group facilitators known to the staff. Efforts were made to reduce bias by ensuring that therapists did not interview staff they had worked alongside.

A significant practical problem encountered, which would have an impact on replication of the study, was the difficulty of reconciling the researchers' requirements with the demands of the shift rota. It became apparent that staff sometimes attended the sessions when they were meant to be off duty. For a future study, careful planning with the home manager would be required to ensure that staff participants be properly supported by being allowed release from their work rather than relying on their goodwill. It is recognised that this could present a real challenge in the care home setting, where staffing levels to cover routine care tasks are often critical.

Although the focus of the study was on the experience of staff, it would have been illuminating to try to gain feedback from residents about their own experiences regarding the sessions and relationships with staff; this should be considered for future studies, notwithstanding the inherent difficulties of interviewing those with cognitive impairment. A further study could also incorporate the therapists' own reflections on their experience of the collaboration with staff as an additional perspective. A record of events, issues and developments, including both positive and negative feedback, could be kept through a reflective diary. This would also help to clarify and validate the role of the therapists' professional training and experience in facilitating discussion and working through the emotional challenges which inevitably arise when working closely with residents.

Further considerations

McDermott *et al.* (2014) have since highlighted the need to identify not only *what* can be achieved through music therapy intervention, but also *why* and *how*. This study offers some clues to understanding *why* MT and DMT may be an effective way of supporting staff development. It seems clear that it was not the media of music and dance alone that contributed to the positive outcomes of this project; the therapists' training and approach also played a vital role. For example, theme 2 indicates that there are certain fundamental elements of the therapists' approach, such as attending to individual pace, and supporting autonomy and choice, that promote good communication and relationships, and that these may be effectively imparted to staff through regular involvement in either MT or DMT sessions and subsequently applied in their own work. Another important factor to consider is the nature of the nursing home environment, which is typically characterised by busy routines of daily care. Staff can feel that they are under intense pressure to complete the essential physical tasks such as washing, dressing and feeding (Froggatt, Davies and Meyer 2009). In contrast, staff taking part in the MT and DMT sessions could spend less pressured time with the residents, engaging with them in shared activities that were often resident led, consisted largely of non-verbal means of communication and did not aim to achieve set goals. The therapists' approach to running the groups enabled residents to take initiatives, to express authentic feelings and to reconnect with capabilities (Shustik and Thompson 2001; Kowarzik 2006), which in turn helped staff to learn more about the personalities and skills of the people they cared for prior to the onset of dementia.

In further considering why and how this project was successful in supporting staff development, it may also be helpful to identify elements of the learning experience offered to participants. This can be described as a process of discovery through participation, observation and reflective discussion which took place over a period of weeks. Actual involvement in the sessions encouraged staff to experience the media of music and dance for themselves, offering new ways of relating to residents, which required immediacy and real emotional engagement. Observing the therapists allowed the staff time away from the practical, task-oriented aspects of care to watch other professionals modelling different approaches to interaction. From this they could develop their own skills. The post-session discussions were an opportunity for reflection and processing of feelings which is not often available to staff in the care home environment. This may have had a significant impact on the development of insight and self-awareness demonstrated by the staff who took part in this project.

The importance of learning from feelings and experiences has been emphasised by dementia care trainers and practitioners (Packer 2000a and 2000b; Bowe and Loveday 2004; Bender *et al.* 2008) drawing inspiration from Kitwood (1997), who extended his person-centred approach to staff, recommending an experiential approach to training embedded in a process of action, reflection and consolidation of better practice.

While it might be thought that staff who participated in DMT and those who took part in MT would have very different experiences, it is notable that the staff appeared to gain similar insights regardless of whether they had attended MT or DMT sessions. The project findings highlight the similarities of the MT and DMT approach: the therapists did not set out to compare and contrast their respective art forms, but rather to focus on their common aims of facilitating emotional expression and the development of connections and relationships with others. This could assist in validating their shared professional profile as arts therapists and supporting their role not only in the long-term dementia care environment but also in a wide range of other health care settings (Health and Care Professions Council 2014).

Future directions, clinical implications and personal reflections

Living Well with Dementia (Department of Health 2009) continues to be the guiding principle in contemporary dementia care; yet translating principles into caring practice is not always straightforward, especially in long-term care. For example, lack of staff training and supervision is highlighted by Bradshaw *et al.* (2012) as one of the barriers to improving relationships between staff and residents in nursing homes. The results of this small project indicate that working alongside professional therapists and people with dementia in MT and DMT sessions was an effective means of supporting care staff and developing their skills. According to the home manager (in a personal communication) it also helped them to feel valued and to value their own work. It follows that if these findings were to be generalised, service managers and care home providers might consider it an advantage to employ music and/or dance movement therapists, not only to benefit their residents but also as a cost-effective means of training and supporting their staff.

These preliminary findings reflect significant developments in music therapy practice in dementia over the past few years, in response to the move towards person-centred care. Alongside increased research in the field of MT and dementia, there has been a flowering of practice development, as evidenced by the *Music Therapy and Dementia Care in the 21st Century* conference held at Anglia Ruskin University in 2015. Here themes of interdisciplinary and multidisciplinary approaches, collaboration, inclusion, involvement of staff and family members, training and skill sharing with other practitioners can be identified throughout the conference programme. This suggests that a greater understanding of the role of music therapy in promoting quality of life, and especially the wider relationship needs of the person with dementia, is bringing about a move towards a more flexible, context-led and dementia-specific approach to therapeutic input.

This is certainly reflected in my own experience. Approaching and adapting to the challenges of working in a long-term dementia care environment has been a formative journey, starting from the need to think much more broadly about the nature of therapeutic practice, and how to provide a service that was effective and sustainable in the setting. This led to the development of the large open group as the centre of my practice in the home, embracing the often fragmented nature of the work, the unpredictability of resident engagement and the benefits and challenges of staff involvement. Closer collaboration with staff through this project greatly influenced my thinking about what is most important in the work, that is, the potential benefits for both residents and staff in maintaining relationships and quality of life. This understanding was also the foundation for developing an approach to evaluating music therapy groups in dementia care (Melhuish 2013), which has enabled me to focus more robustly on outcomes, to communicate more clearly about the work and to foster fruitful connections and collaborations with music therapy colleagues as well as other practitioners working in different settings.

The opportunity to collaborate with Catherine, my DMT colleague, has also been highly significant, allowing us to recognise our common goals and the potential for a collaborative approach to dementia care between arts therapists from different disciplines. This too was highlighted at the recent dementia care conference held by the International Centre for Research in Arts Therapies prior to the MT conference at Anglia Ruskin University in 2015.

Conclusion

In conclusion, it is to be hoped that collaborative efforts will continue to characterise and nurture arts therapies practice. There is undoubtedly scope for continuing to research and develop collaborative practices at all levels to improve caring relationships and quality of life, with potential applications both within and beyond the field of dementia care.

References

Aldridge, D. (2000) 'Overture: It's Not What You Do but the Way that You Do It.' In D. Aldridge (ed) *Music Therapy in Dementia Care*. London: Jessica Kingsley Publishers.

Bender, M., Horton, V., Rees, F. and Butler, A. (2008) 'Where women meet: Aren't we more alike than different?' *Journal of Dementia Care 8*, 6, 20–21.

Bowe, L. and Loveday, B. (2004) 'Strategies for Training and Organisational Change.' In Bradford Dementia Group (ed) *Reflective Practice in Dementia Care*. Bradford: Bradford University Press.

Bradshaw, S.A., Playford, E.D. and Riazi, A. (2012) 'Living well in care homes: a systematic review of qualitative studies.' *Age and Ageing 41*, 429–440.

Bright, R. (1992) 'Music Therapy in the Management of Dementia.' In G. Jones and B. Miesen (eds) *Care-Giving in Dementia: Research and Applications* (Vol. 1). London: Routledge/Tavistock.

Brotons, M. and Marti, P. (2003) 'Music therapy with Alzheimer's patients and their family caregivers: a pilot project.' *Journal of Music Therapy 40*, 2, 138–150.

Brown-Wilson, C. and Davies, S. (2009) 'Developing relationships in long-term care environments: the contribution of staff.' *Journal of Clinical Nursing 18*, 1746–1755.

Clair, A. (1996) 'The effect of singing on alert responses in persons with late stage dementia.' *Journal of Music Therapy 33*, 4, 234–247.

Clair, A. and Ebberts, A.G. (1997) 'The effects of music therapy on interactions between family caregivers and their care receivers with late stage dementia.' *Journal of Music Therapy 34*, 3, 148–164.

Clare, L., Rowlands, J. and Bruce, E. (2008) 'The experience of living with dementia in residential care: an interpretative phenomenological analysis.' *The Gerontologist 48*, 711–720.

Coaten, R. (2001) 'Exploring reminiscence through dance and movement.' *Journal of Dementia Care 9*, 5, 19–22.

Cooper, C., Mukadam, N., Katona, C., Lyketsos, C.G. *et al.* (2012) 'Systematic review of the effectiveness of non-pharmacological interventions to improve quality of life of people with dementia.' *International Psychogeriatrics 24*, 6, 856–870.

Daley, S., Newton, D. and Slade, M. (2013) 'Development of a framework for recovery in older people with mental disorder.' *International Journal of Geriatric Psychiatry 28*, 522–529.

Department of Health (2009) *Living Well with Dementia: a National Dementia Strategy.* London: Department of Health. Available at www.gov.uk/government/publications/living-well-with-dementia-a-national-dementia-strategy, accessed on 28 February 2016.

Douglas, S., James, I. and Ballard, C. (2004) 'Non-pharmacological interventions in dementia.' *Advances in Psychiatric Treatment 10*, 3, 171–179.

Froggatt, K., Davies, S. and Meyer, J. (2009) *Understanding Care Homes: A Research and Development Perspective.* London: Jessica Kingsley Publishers.

Guzmán-García, A., Hughes, J.C., James, I.A. and Rochester, L. (2012) 'Dancing as a psychosocial intervention in care homes: a systematic review of the literature.' *International Journal of Geriatric Psychiatry 28*, 9, 914–924.

Guzmán-García, A., Mukaetova-Ladinska, E. and James, I.A. (2012) 'Introducing a Latin ballroom dance class to people with dementia living in care homes: benefits and concerns – a pilot study.' *Dementia 12*, 5, 523–535.

Health and Care Professions Council (2014) *What Is an Arts Therapist?* London: Health and Care Professions Council.

Hsu, M., Flowerdew, R., Parker, M., Fachner, J. and Odell-Miller, H. (2015) 'The impact of music therapy on managing neuropsychiatric symptoms for people with dementia and their carers: a randomised controlled feasibility study.' *BMC Geriatrics 15*, 84. Available at http://bmcgeriatr.biomedcentral.com/articles/10.1186/s12877-015-0082-4, accessed on 14 April 2016.

Karkou, V. and Meekums, B. (2014) 'Dance movement therapy for dementia (protocols).' *The Cochrane Database of Systematic Reviews 3.* Art. No.: CD011022. Available at 10.1002/14651858.CD011022, accessed on 14 April 2016.

Kitwood, T. (1997) *Dementia Reconsidered: The Person Comes First.* Buckingham: Open University.

Kowarzik, U. (2006) 'Opening Doors: Dance Movement Therapy with People with Dementia.' In H. Payne (ed) *Dance Movement Therapy: Theory, Research and Practice* (2nd ed.). London: Routledge.

Kverno, K.S., Black, B.S., Nolan, N.T. and Rabins, P.V. (2009) 'Research on treating neuropsychiatric symptoms of advanced dementia with non-pharmacological strategies 1998–2008: a systematic literature review.' *International Psychogeriatrics 2*, 5, 825–843.

McDermott, O., Crellin, N., Ridder, H.M. and Orrell, M. (2013) 'Music therapy in dementia: a narrative synthesis systematic review.' *International Journal of Geriatric Psychiatry 28*, 8, 781–794.

McDermott, O., Orrell, M. and Ridder, H.M. (2014) 'The importance of music for people with dementia: the perspectives of people with dementia, family carers, staff and music therapists.' *Aging & Mental Health 18*, 6, 706–716.

Melhuish, R. (2013) 'Group music therapy on a dementia assessment ward: an approach to evaluation.' *British Journal of Music Therapy 27*, 1, 16–31.

Moss, H. (2003) 'Service evaluation: music therapy and medicine for the elderly.' *British Journal of Music Therapy 17*, 2, 76–89.

Newman-Bluestein, D. and Hill, H. (2010) 'Movement as the medium for connection, empathy, playfulness.' *Journal of Dementia Care 18*, 5, 24–27.

Nyström, K. and Lauritzen, S.O. (2005) 'Expressive bodies: demented persons – communication in a dance therapy context.' *Health 9*, 3, 297–317.

Odell-Miller, H. (1995) 'Approaches to Music Therapy in Psychiatry with Specific Emphasis upon a Research Project with the Elderly Mentally Ill.' In T. Wigram, B. Saperston and R. West (eds) *The Art and Science of Music Therapy: A Handbook.* Chur: Harwood Academic Publishers.

Packer, T. (2000a) 'Does person-centred care exist?' *Journal of Dementia Care 8*, 3, 19–21.

Packer, T. (2000b) 'Pass the hot potato: is this person-centred teamwork?' *Journal of Dementia Care 8*, 5, 17–19.

Pavlicevic, M., Tsiris, G., Woods, S., Powell, H. *et al.* (2013) 'The "ripple effect": towards researching improvisational music therapy in dementia care homes.' *Dementia.* Available at 10.1177/1471301213514419, accessed on 15 December 2015.

Powell, H. (2006) 'The voice of experience: evaluation of music therapy with older people, including those with dementia, in community locations.' *British Journal of Music Therapy 20*, 2, 109–121.

Powell, H. (2010) 'Weaving the threads together: music therapy in care homes.' *Journal of Dementia Care 18*, 4, 24–28.

Ridder, H.M. and Aldridge, D. (2005) 'Individual music therapy with persons with frontotemporal dementia: singing dialogue.' *Nordic Journal of Music Therapy 14*, 2, 91–106.

Ridder, H.M., Wigram, T. and Ottesen, A.M. (2009) 'A pilot study on the effects of music therapy in frontotemporal dementia.' *Nordic Journal of Music Therapy 18*, 3, 103–132.

Shustik, L. and Thompson, T. (2001) 'Dance/Movement Therapy: Partners in Personhood.' In A. Innes and K. Hatfield (eds) *Healing Arts Therapies and Person-Centred Dementia Care.* London: Jessica Kingsley Publishers.

Smith, J.A. (1996) 'Beyond the divide between cognition and discourse: using interpretative phenomenological analysis in health psychology.' *Psychology and Health 11*, 2, 261–271.

Smith, J.A., Jarman, M. and Osborn, M. (1999) 'Doing Interpretative Phenomenological Analysis.' In M. Murray and K. Chamberlain (eds) *Qualitative Health Psychology.* London: Sage.

Vink, A.C., Bruinsma, M.S. and Scholten, R.J.P.M. (2013) 'Music therapy for people with dementia.' *The Cochrane Database of Systematic Reviews 4.* Available at 10.1002/14651858.CD003477.pub2, accessed on 28 February 2016.

Further reading

Melhuish, R., Beuzeboc, C. and Guzman, A. (2015) 'Developing relationships between care staff and people with dementia through music therapy and dance movement therapy: a preliminary phenomenological study.' *Dementia.* Available at 10.1177/1471301215588030, accessed on 24 January 2016.

Chapter 7

Caregivers' Dual Role in Music Therapy to Manage Neuropsychiatric Symptoms of Dementia

Ming Hung Hsu

Introduction

Caregivers in dementia care

Caregivers are the backbone of the health and care of people living in dementia care homes. People living with dementia in a care home eventually lose many of their faculties such as memory, language, volition and identity. As cognition declines, simple aspects of day-to-day life, such as eating, drinking, washing and dressing, become extremely challenging for individuals and their caregivers. Many caregivers may echo the experience of their hair being pulled and their arms being scratched during personal hygiene interventions for care home residents. In some more serious situations, they may even require medical attention. Caregiving demands great physical, mental and emotional efforts to manage residents' symptoms and fulfil their care needs; however, time constraints owing to staff shortage or lack of training and support can compromise how caregivers perform their care duty.

The scope of this chapter

Within this context, this chapter discusses how individual music therapy in care homes could support not only residents but also their caregivers. This therapy enhances caregiving by equipping carers with additional skills, knowledge and an extraordinary role in enriching the lives of care home residents by prolonging the effects of music therapy outside therapy rooms on a day-to-day, and even more on a moment-by-moment, basis. The chapter illustrates caregivers' dual role in relation to music therapy, a role which is particularly prominent when managing neuropsychiatric symptoms, a global challenge and major therapeutic target in dementia care. The chapter is based on a doctoral study (Hsu *et al.* 2015), which more widely looked at how music therapy helps reduce neuropsychiatric symptoms of dementia and investigated how music therapy could be embedded in the context of care. The latter aspect of the study is examined here by means of qualitative results from caregivers' interviews.

Neuropsychiatric symptoms of dementia

The delivery of dementia care is challenged not only by the declining cognition of people with dementia, but also by a group of associated non-cognitive neuropsychiatric symptoms of dementia, including agitation, apathy, aberrant motor behaviour and psychosis, as well as mood and emotional disorders including depression and anxiety. These symptoms affect up to 92% of residents in dementia care homes (Margallo-Lana *et al.* 2001; Zuidema *et al.* 2007). The symptoms are associated with faster progression of the disease if untreated (Rabins *et al.* 2011). Different symptoms can develop intermittently during the course of dementia, but more persistent occurrence has been observed for apathy and aberrant motor behaviour such as excessive pacing, wandering and repetitive vocalisation (Aalten *et al.* 2005). The management of these symptoms often consumes a vast amount of staff time and resources. Agitation, for example, can be seen at different times throughout a day such as during personal hygiene interventions, mealtimes and in the late afternoon or evening – identified as sundowning syndrome – and additional staff time is required to ameliorate a resident's distressed feelings, as well as any physical or verbal agitated behaviour. This can disrupt staff work routine and impact on fellow residents who also need staff attention. In more serious cases, administrative workload can also be increased by reporting safeguarding issues to the relevant bodies. Staff stress can be aggravated by time constraints and inefficient levels of staffing, leading to care staff burnout, decreased morale and job satisfaction, increased sickness and turnover, and consequent reduced quality of life for residents. Moreover, inadequate staff coping strategies in the past have caused inappropriate use of psychotropic medications and physical restraints, as reported in media stories and health inspections.

Pharmacological and non-pharmacological interventions

Since the management of neuropsychiatric symptoms has become a pandemic issue in dementia care, attention has turned to understanding the causes of such symptoms as well as identifying preventive and coping strategies. So far, the pathogenesis of symptoms has been understood as derived from a complex interplay of psychological, social and biological factors (Cerejeira, Lagarto and Mukaetova-Ladinska 2012) with an emphasis on the role of neurochemical, neuropathological and genetic factors underlying the clinical presentation. Pharmacological interventions, including antipsychotics and anti-dementia drugs, have only demonstrated moderate effects. Additionally, reviews suggest that improvements in quality of life cannot be presumed from symptomatic reduction (Cooper *et al.* 2013).

Recent research has investigated the effectiveness of non-pharmacological interventions, often referred to as psychosocial interventions (Vernooij-Dassen *et al.* 2010; Lawrence *et al.* 2012; Orrell 2012; Dugmore, Orrell and Spector 2015). These include an array of sensory, psychological and behavioural interventions such as staff education, behavioural management techniques, pet therapy, aromatherapy, snoezelen, cognitive stimulation therapy and arts therapies. These interventions have been recommended as first-line treatment (Howard *et al.* 2001). Growing evidence suggests a positive impact on neuropsychiatric symptoms, cognition and quality of life (Spector *et al.* 2003; Livingston *et al.* 2005; Patel *et al.* 2014). These interventions attribute behaviours to unmet needs, environmental overload and interactions between individual, caregiver and environmental factors. For example, apathy can be seen not only as a symptom but also a prevalent phenomenon in care homes when residents are under-stimulated and spend most of the day dozing. Agitation and associated behaviours arise when residents experience undetected pain or distress in a noisy environment but cannot communicate this. Carers' vocal, facial and bodily expressions that are not adjusted to facilitate communication with residents can escalate residents' challenging behaviour. Addressing the causal relationship between factors and behaviours is key to these non-drug approaches, with prevention, symptom relief and reduction of caregiver distress the ultimate goals (Gitlin, Kales and Lyketsos 2012).

Music therapy in dementia care

Music therapy is a psychosocial intervention showing potential alleviating effects on symptoms of dementia (Livingston *et al.* 2005; Robinson *et al.* 2007; Olazarán *et al.* 2010; Dickson *et al.* 2012; Seitz *et al.* 2012). However, only short-term effects during and immediately after sessions are well evidenced (Livingston *et al.* 2005). Robust evidence of long-term effects remains scant (Vink, Bruinsma and Scholten 2003; Livingston *et al.* 2005; McDermott *et al.* 2013). Moreover, the term 'music therapy' is flexibly defined in review studies, referring either to interventions and activities delivered by nursing and research staff, such as listening or exercising to recorded music and singing or playing instruments along with recorded music (Ragneskog *et al.* 1996; Gerdner 2000; Sung *et al.* 2006; Cooke *et al.* 2010), or to formal therapy delivered by qualified music therapists, focused on developing an interpersonal relationship between the client and therapist through active music-making (Odell-Miller 1995; Svansdottir and Snaedal 2006; Raglio *et al.* 2008, 2010; Ridder, Wigram and Ottesen 2009; Solé *et al.* 2014).

Issues within the therapist-led intervention, such as limited knowledge of the mechanisms of therapy sessions, the role of music therapists and the theoretical model, may have contributed to blurring the line between music therapy and other music interventions (McDermott *et al.* 2013). How different music therapy methods or techniques relate to patients' context of care is also unclear (Guetin *et al.* 2012); therefore, the need for qualified music therapists in providing such therapy has been questioned. If singing or listening to singing is therapeutic, do patients need a music therapist to help them do so? Is active joint music-making between music therapist and client necessary, and how does this improve patient care? What difference can a music therapist make instead of a professional musician or someone with some musical training?

While these questions warrant further investigation, Ridder *et al.* (2013) and Hsu *et al.* (2015) both report a difference which individual music therapy can potentially make to staff perception of residents' symptoms. Ridder and colleagues found that twice weekly individual music therapy sessions over 6 weeks did not significantly reduce the frequency of agitation, but that staff perceived disruption from residents' agitated behaviours as significantly reduced. Hsu and colleagues found that weekly individual music therapy plus post-therapy communication with caregivers over 5 months also decreased caregivers' perception of residents' disruptiveness. The effects were found 2 months after the cessation of the interventions. These findings suggest that although individual music therapy may or may not change the intermittent presence of symptoms, it can impact over a prolonged period on how caregivers manage residents' symptoms. Hsu and colleagues emphasise the need for music therapist–caregiver communication. Systematic sharing of video excerpts from the sessions with caregivers allowed music therapists to relay preventive and coping strategies for neuropsychiatric symptoms to caregivers, thus sustaining a positive change in the care environment. The study noted that the effectiveness of this communication was dependent on music therapists' understanding of cognitive functions.

Staff training

Care home residents receive more contact time from caregivers than from any other health care professionals. This understandably puts caregivers at the forefront in managing residents' symptoms. Consistent evidence of effectiveness has been found in interventions involving behavioural management techniques centred on either patients' or caregivers' behaviour (Livingston *et al.* 2005). Among these training interventions, psychoeducation and teaching caregivers to change their interaction with patients appear to have lasting effects. This corroborates the findings of another staff training review (Spector, Orrell and Goyder 2013) that a change in staff behaviour can impact on residents' symptoms. The positive effects of changes to care practices can usually be maintained over time; however, an ongoing supervision system is needed to prevent staff from reverting to previous styles of care practice. As the review advises: 'Organisational factors, including management style, care culture, and rifts between staff groups, should also be considered when making changes to care practice' (p.363). Providing staff with sufficient skills and support to manage neuropsychiatric symptoms is essential to the safety and quality of life of people with dementia (Banerjee 2009). If caregivers' practice is the key to managing symptoms, embedding music therapy in care practice should maximise the effects. Music therapy requires care staff involvement as the key to successful implementation in care homes (Lawrence *et al.* 2012).

Integrating music therapy into care

Simply providing music therapy sessions in a care home does not constitute integrating music therapy into daily care. Music therapy clearly cannot work wonders when it is solely delivered to temporarily relieve symptoms. Symptoms may reappear after weekly music therapy sessions. What can caregivers do during this time? As psychosocial interventions work best when embedded into daily care (Vernooij-Dassen *et al.* 2010; Lawrence *et al.* 2012), music therapy should be delivered with a view to enhancing multidisciplinary working and influencing caregivers' thinking and action in their daily care practice. In the end, better quality of care and life for residents will validate this notion.

Regular and systematic communication between music therapists and caregivers is mutually beneficial, enabling music therapists to be seen as a necessity in the care team rather than as visiting professionals who only deliver services as required. Caregivers can obtain help from music therapists to better deliver individualised care. Music therapists can use caregivers' feedback to establish better working strategies with individual residents. Three elements require attention when establishing this communication. First, the content of the communication which can benefit caregivers' work should be clearly defined. Second, the most impactful and realistic method to bring about a consistent influence on care practice should be thoroughly sought and tested. Finally, this communication should be supported on an organisational level, for example, by making and renewing policies and procedures for staff to make use of psychosocial interventions (Lawrence *et al.* 2012; Orrell 2012; Dugmore *et al.* 2015). Time should be allowed for music therapist caregiver communication. Then caregivers can try out what they have learned from music therapists and incorporate the new ideas and methods into their practice. Most importantly, ongoing support should be available to help resolve difficulties and evaluate effectiveness. These elements will now be illustrated by examining the theoretical framework and set-up of a music therapy programme in care homes, to reveal caregivers' dual role, before and after individual music therapy sessions. Extracts from caregivers' interviews will elucidate the changes brought to care practice by music therapy.

Methodist Homes

Methodist Homes (MHA), a charitable care organisation supporting older adults, was founded by members of the Methodist Church in 1943. Today it provides care, accommodation and support services for more than 16,000 older people throughout Britain. Inspired by Christian concern, the charity's mission is to improve the quality of life of older people. In 2008, a music therapy programme was piloted and incorporated into the dementia care service in the charity's care homes. The programme currently runs in 54 dementia care homes. Residents receive weekly music therapy from 18 music therapists employed by the charity. The doctoral study behind this chapter was funded by MHA in collaboration with Anglia Ruskin University. The study employed a cluster randomised controlled trial to test the feasibility of embedding a music therapy programme in the dementia care services of two care homes. This is now a model being implemented in all 54 homes. The music therapy service was awarded a LaingBuisson Award in 2015 for achieving excellence in dementia care, and the charity is presently seeking funding to enable more frequent access to music therapy sessions.

MHA care homes

The indoor and outdoor layout of care homes varies, but all are purpose-built with facilities designed to support individuals with dementia nursing and residential care needs. The care homes involved in the study have *en suite* bedrooms. The accommodation can be located on different floors. Each home has communal areas such as main lounges, small quiet lounges and separate dining areas with fully fitted kitchens. Each care home has a hairdressing salon, a holistic therapy room, a cafe and a large living room leading out into an enclosed therapeutic garden.

Individual music therapy sessions are normally held in a small quiet lounge or a holistic therapy room away from the main living area. A keyboard, a guitar and a set of percussion instruments, including drums, cymbals, xylophones and metallophones, are provided for therapy sessions. Some ethnic or unique instruments, such as a sounding bowl, African djembes and small handheld instruments, may also be offered. In line with health and safety, the rooms have emergency buzzers and are clutter free to prevent trip hazards and allow sufficient space for residents in large reclining chairs.

Residents

Most of the residents are over 65 years of age and have a wide range of dementia nursing and residential care needs. Each resident receives individualised care according to care plans concerned with general health, tissue viability, nutrition, spiritual needs, mental health and so forth. Diagnoses of their dementia include Alzheimer's, vascular, Lewy Body and frontotemporal, as well as rarer conditions such as Korsakoff syndrome. The Mini Mental State Examination and the Global Deterioration Scale are used to assess functioning. Neuropsychiatric symptoms are assessed with various measures including the Neuropsychiatric Inventory and the Cohen-Mansfield Agitation Inventory.

The wider care home community

The care team, volunteers and residents' families are part of the wider care home community. Every member of staff is part of the care team. The care home manager, an administrator, carers, nurses and kitchen and maintenance staff can all contribute to residents' well-being; therefore, all staff members are provided with training in care delivery, health care standards and regulations. Alongside the above staff, a music therapist is appointed to the department of emotional and social well-being support in each home, which includes a chaplain, an activity coordinator and a reflexologist. Volunteers are recruited to assist the care team in various day-to-day jobs including helping residents during mealtime, helping with gardening and sometimes providing group activities. Some volunteers assist music therapists in therapy sessions.

Although not directly members of the care team, residents' families are at the core of the care homes. Families' knowledge of their loved ones, their opinions about the care provided, and their assistance and observations are highly valued. Regular support meetings for relatives, chaired by the care home manager or a member of staff, and sometimes attended by music therapists, are beneficial to the spouses of residents, who may feel isolated since their loved one came into care.

Theoretical framework of the MHA music therapy programme

Derived from the tradition of music therapy training in the UK since the 1960s, the programme is informed by psychoanalytical, psychodynamic, developmental and humanistic theories (Odell-Miller 1995). The therapy sessions delivered are akin to the work of Odell-Miller (1995, 1997, 2002) and Ridder et al. (2013). Insights from neuroscience and neuropsychology have further strengthened the clinical framework as recent advances in imaging techniques, such as functional magnetic resonance imaging and positron emission tomography, have yielded new understanding of the human brain and behaviours. Neurology and psychiatry may be the same speciality after all, as mounting evidence suggests a biological basis for functional disorders (Burton 2010, p.145). Dementia, a neurodegenerative disease, sits pertinently within this neuropsychiatric paradigm. It has therefore become increasingly necessary for music therapists working in the field to acquire a new language in order to communicate their work in relation to patients' health.

In a therapy session, a therapist can be seen as offering multiple sensory stimuli, giving his or her vocal, facial, bodily and musical expressions as social, affective and musical stimuli to a patient who could be viewed as the human brain. A key facet of therapist–patient communication is observing how the patient (the human brain) responds to the therapist (multiple sensory stimuli). Based on the therapist's observations during therapy, a patient's health status can be explained after sessions, when the basic understanding of neuropsychological constructs comes into play. The taxonomy of higher and lower cognitive functions, including thoughts, volition, types of attention, types of memory, sensorimotor modalities and emotions, are the major aspects to be identified and communicated. It is the music therapist's duty of care to provide feedback on any change observed to enable other health professions, such as carers, nurses, doctors and psychiatrists, to deliver better and safer care.

Music therapists in this setting should understand these basic neuropsychological constructs; otherwise, they would not know what to observe, what changes to identify, what functions a resident retains and what to communicate to staff. Adverse consequences, such as inappropriately starting or stopping certain medications, can happen when accurate information is not relayed between all the health professionals involved. The ethos of this programme is the use of music therapy and music therapists' knowledge to improve multidisciplinary communication. Patient safety always lies within the core of music therapists' practice as clinicians. This involves understanding diagnoses, prognosis, medications and risk assessments of patients' tissue viability, mobility and dexterity. Evaluation of clinical outcomes requires appropriate validated outcome measures so that care planning and delivery can be tailored to meet individual residents' levels of needs and thus improve quality of life.

Emotion regulation

Emotion regulation is a core aspect of the music therapy programme, as of all cognitive and behavioural therapies (Phan and Sripada 2013, p.396), which highlights the need to understand what cognitive functions are still accessible to a resident and utilise these functions to make emotion regulation work. Emotion regulation is a growing area for research in the field of affective neuroscience. An emotion can be seen as a transition from perception and appraisal to response. Emotions, when triggered, can generate changes across multiple cognitive and physiological systems and specific action tendencies (Phan and Sripada 2013, p.376). The subsections below describe the four-stage model of emotional regulation proposed by Gross and Thompson (2007).

Situation selection and modification

This initial stage focuses on how a person chooses or avoids situations leading to desired or undesired emotions, respectively, and modifies situations to reduce emotional impact. With dementia, a resident may be unable to avoid entering a lounge where the noisy TV triggers agitation, and to remove herself from the noisy environment. Residents therefore rely on caregivers to help select and modify situations such as preventing environmental overload.

Attentional deployment

Attention is the gateway to emotional responses. Directing attention towards or away from emotionally provocative stimuli can lessen emotional impact. Distraction is a key strategy to modulate the activation of brain regions such as the amygdala, ventral stratum, nucleus accumbens, insula, ventral prefrontal cortex and orbital frontal cortex (Phan and Sripada 2013, p.381), the areas generally thought responsible for emotional appraisal, generation and responding. For example, directing an agitated resident's attention away from the therapist's facial expressions may reduce agitation by reducing amygdala emotional reactivity (Fusar-Poli *et al.* 2009). Engaging a client with anxiety in retrieving positive autobiographical memories incongruent with their current negative emotional state can also serve as a distraction technique.

Cognitive change

Giving a new meaning to a situation can change its emotional significance. Reappraisal reframes the meaning of an aversive situation from a negative interpretation to a positive one and has been found to reduce negative affect (Phan and Sripada 2013, p.383). In therapy, a resident showing signs of disorientation and anxiety may feel that she is lost in a strange place and that the police are searching for her. Using facts about the care home, the people she knows, her family's visits or facts about herself can help her reinterpret the situation. This strategy requires good knowledge of a resident's history and what components of cognitive process, such as working and semantic memory, are accessible to a resident.

Response modulation

This final stage involves techniques, such as suppression, to change a person's reaction after the emotional or behavioural response has been generated. Response modulation also involves directly altering cognitive, behavioural and physiological responses such as heart rate, respiration and facial expression (Phan and Sripada 2013, p.390). This makes music a highly versatile tool to help implement this strategy. Music can be broken down into elements such as melody, timbre, pitch and rhythm which, when manipulated, have been reported to influence heart rate, skin conductance, respiration, stress, immunity, social affiliation and emotion including reward and motivation (Chanda and

Levitin 2013; Salimpoor and Zatorre 2013; Koelsch 2014; Krabs *et al.* 2015). This underpins the uniqueness of music therapy as an emotion regulatory intervention.

When verbal cues fail to engage a resident displaying low mood, the familiarity of a song or piece of music can mediate arousal and emotional responses (Van Den Bosch, Salimpoor and Zatorre 2013). This may lead to the retrieval and discussion of certain autobiographical memories (Haj, Postal and Allain 2012). To counter apathy, the therapist may consider producing a percussive sound and quickening tempo to increase a resident's heart rate and skin conductance (van der Zwaag, Westerink and van den Broek 2011). These physiological manifestations are associated with motivational and orienting responses (Bradley 2009).

The above stages provide a brief view demarcating the regulatory principles. Hsu and colleagues (2015) identified talking, well-known songs, joint improvisation and the therapist's vocal, facial and bodily expressions as the main visual and auditory stimuli employed intuitively to implement the regulatory strategies.

Interventions aimed at improving emotion regulation can lead to physical and psychosocial improvement (Smyth and Arigo 2009) and extend beyond 'psychiatric' illness to a broader sense of well-being (Phan and Sripada 2013). The delivery of music therapy sessions in the setting follows this rationale.

The role of music therapists

It is reasonable to assume that a music therapist's main duty in a care home is to provide individual or group music therapy; however, the success of non-drug interventions relies on embedding them in daily care. Hsu and colleagues (2015) have explored this under-researched area by examining the use of video excerpts from music therapy sessions to assist post-therapy communication with care home staff. Using the Dementia Pathway (NICE 2006), after a thorough review of videoed sessions, therapists can extract one or two video clips to show caregivers how residents' symptoms are reduced during sessions. This weekly video presentation also allows music therapists and caregivers together to identify any observed possible causes of symptoms. Video clips can pinpoint components of residents' retained attention, memory and sensorimotor skills so that caregivers can utilise these skills to manage residents' symptoms and regulate their emotions. The music therapist must therefore establish this regular communication and advise on emotion regulatory strategies for implementation in daily care. Then caregivers can gain new insights, awareness and skills to enhance their interaction with residents. Once again, this highlights the need for music therapists to communicate from outside the 'music therapy box' rather than solely thinking about using instruments and music. Music therapists need up-to-date knowledge of dementia research into cure, cause, care, prevention and governmental policies. Understanding the taxonomies of emotion, attention, memory and sensorimotor coupling in the field of neuropsychology helps music therapists bring their clinical expertise to the care team. These broad knowledge sets cannot be adequately covered in the 2 years of music therapists' qualifying training. Employers may need to provide training opportunities as part of the continuing professional development for their music therapy staff. This organisational support will improve music therapy practice, enhance caregivers' knowledge and skills, and hence improve care delivery.

Caregivers' role before music therapy

Staff involvement is the key to successfully implementing psychosocial interventions such as music therapy in care homes. Several matters, including the understanding of individual music therapy, referral process, scheduling and so forth, merit caregivers' attention if they are to enable residents to obtain music therapy treatment. These matters are crucial when music therapy is first introduced into an existing care context. On an organisational level, guidance and support need to be provided to caregivers before commencing individual music therapy sessions if they are to fulfil a supportive role to residents and music therapists.

The subsections below discuss the essential characteristics of this supportive role and how they are harnessed to prepare caregivers for a proactive and leading role in the provision of music therapy that enables person-centred care.

Understanding the value of individual music therapy

Caregivers' understanding of music therapy can be a predictor of the effectiveness of this therapy. Caregivers may mistakenly believe that the musical entertainment, background music, singing and exercising to music already found in care homes constitute music therapy. Seeing a 'magic moment' where residents respond to music by singing or tapping their feet may be interpreted as the effect of music therapy. Although positive feelings can be generated by witnessing such an event, this does not itself improve caregivers' capability of managing residents' symptoms. It is necessary to help caregivers see beyond these predominantly response-based magic moments to understand music therapy as a long-term facility they can turn to when difficulties arise from residents' symptoms, which helps them relate the therapy to their job.

To reinforce understanding of music therapy as a clinical intervention, information about the potential adverse effects of music can be included, so that caregivers see music as a tool to be used cautiously. The volume of music or constant exposure to ambient music can trigger residents' symptoms through environmental overload or have an habituating effect. Caregivers' beliefs about the potential of the intervention to benefit or harm participants have been noted as a factor affecting the delivery of the intervention (Hope and Waterman 2004). In Methodist Homes, music therapists give music therapy workshops and presentations as an organisational support for both caregivers and music therapists when the therapy is newly introduced. Caregivers are thereby able not only to experience a snapshot of music therapy but also to voice their concerns or questions about the intervention. They often suggest a list of residents who might benefit from music therapy. With the music therapist's assistance, they can further reflect upon their observations and identify any pros and cons of music therapy in residents' best interest. The organisation recognises this collaborative method as a strategy to engage staff by upholding their perspectives and expertise from the outset (Lawrence and Banerjee 2010), thus increasing their willingness to make use of the intervention.

Referral process

Caregivers are also involved in the referral process. They need to understand that music therapy is not offered to residents because of their great love for music but because of their needs. This process is furthered if caregivers spontaneously exercise their knowledge of the purpose of music therapy. Their abilities to access criteria for referral and timely seek music therapy input as a resource should be developed during their daily practice. For example, instead of using prescribed-as-required medications, such as benzodiazepines, to manage acute restlessness, staff should consider a drop-in music therapy session as a better treatment option. This notion should be introduced in staff inductions and reinforced later in further training opportunities. As well as seeking music therapists' assistance in identifying reasons for referral, care staff can refer to specially written policies and procedures. Developing policy and treatment guidelines is necessary to sustain good staff practice (Aylward *et al.* 2003).

Music therapy care plan

Music therapy recipients in the homes go through a referral and assessment process. A care plan is completed by a music therapist in consultation with a resident's key worker, named nurse, representative and, if possible, the resident herself, and is periodically reviewed and updated as a result of changes to the resident's health. It is important that it be written in plain language to explain clearly what should be done to enable a resident to participate in music therapy. The care plan should provide clear reasons why a resident would benefit from music therapy. The time and space for therapy should be specified and pre-therapy preparation, such as medications, hoisting and transferring methods, outlined. The plan should also cross-reference with other care plans, such as mobility, dexterity and tissue viability, to prevent risks and hazards, outlining the music therapist's and the care team's health and safety requirement before, during and after a therapy session, including specifying the number of staff required to escort a resident to the therapy room to prevent risks such as falls. The care plan should enable any caregivers who have not previously worked with a resident to carry out all tasks necessary to enable attendance at a session. For example, a resident might need proactive encouragement from the staff to attend therapy sessions. Caregivers' awareness of the care plan is the key to undertaking the actions required to ensure the safety and consistency of therapy sessions.

Effective encouragement and scheduling

Caregivers' help in encouraging residents and scheduling sessions is invaluable. These seemingly simple aspects can become effortful at times. Without identifying effective methods, sessions may not take place, especially when residents display resistive behaviour or experience changes to symptoms and health. Effective methods depend on caregivers' insights into residents' individual daily routines, preferences and behavioural or emotional traits. Then caregivers are able to notice a resident's non-verbal implied consent for a therapy session or relate drowsiness to a change in medication and recommend re-scheduling the session from morning to afternoon, when the resident is more able to attend therapy. The fact that a cup of tea can enable a resident to settle in a quiet lounge for a therapy session is something a therapist might overlook. Such examples of encouragement and scheduling are often uniquely advantageous to individual residents. They exemplify caregivers' supportive role in pursuing the consistency of music therapy sessions, based on their unique caring skills and expertise.

Caregivers' role after music therapy

The following subsections depict a change brought to the care home since the presence of music therapy. This change can be manifested in caregivers' increased awareness of residents' needs and enhanced caring skills by which they are enabled to take a proactive and leading stance in managing symptoms and promoting a sense of well-being for care home residents. The content of these subsections derives from the results of semi-structured interviews from a doctoral study. The quantitative results have previously been reported in the feasibility study by Hsu and colleagues (2015).

Witnessing a change

Music therapy is often perceived as hidden behind closed doors, particularly when caregivers are not present in individual music therapy sessions. Despite their participation in workshops or presentations during their induction, caregivers are unlikely to relate to such an intervention without witnessing an actual therapy session. However, difficulties arise when caregivers' time is spent on participating in therapy sessions instead of carrying out other essential duties. This can affect staff-to-resident ratios and put a strain on work routine especially when there are staff shortages. Moreover, it is hard to maintain confidentiality between a resident and therapist in individual sessions when a caregiver is present. Considering these factors, video presentation by music therapists has been identified as the most effective method to involve caregivers. By selecting and showing two significant video clips from a resident's sessions, music therapists are able to filter out sensitive information. Video presentation can efficiently convey the most useful message regarding residents' symptoms within 15 minutes. The results of the caregivers' interviews (Figure 7.1) demonstrate the acceptability of this video-assisted method and indicate that the most pronounced change was perceived in residents' mood, emotion and sensorimotor functions.

Have you seen a change in residents' symptoms in response to music therapy?

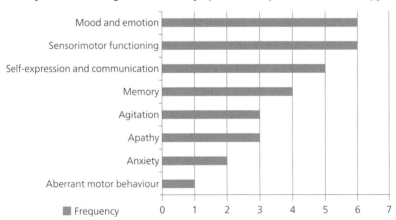

Figure 7.1 Care staff perceptions of music therapy's effect on residents

One caregiver commented on a resident's mood and emotion:

Music therapy gives her so much joy…such a release of like, coming away from such noise and hectic and, you know…to somewhere actually sit down and concentrate on her, and it's all about her, she really, really enjoys that…

Some of the activated functioning in the videos surprised one caregiver:

> When we do her [personal care], she just sits there and there's nothing, she'll just stare at you, there's just nothing to me, there just seems nothing there, but with music you got the tappin', you know, some movement in her arm, and the odd word would come out...

These observations demonstrate how effectively video excerpts help caregivers perceive changes in residents. Witnessing changes is central to the rationale behind the video presentation, as it can increase caregivers' motivation and confidence in making use of such intervention. By building on these observations, music therapists can communicate further aspects regarding the causes and prevention of symptoms.

Awareness of symptom causes and prevention

Enabling caregivers to see a difference made by music therapy is an important aspect in the role of music therapists; however, in order to induce a long-term change in care practice, NICE's Dementia Pathway addresses the need for early assessment to identify factors causing non-cognitive symptoms. These factors include physical health, depression, possible undetected pain or discomfort, side effects of medication, individual biography, psychosocial factors and physical environmental factors (NICE 2006). These factors are the focus to address in the video presentation to caregivers. The interview results reveal the impact of the video presentation on caregiving (Figure 7.2).

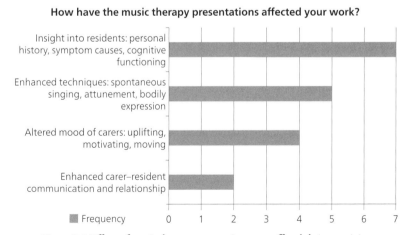

Figure 7.2 *Effects of music therapy presentations on staff and their caregiving*

All seven caregivers interviewed reported increased insight into residents' personal history, causes of symptoms and cognitive functioning. One caregiver commented on how she learned more about a resident's personal history:

> …and with R (a resident), the memories of her husband…'cause she was talking to T (a therapist) that time about that song. I think it's called 'Red Sails in the Sunset' or something, and even I didn't know that about R – and I was her key worker.

As discussed earlier, the retrieval of positive autobiographical memory can distract attention from current negative emotion or mood. The caregiver could therefore use this song and the ensuing verbal discussion during the resident's episodes of anxiety or low mood.

In regard to the causes of symptoms, a caregiver mentioned how she learned to prevent a resident's agitation:

> I didn't realise how she can be sensitive to noise… Yeah! I don't know if she's suspicious of people, but it did make me realise that you do need to approach her quite calmly and quite softly and ease your way in.

This underlines the fact that caregivers' speech prosody can be an effective preventive technique involving distinctive modulation of vocal pitch, quality, loudness and speech rhythm (Banse and Scherer 1996). Prosodic acoustic cues that enrich given information can surprise or enrage a resident during communication. These acoustic signals are complemented by facial expressions to trigger audiovisual binding (Pourtois *et al.* 2000) that influences emotion judgements. Residents with deteriorating cognition benefit from sufficient contextual cues for communication.

Another caregiver observed a resident's cognitive and motor functions being activated during engagement in drumming:

> …the one with M (a resident)…which was tapping the drum along to…T (a therapist). T was changing the tempo of the songs, and then you could see M working it out, and changing tempo with her to keep in tempo. That's a really good one.

These observations by caregivers demonstrate that video presentation, when implemented regularly, may sustain and enhance staff awareness of symptom causes and prevention. Literature reviews also note that interventions involving life review and music help caregivers see residents beyond symptoms of dementia (Lawrence *et al.* 2012, p.348).

Interaction techniques

A major impact of video presentation was caregivers' enhanced interaction techniques. This transformed caregivers from a supportive stance to an autonomous and active role in prolonging the effects of music therapy. Caregivers were more aware that by adjusting their vocal, facial and bodily expressions, they were able to attune to the residents and thus ameliorate symptoms such as agitation:

> Tinkering on the edge sometimes, you see the agitation starting to build, and we will say to her, 'Come on B (a resident), play us a tune!' And even doing this business with your fingers (mimes playing piano) will bring a smile to her face.

Spontaneous singing has also emerged as a distinctive technique adopted in various aspects of care delivery such as during residents' hygiene care and general communication. A caregiver mentioned how she used the songs:

> Different residents like particular songs, or maybe a particular pace of song – maybe a slower song, especially before personal care if they're agitated, a slower song sang nice and softly. But then, once they're in a good mood, they're up for a nice fast song and clap or dance around the room.

This example shows that the caregiver not only sang the songs but also considered their selection and how they should be sung. Varying the tempo of the songs may perceptibly modulate residents' reaction when their affective behaviours appear. How music therapists select and explain video excerpts is pivotal in the post-therapy communication.

Here is another example of a caregiver using spontaneous singing to ameliorate apathy:

> T (a therapist) sometimes slowed down some of the songs, and almost to a stop, to see if it prompted that person to put the words in…'cause that's what we do with D (a resident) now – we sometimes slow the song down to see if she'll say the words…sometimes she does, sometimes she doesn't. It's not just about playing a tune, it's…the body language.

Evidently, the emotion regulatory strategy has been adopted in caregivers' day-to-day thinking and action, and can therefore be implemented whenever signs of symptoms arise. The interviews further reveal that the videos allowed caregivers to appreciate certain aspects of their job:

> It lifts your mood as well – it's not just the resident. It lifts my mood. I love to see them come back from a session if they're really smiley and happy – or to hear them sing back to me when I'm singing a song.

Video presentation, implemented effectively, has the potential to motivate regular staff communication. It is the catalyst for a unique role for caregivers, enhancing a resident-centred care model. This role mirrors the role of music therapists and illuminates the possible working mechanisms of individual music therapy sessions in dementia care.

Conclusion

Unlike some other psychosocial interventions, music therapy requires a trained clinician to deliver this unmanualised intervention; however, without staff participation in individual therapy sessions, it is difficult to embed this therapy in daily care. This chapter demonstrates effective methods of introducing active staff involvement in the provision of individual music therapy. This helps manage care home residents' neuropsychiatric symptoms and enhances caregiving. Components of individual music therapy sessions, including the concept of emotion regulation, interaction techniques, singing and the awareness of symptom causes, can be transferred to caregivers via video presentation. These skills, as well as the knowledge, thinking and attitudes, can be applied as soon as a need or opportunity arises. For instance, singing can be delivered as soon as a resident's agitation appears during personal care. It can also be implemented as part of carer–resident communication.

The provision of music therapy, like many psychosocial interventions, can be limited by time pressure, low staff-to-resident ratios, limited staff abilities and organisational culture. Where physical and medical care outweigh social and emotional care, a task-oriented model can dominate care settings and impede the provision of such an intervention. However, these limitations can be overcome if clinicians research and implement innovative approaches to influencing both staff and organisation, changing the landscape of dementia care by using the unique parameters of music therapy.

References

Aalten, P., de Vugt, M.E., Jaspers, N., Jolles, J. and Verhey, F.R. (2005) 'The course of neuropsychiatric symptoms in dementia. Part I: Findings from the two-year longitudinal Maasbed study.' *International Journal of Geriatric Psychiatry 20*, 6, 523–530.

Aylward, S., Stolee, P., Keat, N. and Johncox, V. (2003) 'Effectiveness of continuing education in long-term care: a literature review.' *Gerontologist 43*, 259–271.

Banerjee, S. (2009) *The Use of Antipsychotic Medication for People with Dementia: Time for Action.* London: UK Department of Health.

Banse, R. and Scherer, K.R. (1996) 'Acoustic profiles in vocal emotion expression.' *Journal of Personality and Social Psychology 70*, 3, 614–636.

Bradley, M.M. (2009) 'Natural selective attention: orienting and emotion.' *Psychophysiology 46*, 1, 1–11.

Burton, N. (2010) *Psychiatry.* Oxford: Wiley-Blackwell.

Cerejeira, J., Lagarto, L. and Mukaetova-Ladinska, E.B. (2012) 'Behavioral and psychological symptoms of dementia.' *Frontiers in Neurology 3*, 73.

Chanda, M.L. and Levitin, D.J. (2013) 'The neurochemistry of music.' *Trends in Cognitive Sciences 17*, 4, 179–193.

Cooke, M.L., Moyle, W., Shum, D.H., Harrison, S.D. and Murfield, J.E. (2010) 'A randomized controlled trial exploring the effect of music on agitated behaviours and anxiety in older people with dementia.' *Aging & Mental Health 14*, 8, 905–916.

Cooper, C., Mukadam, N., Katona, C., Lyketsos, C.G. *et al.* (2013) 'Systematic review of the effectiveness of pharmacologic interventions to improve quality of life and well-being in people with dementia.' *The American Journal of Geriatric Psychiatry 21*, 2, 173–183.

Dickson, K., Lafortune, L., Kavanagh, J., Thomas, J., Mays, N. and Erens, B. (2012) *Non-Drug Treatments for Symptoms in Dementia: An Overview of Systematic Reviews of Non-Pharmacological Interventions in the Management of Neuropsychiatric Symptoms and Challenging Behaviours in Patients with Dementia.* London: London School of Hygiene and Tropical Medicine.

Dugmore, O., Orrell, M. and Spector, A. (2015) 'Qualitative studies of psychosocial interventions for dementia: a systematic review.' *Aging & Mental Health 19*, 11, 955–967.

Fusar-Poli, P., Placentino, A., Carletti, F., Landi, P. *et al.* (2009) 'Functional atlas of emotional faces processing: a voxel-based meta-analysis of 105 functional magnetic resonance imaging studies.' *Journal of Psychiatry & Neuroscience 34*, 6, 418–432.

Gerdner, L.A. (2000) 'Effects of individualized versus classical "relaxation" music on the frequency of agitation in elderly persons with Alzheimer's disease and related disorders.' *International Psychogeriatrics 12*, 1, 49–65.

Gitlin, L.N., Kales, H.C. and Lyketsos, C.G. (2012) 'Nonpharmacologic management of behavioral symptoms in dementia.' *The Journal of the American Medical Association 308*, 19, 2020–2029.

Gross, J.J. and Thompson, R.A. (2007) 'Emotion Regulation: Conceptual Foundations.' In J.J. Gross (ed) *Handbook of Emotion Regulation.* New York, NY: Guilford Press.

Guetin, S., Charras, K., Berard, A., Arbus, C. *et al.* (2012) 'An overview of the use of music therapy in the context of Alzheimer's disease: a report of a French expert group.' *Dementia 12*, 619–634.

Haj, M., Postal, V. and Allain, P. (2012) 'Music enhances autobiographical memory in mild Alzheimer's disease.' *Educational Gerontology 38*, 1, 30–41.

Hope, K.W. and Waterman, H.A. (2004) 'Using multi-sensory environments (MSEs) with people with dementia: factors impeding their use as perceived by clinical staff.' *Dementia 3*, 1, 45–68.

Howard, R., Ballard, C., O'Brien, J. and Burns, A. (2001) 'Guidelines for the management of agitation in dementia.' *International Journal of Geriatric Psychiatry 16*, 7, 714–717.

Hsu, M.H., Flowerdew, R., Parker, M., Fachner, J. and Odell-Miller, H. (2015) 'Individual music therapy for managing neuropsychiatric symptoms for people with dementia and their carers: a cluster randomised controlled feasibility study.' *BMC Geriatrics 15*, 1. Available at http://bmcgeriatr.biomedcentral.com/articles/10.1186/s12877-015-0082-4, accessed on 30 December 2015.

Koelsch, S. (2014) 'Brain correlates of music-evoked emotions.' *Nature Reviews Neuroscience 15*, 3, 170–180.

Krabs, R.U., Enk, R., Teich, N. and Koelsch, S. (2015) 'Autonomic effects of music in health and Crohn's disease: the impact of isochronicity, emotional valence, and tempo.' *PloS One 10*, 5. Available at http://journals.plos.org/plosone/article?id=10.1371/journal.pone.0126224, accessed on 30 December 2015.

Lawrence, V. and Banerjee, S. (2010) 'Improving care in care homes: a qualitative evaluation of the Croydon Care Home support team.' *Aging & Mental Health 14*, 416–424.

Lawrence, V., Fossey, J., Ballard, C., Moniz-Cook, E. and Murray, J. (2012) 'Improving quality of life for people with dementia in care homes: making psychosocial interventions work.' *The British Journal of Psychiatry 201*, 5, 344–351.

Livingston, G., Johnston, K., Katona, C., Paton, J. and Lyketsos, C.G. (2005) 'Systematic review of psychological approaches to the management of neuropsychiatric symptoms of dementia.' *The American Journal of Psychiatry 162*, 11, 1996–2021.

Margallo-Lana, M., Swann, A., O'Brien, J., Fairbairn, A. *et al.* (2001) 'Prevalence and pharmacological management of behavioural and psychological symptoms amongst dementia sufferers living in care environments.' *International Journal of Geriatric Psychiatry 16*, 1, 39–44.

McDermott, O., Crellin, N., Ridder, H.M. and Orrell, M. (2013) 'Music therapy in dementia: a narrative synthesis systematic review.' *International Journal of Geriatric Psychiatry 28*, 8, 781–794.

National Institute for Health and Care Excellence (NICE) (2006) *NICE Guidelines 42: Dementia.* Available at http://pathways.nice.org.uk/pathways/dementia, accessed on 30 December 2015.

Odell-Miller, H. (1995) 'Approaches to Music Therapy in Psychiatry with Specific Emphasis upon a Research Project with the Elderly Mentally Ill.' In T. Wigram, B. Saperston and R. West (eds) *The Art and Science of Music Therapy: A Handbook.* Chur: Harwood Academic Publishers.

Odell-Miller, H. (1997) 'Music Therapy and the Functions of Music with Older Mentally Ill People in a Continuing Care Setting.' In M.J. Denham (ed) *Continuing Care for Older People.* Cheltenham: Stanley Thornes.

Odell-Miller, H. (2002) 'Musical Narratives in Music Therapy Treatment for Dementia.' In L. Bunt and S. Hoskyns (eds) *The Handbook of Music Therapy.* Hove: Brunner-Routledge.

Olazarán, J., Reisberg, B., Clare, L., Cruz, I. *et al.* (2010) 'Nonpharmacological therapies in Alzheimer's disease: a systematic review of efficacy.' *Dementia and Geriatric Cognitive Disorders 30*, 2, 161–178.

Orrell, M. (2012) 'The new generation of psychosocial interventions for dementia care.' *The British Journal of Psychiatry 201*, 5, 342–343.

Patel, B., Perera, M., Pendleton, J., Richman, A. and Majumdar, B. (2014) 'Psychosocial interventions for dementia: from evidence to practice.' *Advances in Psychiatric Treatment 20*, 5, 340–349.

Phan, K.L. and Sripada, C.S. (2013) 'Emotion Regulation.' In J. Armony and P. Vuilleumier (eds) *The Cambridge Handbook of Human Affective Neuroscience.* Cambridge: Cambridge University Press.

Pourtois, G., de Gelder, B., Vroomen, J., Rossion, B. and Crommelinck, M. (2000) 'The time-course of intermodal binding between seeing and hearing affective information.' *Neuroreport 11*, 6, 1329–1333.

Rabins, P., Schwartz, S., Tschanz, J., Corcoran, C. *et al.* (2011) 'Risk factors for severe dementia from a population-based sample of incident Alzheimer's disease: the Cache County Dementia Progression Study.' *Alzheimer's & Dementia 7*, 4, S356.

Raglio, A., Bellelli, G., Traficante, D., Gianotti, M. *et al.* (2008) 'Efficacy of music therapy in the treatment of behavioral and psychiatric symptoms of dementia.' *Alzheimer Disease & Associated Disorders 22*, 2, 158–162.

Raglio, A., Bellelli, G., Traficante, D., Gianotti, M. *et al.* (2010) 'Efficacy of music therapy treatment based on cycles of sessions: a randomised controlled trial.' *Aging & Mental Health 14*, 8, 900–904.

Ragneskog, H., Kihlgren, M., Karlsson, I. and Norberg, A. (1996) 'Dinner music for demented patients: analysis of video-recorded observations.' *Clinical Nursing Research 5*, 3, 262–277.

Ridder, H.M., Stige, B., Qvale, L.G. and Gold, C. (2013) 'Individual music therapy for agitation in dementia: an exploratory randomized controlled trial.' *Aging & Mental Health 17*, 6, 667–678.

Ridder, H.M., Wigram, T. and Ottesen, A.M. (2009) 'A pilot study on the effects of music therapy on frontotemporal dementia: developing a research protocol 1.' *Nordic Journal of Music Therapy 18*, 2, 103–132.

Robinson, L., Hutchings, D., Dickinson, H.O., Corner, L. *et al.* (2007) 'Effectiveness and acceptability of non-pharmacological interventions to reduce wandering in dementia: a systematic review.' *International Journal of Geriatric Psychiatry 22*, 1, 9–22.

Salimpoor, V.N. and Zatorre, R.J. (2013) 'Neural interactions that give rise to musical pleasure.' *Psychology of Aesthetics, Creativity, and the Arts 7*, 1, 62–75.

Seitz, D.P., Brisbin, S., Herrmann, N., Rapoport, M.J. *et al.* (2012) 'Efficacy and feasibility of nonpharmacological interventions for neuropsychiatric symptoms of dementia in long term care: a systematic review.' *Journal of the American Medical Directors Association 13*, 6, 503–506.

Smyth, J.M. and Arigo, D. (2009) 'Recent evidence supports emotion-regulation interventions for improving health in at-risk and clinical populations.' *Current Opinion in Psychiatry 22*, 2, 205–210.

Solé, C., Mercadal-Brotons, M., Galati, A. and De Castro, M. (2014) 'Effects of group music therapy on quality of life, affect, and participation in people with varying levels of dementia.' *Journal of Music Therapy 51*, 1, 103–125.

Spector, A., Orrell, M. and Goyder, J. (2013) 'A systematic review of staff training interventions to reduce the behavioural and psychological symptoms of dementia.' *Ageing Research Reviews 12*, 1, 354–364.

Spector, A., Thorgrimsen, L., Woods, B., Royan, L. *et al.* (2003) 'Efficacy of an evidence-based cognitive stimulation therapy programme for people with dementia: randomised controlled trial.' *The British Journal of Psychiatry 183*, 3, 248–254.

Sung, H.C., Chang, S.M., Lee, W.L. and Lee, M.S. (2006) 'The effects of group music with movement intervention on agitated behaviours of institutionalized elders with dementia in Taiwan.' *Complementary Therapies in Medicine 14*, 2, 113–119.

Svansdottir, H.B. and Snaedal, J. (2006) 'Music therapy in moderate and severe dementia of Alzheimer's type: a case-control study.' *International Psychogeriatrics 18*, 4, 613–621.

Van Den Bosch, I., Salimpoor, V.N. and Zatorre, R.J. (2013) 'Familiarity mediates the relationship between emotional arousal and pleasure during music listening.' *Frontiers in Human Neuroscience 7*. Available at http://journal.frontiersin.org/article/10.3389/fnhum.2013.00534/full, accessed on 30 December 2015.

van der Zwaag, M.D., Westerink, J.H. and van den Broek, E.L. (2011) 'Emotional and psychophysiological responses to tempo, mode, and percussiveness.' *Musicae Scientiae 15*, 2, 250–269.

Vernooij-Dassen, M., Vasse, E., Zuidema, S., Cohen-Mansfield, J. and Moyle, W. (2010) 'Psychosocial interventions for dementia patients in long-term care.' *International Psychogeriatrics 22*, 7, 1121–1128.

Vink, A.C., Bruinsma, M.S. and Scholten, R.J. (2003) 'Music therapy for people with dementia.' *Cochrane Database of Systematic Reviews 2003*, 4, Art. No. CD003477. Available at http://onlinelibrary.wiley.com/doi/10.1002/14651858.CD003477.pub2/abstract, accessed on 30 December 2015.

Zuidema, S.U., Derksen, E., Verhey, F.R. and Koopmans, R.T. (2007) 'Prevalence of neuropsychiatric symptoms in a large sample of Dutch nursing home patients with dementia.' *International Journal of Geriatric Psychiatry 22*, 7, 632–638.

Chapter 8

Psychodynamic Group Music Therapy Facilitates Carers to Become Auxiliary Music Therapists

A Case Study and Methodological Analysis

Anthi Agrotou

Introduction

This chapter is a detailed analysis of a single case study spanning a period of 3.5 years.[1] It describes a radical approach to involving carers in music therapy groups, whereby they gradually acquired therapeutic skills through spontaneously forming attachment bonds within the therapy setting. The methodology and processes of one music therapy group, consisting of three women with profound learning difficulties, four carers and myself as music therapist, are briefly outlined, and a few mutative moments in the group's process are described in greater detail.

The clinical work evolved in the way described in response to my situation as the only constant therapist in an isolated institution outside Nicosia, the Cypriot capital. Here staff and residents lived estranged lives, with little emotional contact between them. The residents, classified as profoundly learning disabled, had spent their days since early childhood in one room with nothing to do, and the majority of carers, untrained and unsupported, believed the people they were caring for felt little and thought even less.

---

1   This chapter is based on my doctoral thesis (Agrotou 1998) and my presentation, 'Novel Methodology in Psychodynamic Group Music Therapy: Treating the Patients, Training the Carers', given at the Tenth World Congress of Music Therapy, 23–28 July 2002, Oxford, England.

Desperate to alleviate my own isolation and that of the institution's population, I decided to create groups with stable resident and carer membership and devise a methodology for developing untrained carers into auxiliary therapists by facilitating attachment bonds between estranged carers and residents, thus addressing at source the residents' isolating and handicapping symptoms.

The carer members were randomly selected to alleviate staff envy and persecutory feelings towards me as someone who chose some and rejected others. Four carers were selected, three as permanent members and the fourth as a substitute, in case of absences.

After discussions with the selected carers, the psychologist and the director, three women residents were chosen to join the group, all aged about 20 years when we first met in April 1994. They had spent their entire life in isolation. They had never had speech, nor played or occupied themselves with anything; they had never been attached to anyone in particular in the institution where they had lived since the age of 5 years. Each carer was asked to choose the patient to whom they desired to channel more attention than to anyone else, and was then allocated to that patient for the whole span of the group's life. She was initially directed to give full attention to her allocated patient, while keeping an awareness of the whole group, and to be that patient's special facilitator, her auxiliary hand and mind.

Participants

In this chapter I use first-name aliases for the patients, to preserve confidentiality, and the carers' actual surnames. In the sessions, however, we all used first names, in keeping with the institution's existing practice.

Sarah

Sarah was characterised by a piercing look of screaming intensity, which she gave each passer-by, always with a stereotypical smile. When she actually screamed, it felt as if the sounds poured from her eyes. Her frail body needed to bend and lean on others in order to stand up, sit down or make any step. Whenever she sat or walked with someone's support, her body stooped forwards, as though on the brink of a fall. Any soft toy was the only object for which she expressed an emotional need.

Ms Antouna

Ms Antouna was Sarah's allocated carer. A shy person in the early life of the group, she hid the sensitive part of her personality behind stereotypical ways acquired in the institution. Her observant and perceptive abilities flourished very quickly, though she would keep most of her thoughts to herself. Her naturally slow rhythm facilitated her bonding with Sarah.

Jenny

Jenny's doll-like face and slim, able body granted her an attractiveness which differentiated her from most of the residents. She usually sat passively for hours, staring into space; or she moved about aimlessly, sometimes laughing or vocalising, while turning her head from side to side. Often she ground her teeth or abandoned herself to stereotypical sounds and movements, all strong autistic features.

Ms Demetriou

Ms Demetriou was Jenny's allocated carer. She proved a suitable companion, having a rather 'hyperactive' temperament, a liveliness and an immediacy in her approach to people, when she was in the appropriate environment. Such personality features helped her eventually cut through Jenny's autistic mannerisms; however, her rebelliousness, though refreshing towards the mature stage of the group, at first hampered her trust and commitment to the group.

Pamina

Pamina spent her days in the institution unnoticed by all, wheelchair bound and totally silent in quiet anonymity, permanently wearing a plastic helmet to protect her head from injury in case of grand-mal fits. Abandoned in infinite silence or a comatose kind of sleep, she was one of the most isolated people I have ever encountered.

Sometimes she appeared anguished and her whole body moved as she hyperventilated, as if suffocated by a hidden anxiety. This usually occurred when moving her wheelchair around the room, which was her only sign of being alive.

Ms Kazakaiou

Ms Kazakaiou was Pamina's allocated carer. Having a similar temperament and rebellious disposition as Ms Demetriou, she also doubted that the actions of people with learning disability have psychological meaning, and once said during the early months, '... it is ridiculous to think that people like Pamina have feelings and thoughts'.

Ms Lovari

Ms Lovari was the supplementary carer. Of an innately gentle temperament, she was sometimes mentally absent in the sessions, particularly during the group's first years.

Mr Loizou

Mr Loizou, the assistant physiotherapist, who was treated as a constant member of the group, did the filming.

CASE STUDY: SOUNDS AND MEANING

The beginning of the group

Our half-hour weekly sessions began in April 1994. The first months were characterised by silence and isolation, but also deeply buried expressions of agony in the patients, who displayed what attachment theorists classify as 'anxious avoidant attachment'. Expecting nobody to be there to receive their signals of attachment needs, they lived as if the comfort of human intimacy did not matter (Bowlby 1988). The carers' anxiety was manifested in indifference and frequent absences.

None of us could have predicted that it would be Pamina – in the early stages she often appeared still, motionless, comatose, even nearing life's end – who would be the first to lead the group towards communicative expression.

Awakenings

Right from the beginning of the session of 15 July 1994, 3 months after our first session, Pamina communicates for the first time using her mouth, by forcefully pressing her tongue on her hard palate from behind a slowly lifted palm, creating a sound that the carers have not previously heard in the institution. I choose the temple blocks for their undefined, watery sound, resembling Pamina's sound, and respond with a quick quaver–crotchet figure, aiming to reflect the two elements of her action: the tongue movement and the resultant sound.

Almost at once Pamina recognises that someone is responding to her and creates rhythmical themes and variations in her own part, prefacing the accentuated sound just described with four quaver-length sounds created by moving her tongue inside her mouth. Gradually, she takes part in a dialogue, expecting my responses 1 second after the end of her own part. She acts as though my sounds originate from her allocated carer, turning her head towards her while dropping her hand from her mouth, only to lift it again for her next phrase once the desired response is heard (Figure 8.1). This is probably partly due to their evolving relationship, and also to Ms Kazakaiou's physical proximity and her tambourine phrases, as she tries to pick up motives and play them in synchrony with mine. However, the main cause must lie in Ms Kazakaiou's concentration and attention, channelled into a desire to meet Pamina, which enables her to listen both to Pamina's phrases and to my responses.

Figure 8.1 Pamina's first musical communication

Within 2 minutes, Jenny reacts: it seems hard for her to be present during this first, clear communication initiated by a group member, and she heads for the door. To ease Jenny's jealousy, as well as enhance the evolving intimacy between Pamina and Ms Kazakaiou, I hand over the temple blocks to Ms Kazakaiou, signalling her to use them while I try to keep Pamina's interest alive by adding melodic phrases on the metallophone. This gives direction to Ms Kazakaiou's temple-block phrases, helping her learn to respond to Pamina on the spot. Pamina succeeds in maintaining her own part for another 10 minutes continuously. The other two carers, touched by Pamina's communicative moments, desire to facilitate her even more. Their playing is timid and simple, yet affectively appropriate: some soft cymbal touches by Ms Lovari and bongo-drum touches by Ms Demetriou offer an unobtrusive humanly created sound presence.

Pamina's sustained initiative has an impact on the other two resident members. Jenny leaves the door and goes to the piano for her own first sounds. Her final accentuated cluster brings Sarah to her feet for the first time. Sarah's desire to stand and her initiative in seeking help to do so from Ms Lovari seated beside her are something new, never before witnessed. We clearly see from all group members' responses that this is a mutative moment in which a transformation has occurred.

Attachment and the use of a rhythmical part to open each session

The work employed a methodology focused on creating a therapeutic environment that would facilitate the formation of affectional bonds between the carers and the patients. According to Bowlby (1988), humans are born with a natural propensity to form affectional bonds to particular others, and not only the care seeking but also the caregiving state of mind are basic components of human nature; their character arises from internal working models developed through early attachment experiences, and they naturally emerge in human interactions.

When the carers first entered the group, they were operating like mothers of anxiously attached infants, having within them no mental space to receive the patients' signals, being emotionally unresponsive and feeling no commitment towards the residents. Several methods were used to elicit a care-seeking state in the patients and a care-giving stance in the carers. One was to begin every session with a rhythmical part in which for 5 to 7 minutes each carer would focus predominantly on her allocated patient, observing very closely her every gesture and expression and responding to her rhythmically, but only after the patient had first expressed rhythm through her voice or body language. The carer's response had to be based closely and directly on the patient's rhythmical 'repertoire'.

This isolation of the rhythmical element at the beginning of every session had multiple benefits: it gave the patients a special kind of quiet space and a certain security at receiving undivided, exclusive attention. It also facilitated the carers' closer experience of the patients' world by cultivating a stance of observation and abstinence from impulsive action. The carers were enabled to discover aspects of music therapy techniques through unconscious or conscious observation of my responses and of cues received from the patients, and by witnessing the patients' evolving attachment behaviour which, though still nascent, was unprecedented in the carers' experience of the patients. This gave them both stimulus and incentive, and elicited the beginnings of their innate 'caregiving' behaviour (Bowlby 1988).

The excerpt analysed above was an example from the rhythmical part of a session. During free discussion later that day Ms Kazakaiou said, 'I feel as if my mind gets gradually located inside Pamina.'

Foundation matrix and dynamic matrix

It was interesting to find this patient group functioning similarly to groups with verbally fluent people as described in the work of the group analyst S.H. Foulkes. Like patients who meet in the context of a group-analytic situation, members of the music therapy group created a shared psychic life, a psychic network of communication, 'a mother soil (matrix) in which all dynamic processes operate' (Foulkes 1990a, p.185). From the beginning, mental aspects of their personalities interacted instinctively, intuitively and basically unconsciously in what Foulkes (1990b) called a 'foundation matrix'. But the foundation matrix of this group was one of autistic isolation shared by each member in her own way. In the initial stages, Pamina's typical comatose state, constituting a shell of isolation and protection from an unpredictable and threatening outside world and a tormenting inner world, was interconnected to the inner world of the other two women. A similar shell-like encapsulation characterised Sarah and Jenny, through their continuous fiddling over their own skin or the soft surfaces of objects. By concentrating on sensations engendered by their own bodies, they constructed a protective shelter that allowed neither the externalisation nor the reception and processing of information. Such autistic experiences have been illuminated by the work of Tustin (1986, 1990).

Jenny even seemed to have been using her voice towards a similar end. Her repeated vocalisations – whether emitted softly or forcefully – were a continuous flow that formed a barrier which distracted her attention not only from everything around her, but also from everything inside her. They may be regarded as 'autistic sounds' (Figure 8.2).

Figure 8.2 Jenny's autistic vocalisations

Foulkes (1990b) writes that, as the relationships of the members of a group become more intimate over time, 'they also form a current, ever-moving, ever-developing *dynamic matrix*' (p.228). The individuals are the foreground, the nodal points in this network, while the group is its background. The whole allows members' psychological processes to interact as 'transpersonal mental processes' which permeate each individual's psyche as X-rays permeate the body. Yet each individual resonates such processes in his own key, 'elaborates them and contributes to them and modifies them in his own way' (Foulkes 1990b, p.229). Whatever happens to the individual concerns the group, and whatever happens to the group concerns the individual members. They all form part of an intertwined whole.

In this group, the dynamic matrix was set going the moment that Pamina first allowed herself to communicate. This dynamic matrix concerned the conflict between externalising affective states and isolating the self, and between the need for relationships of intimacy and the fear of such relationships; and the conflict between feelings of trust in our benevolent and reliable presence and mistrust in it – a conflict that characterised the group's life from that first group awakening evoked by Pamina's *mouth repertoire*, and moved ever deeper in parallel to the deepening of trust.

CASE STUDY CONTINUED

Loss and abandonment expressed in the patients' shared body language

It is 7 November 1994, 6 months into the group's life. Pamina makes continuous circles with her wheelchair, keeping Ms Kazakaiou as a focal point. She seems to be acting out a series of endless appearances and disappearances. Every time she turns towards Ms Kazakaiou she reappears; every time she turns her wheelchair away, she disappears. Pamina seems to become the active creator of the drama of which she had been the passive recipient in the hands of others: that of repeated abandonment. This active drama can only be performed because Pamina has experienced within her some trust in the group and Ms Kazakaiou.

Sarah's murmurs, as they take a shape of bursts and pauses, are another pattern of repeated appearances and disappearances. It is these sounds that I first take in, during the music I address to Pamina and the group; my piano phrases are a response and an expansion of every one of Sarah's murmurs. But my main aim is to create a humanly invested presence, a voice that calls the patient back to life. Alvarez (1992) writes that in treating severely depressed children who have lost hope, it is necessary for the therapist to bring the patient back to life. The carers' rhythmical accompaniments reinforce this aim – in particular, Ms Kazakaiou's accurate and steadfast rhythmical beat, which follows Pamina's every movement.

There comes a moment when Pamina's torso becomes even more stooped, while Sarah seems concerned; I feel that it is appropriate to strengthen my presence in the room and to be close to the group through more intimate music. As soon as my first slow, plaintive vocal phrases with piano accompaniment are heard, Pamina's circles become differentiated. Her torso becomes all the more stooped, her body curled up and even more handicapped, like a dropped, ailing body and soul that drives itself into unending, aimless circles. Every push comes with a struggle, the result of an effort; a struggle to push, a struggle to pause, a struggle as she becomes stuck at the wall, a struggle turning towards Ms Kazakaiou, a struggle colliding with the xylophone.

Within seconds, the group experiences clearly a shared affective intensity. Jenny positions her body on her own chair in a posture mirroring that of Pamina. Sarah assumes an expression of piercing pain, as she keeps glancing between Pamina and myself and the rest of the group. Her murmurs form the basis of my vocal phrases (Figure 8.3).

Figure 8.3 Answering Sarah's vocalisations

We see here the group's shared body language, brought to the foreground by Pamina, through which they seemed to me to 'speak' about the fate of being pushed and dragged day by day, about the agony of being imprisoned by despair, about repeated losses and abandonment.

Sarah's beater episodes and manic defences

The beaters had acquired a particular significance from the first months of the group's life. Discovered by Pamina as a means for the creation of sound, and used by Jenny as autistic objects or as a means of attacking another's creations, they elicited particular reactions in Sarah, which reached a climax in March 1995. Time and time again she would grasp as many beaters as possible from Ms Antouna's hands and throw them onto specific targets: towards the instruments, creating loud sounds, or towards specific persons, like her carer or Jenny, or deliberately missing the instruments so that the beaters landed on the floor. This hunger for objects is characteristic of manic states, as described by Klein (1988a). It had a sadistic component as she threw beaters at Ms Antouna's body, and in her apparent pleasure in getting Ms Antouna to bend down to collect them for her, shown by the character of her 'laughter' after each throw, which sounded closer to an explosive scream. Klein (1988b) sees manic defences as the person's way of defending against her dependence on a good object, and her fear that her aggressive wishes could destroy this valued object. By this time, Ms Antouna had already become a valuable and needed person for Sarah.

The free-discussion group and the methodology of affirming and empowering the carers

The carers did not at first see Sarah's behaviour as a manic defence; on the contrary, Ms Antouna, Sarah's allocated carer, said, '…her laughter and her joy give me satisfaction; it is the satisfaction of seeing someone who is totally passive in the institution become active here'. Such attitudes were not corrected by didactic methods. Instead, space was given for the carers themselves to search for meaning in their patients' signals, and for their own true feelings and attitudes. For this reason, a special meeting between the carers and myself took place after every music therapy session. These 'free-discussion group meetings', as I called them, were aimed at allowing the carers' thoughts and feelings to emerge freely and uncritically. I was there only as a facilitator, raising the questions, and trusting the group with my own anxieties, ambivalence and countertransference reactions.

During these free-discussion group meetings, the video-recorded sessions were analysed, gradually introducing the language of sound and music therapy techniques, drawn from the real-life experiences of the music therapy sessions – the feedback or the difficulties we had faced. New music therapy techniques were explained slowly, as I sensed their growing faith that I trusted them as competent and valuable professionals. I encouraged them to take initiatives, giving them space to discover by themselves ways of being and relating to the patients. Their search would throw light on my approach, and many were the times when their interventions and insight saved me from a lot of problems.

It was important that the carers should find themselves in a creative and responsible role from the start. Like the traumatised and vulnerable parents of a handicapped child, they were sensitive to criticism and could have unconsciously experienced a responsibility and guilt for the residents' handicapping condition. This guilt required management, as did their envy at realising they lacked skills and knowledge, having never received any training for the kind of work they were doing. Thus, they envied my position as someone they fantasised as fortunate to be filled with skills and knowledge. This envy was largely mitigated by an approach geared towards the formation of bonds between patients and their carers. When it became apparent that a patient was developing an attachment behaviour towards her allocated carer, I emphasised this in the free-discussion group meetings. As such patient behaviour was unprecedented in her long life in the institution, the carers would rightly experience such change of attitude as their own achievement. I then emphasised that the appropriate and sensitive way of being near someone, which they had proved they had in abundance, was the key skill; musical skills were secondary and would develop with time.

I acknowledged that the carers' presence saved me from slipping into states of numbness and softened my own anxieties about not knowing in a lot of situations. Their anxiety about not knowing was a shared one and they had a valuable role in ameliorating mine. I shared with them my unexpected discovery that this way of working with them in group music therapy was the most satisfying, rewarding and enriching working experience I had ever had; furthermore, that the moments of bonding occurred earlier and regressions were less prolonged than in the individual therapies I had so far conducted (e.g. Agrotou 1993, 1994).

Gradually, these free-discussion group meetings developed a special atmosphere of frankness, shared self-questioning, trust about admitting and sharing our doubts and our difficulties, and searching together for possible answers. Thus, the general principle was that of 'free discussion' of shared problems, as Foulkes (1975, p.8) wrote of some groups which, though not psychotherapeutic, contain certain features of psychotherapy. Ms Demetriou's growing therapeutic awareness elicited from Pamina, on 9 October 1995, skills that she had never manifested in her whole institutionalised life, as described below.

CASE STUDY CONTINUED

Pamina's new form of expression

Pamina wheels herself close to the xylophone, and Ms Demetriou recalls and reproduces the xylophone phrase that invited Pamina to play 3 months previously when she revealed an interest in the instrument. Pamina holds the beater softly, drops it on the xylophone and then wheels herself towards Ms Lovari. She takes another beater from Ms Lovari's hands and initiates a more complex musical structure. While playing the tambourine offered by Ms Lovari, she manages to stamp with her paralysed foot, combining the rhythm, tempo and volume of her stamps with the timbre of her tambourine notes. Through rhythm, tempo and volume, she initiates and maintains an intense communication in dialogue with the music of the carers and myself, including the playful trick of almost hitting the floor with her foot and then delaying it for a split second. This creates a communication with a far more developed content than that of her mouth repertoire. Jenny responds to Pamina's evolution with looks of indifference alongside her loud autistic vocalisations. Sarah reacts with intense fear, screaming in mock laughter every time that Pamina drops the beater on the tambourine. All this is incorporated into the whole music created by the carers and myself (Figure 8.4).

The movement of Pamina's limbs, previously considered paralysed by the carers, moved them all to tears. This was a period when the carers felt strongly attached to all the patients in the group, trusted their potential and felt indignant at the contemptuous attitude towards them of other workers. In our free-discussion group meetings, this indignation was turned into deeper commitment and inner confidence to bring out patients' unprecedented skills.

Figure 8.4 Integrating Pamina's and Sarah's contrasting expressions

Internal worlds of fear and persecution: The paranoid-schizoid position

By now it was becoming ever clearer that each group member's actions, movements and creations were perceived as threatening by the others, or were intended to be threatening. Sarah had difficulty creating a note for fear of what might befall her from all sides; Jenny would either throw the other patients' beaters to the floor or emit her loud autistic vocalisations in order to destroy another's creations; Pamina could even use her wheelchair to dislodge another member. Such attacks were less in the realm of objective reality than in that of unconscious fantasy, which loomed very real for these patients. Having never experienced a benign and emotionally responsive primary caregiver, they peopled their inner worlds with hostile and aggressive objects. According to Klein (1988c), the absence of the breast is not experienced as absence, but as a presence of a bad breast. When there is nobody emotionally present to receive your fears, anxieties, hatred and aggression, the impact of these emotions rebounds into the self, so that they get magnified and distorted.

The patients brought to the group a psychic world tormented with projections and introjections of persecutory and life-threatening objects. As Sinason (1992, 1997) writes, for many learning-disabled people, the threat of annihilation and other people's wish that they were dead or had never been born have a basis in their real-life experiences, as well as their fantasy. This exacerbates the persecutory anxiety characteristic of the paranoid-schizoid position, which was another aspect of the group matrix.

As the patients formed attachment bonds with their allocated carers and with the group, and as the carers became more sensitive to their signals, the feelings of horror and persecution were even more clearly expressed. Thus, from February 1996, to Sarah's dropping beaters was added something far more internal: endlessly repeated belches and emissions of wind, as if evacuating her whole body, mainly directed towards me but also towards any other members of the group who were active in some way. As she belched, Sarah would let her body waver in mid-air, so to speak, as she stooped and stretched out her fingers. The facial muscles would get tense and the eyes would widen in terror, then there would immediately follow her stereotypical smile.

The depressive position and the surfacing of new skills

The group's dynamic matrix, to use an object-relations theoretical framework (Klein 1988b and 1988c; Ganzarain 1989), fluctuated between the paranoid-schizoid and the depressive position. Every regression to the paranoid-schizoid position revealed more clearly the fragmented, terrifying, part-object world of the patients, and every movement forwards revealed more strongly the progress towards integration, greater tolerance for one another, sadness and a desire to master and control their actions creatively, which all characterise the depressive position. Every return to the depressive position brought to the surface new skills of creative achievement, hitherto unthinkable in the patients' life in the institution. One of the first significant changes was Sarah's ability to walk. She had always had to lean her body on her carer in order to walk, yet by June 1995, 14 months into the group's life, she was able to walk unaided. This transformation gave the carers hope and a feeling that it was due to their work that Sarah was able to walk.

The excerpt below from 17 June 1996 shows yet another stage of synthesis and integration in Sarah.

CASE STUDY CONTINUED

Sarah's achievement of mastery and control

Sarah's tentative touches on the piano keys, fearing whatever was happening around her, convert into a creative effort to control her handicapped fingers. She initiates the rhythmical motif 'short–long', corresponding to the rhythm of Pamina's wheelchair movements. Thus, Sarah's creation connects her with Pamina, and we keep this rhythm as a form and reminder of their own repertoires, which are interrelated. It becomes the leitmotif binding the music formed between Sarah and Ms Antouna on the piano, the pulse of Pamina's wheelchair movements and hyperventilation, and their reflection by Ms Kazakaiou on the bass drum and myself on the piano. Sarah succeeds, seemingly intentionally, in playing single notes repeatedly. Her fingers have usually fidgeted with each other, never properly grasping an object, so it is an enormous achievement to control the position of arm, hand and fingers, so as to press one single note. Ms Antouna looks so proud.

Many of Sarah's phrases employ the rhythmical leitmotif within the tempo of the music, meaning that she can focus on a musical thought and control her actions so as to create it. Her belches and her musical phrases meet one another, until the phrases themselves replace and sublimate the anxiety of her internal evacuations.

Evolution of Jenny's communication skills

From the secure base of her attachment to Ms Demetriou, Jenny frequently visited the piano, sat next to me and played. For over 2 years she would play through my hand, but from October 1996 she would explore single notes or clusters in various dynamics and durations with her own hands. During such moments, she would gradually stop swinging her head or grinding her teeth. As she began to function outside her autistic shell, her liveliness surfaced and her isolation decreased. At the same time, Jenny's autistic sounds became, paradoxically, part of her communicative repertoire, as if the autistic and the non-autistic aspects of her personality coexisted. The description below from 2 December 1996 is an example of Jenny's use of vocal sounds.

CASE STUDY CONTINUED

Jenny's use of vocal sounds

Pamina wheels herself near the xylophone, lifting her right hand to indicate a desire for the beater. Ms Kazakaiou puts a beater over the xylophone keys. Pamina takes it instantly and throws it near the xylophone keys. As she does so, Jenny makes repeated 'tsou' sounds (a Greek colloquial expression for 'no'). The second time Pamina is ready to receive the beater, Jenny makes her high-pitched, destructive-sounding vocalisation. Ms Kazakaiou plays a xylophone phrase to invite Pamina to play, and immediately Jenny utters a prolonged 'Ah' from closed vocal cords. She repeats this at exactly the moment Pamina next gets the beater in her hand. The underlying meaning of her sounds becomes clear as she takes more direct action, getting up quickly and noisily from her chair, bending over the xylophone keys and, while looking at Pamina, throwing her beater from the xylophone onto the floor.

Like Sarah's belches, Jenny's sounds formed an aggressive attack against another's existence; but whereas Sarah 'threw up' the other's existence, Jenny denied it, refusing to stomach it for even a few seconds.

Ameliorating the patients' envy

Sarah had never used her hands for anything purposeful in her whole life, yet in music therapy she could grasp a beater and press the piano keys; she had never walked without physical support, yet in music therapy she had walked unsupported. What had previously deterred her from revealing her abilities and making use of them?

Sinason (1986, 1992) describes a type of secondary handicap which the handicapped person uses to deal with the pain of their difference from the normal population. This entails an attack on their own abilities, through which they deny this pain and envy of what others have and they lack. By becoming more handicapped, there can be no comparison.

In the music therapy groups, the patients' envy of the non-handicapped persons, natural within the unsupported institutionalised environment, was eased in multiple ways. They each had an allocated carer, giving them exclusive attention, allowing them to make a split between a good and a bad object: either I or their carer could become the bad, persecuting object to whom they could project their hostile feelings, without endangering the other object, which they would keep as good. The existence of an exclusive relationship with an allocated carer within the group also alleviated the patients' envious attacks upon each other. The fact that their allocated carers played what they themselves could have played, or imagined playing, facilitated their identification with the carers. They could easily introject their carers' musical function. This brought them a step closer to my level of skill, making it easier to receive the music coming from me. They could also identify with the path that their carers were traversing in music therapy: a path of greater openness to communication and understanding of non-verbal language, leading to a richer use of the sound medium. The reduction of their carers' shame in exploring a new medium without previous knowledge brought the reduction of the patients' shame in doing the same. Being enabled to create sounds themselves alleviated their envy of the conductor's sounds.

The setting facilitated both the formation of attachment bonds between the patients and their allocated carers, and the internalisation of the group as one whole good object. The group and my role as a conductor were together both the supportive ambience and the supervising eye, encouraging the evolution of those bonds.

Changes in the group

From February 1996, after a long preparation, sessions were reduced to once monthly. In December 1996, Sarah and Jenny, with Ms Antouna and Ms Demetriou, moved together into the first state community home created in Cyprus. Moving patients and their carers together acknowledged their attachment bonds as an outcome of music therapy participation. The reduced session frequency did not halt the group's process.

CASE STUDY CONTINUED

Sarah's cry

On 5 May 1997, Sarah entered the room and walked to the piano, while looking intensely at Ms Lovari, the only carer in the room from whom she had been parted by moving into the community home. From open smiling lips, she let out intense vocalisations that soon shifted into an endless wailing, with tears pouring out of her eyes for the first time in her known life. It was that awful wail of someone whose soul and body was burning from an aching pain reaching all the corners of her existence; the cry that never was; that never had a right to be. In the history of the sessions, in a meaningful sequence, had come the smile that was not a smile, the laughter that was not laughter, the endless belches and emissions of wind, and at last this cry, her first tears, expressing whatever remained hidden behind everything else. Sarah continued crying for 30 minutes, finally glancing towards all of us, as the carers and I played music for her. Her murmurs then became part of our musical phrases, as she revealed the relief she was experiencing at our collective existence around her.

It was the symbolic benevolent existence of us inside Sarah that allowed her to cry. (Such tears can flow when a person has internalised a compassionate companion in life.)

CASE STUDY CONTINUED

Pamina's evocation of a harmonious ensemble from the carers

Right from her entry into the room on 6 October 1997, Pamina wheeled herself to the synthesiser, placing her body in such a way as to be able to strike the keys. She instantly started playing the synthesiser, pressing the keys with any means she had (elbow, fingers), even before we were all in the room to start the session. It seemed that she had been ready for it for a long time, that her thoughts were clear and organised – and her determination to play the synthesiser preconceived and inevitable. She played almost continuously for the whole 30 minutes of the session. The physical effort must have been gigantic for a person with her physical disabilities – to have kept her elbow lifted and her fingers in a position to strike the keys. Her emotional need to achieve and create must have been outstanding. It required an even greater physical effort to play with her right elbow so that leaning on it she could lift her left hand onto the synthesiser keys and play with both hands. It was very moving to witness her efforts to play with her fingers, sometimes achieving what she seemed to have intended: to play single notes. Her phrases were coherent and consisted of a meaningful array of notes. Jenny's and Sarah's softly uttered vocalisations joined Pamina's phrases. The whole music, created by Ms Kazakaiou on the chimes, Ms Demetriou on the xylophone and bongo drums, Ms Antouna on the metallophone and myself on the piano, contextualised Pamina's phrases alongside Jenny's and Sarah's utterances (Figure 8.5).

Figure 8.5 Pamina's supreme effort to play the keyboard

Around the middle of the session, while still playing the synthesiser with her right hand, Pamina decided to add her mouth repertoire over her left hand. It seemed that she desired to create melody through the synthesiser and rhythm through her mouth repertoire at the same time. Then she immersed herself in just her mouth repertoire for 4.5 minutes, facing Ms Kazakaiou, who responded by creating variations of Pamina's phrases on the temple blocks. In response to Pamina's music, each of the carers simultaneously sustained with confidence and originality a lengthy melodic and rhythmical part. The resultant, well-harmonised music that we all created provided a context for Pamina's phrases, so that her notes were falling into a meaningful musical whole.

Pamina continued to play in this way in most of the remaining sessions. Within the group's 'secure base' she had discovered her own independent part through exerting momentous efforts to surpass her physical limitations. While doing so, her ear was tuned to the group's responses, as she knew that in the music therapy room whatever happened was interrelated.

Conclusion

Patients' development

The group music therapy methodology briefly described in this chapter enabled the patients to find attachment figures and trusted companions in both the music therapy sessions and their everyday lives. Their relief from life's pain was enormous, and their capacity for exploring inner affective states recovered greatly along with the means of expressing them through sound; buried skills saw the light of day. For this reason, in the later period of the group, the patients functioned within the depressive position more than ever before. Expressions of sadness were accompanied by unprecedented independence and creative achievements as well as greater tolerance for each other's creations. The behaviours that had begun as obscure, non-verbal signals were increasingly being clarified as a clear language with specific intentions.

It was extraordinary to realise, through second-by-second analysis of hundreds of video-recorded sessions, that although individuals' available repertoire of behaviour was minimal, there was no sound, no gesture, no movement that occurred that did not form a resonance, an associative link, with another's way of being. It was such links that we tried to receive within us and bind together through a live musical creation. One member's movement became the rhythm, another's murmurs became the melody and yet another's twists and turns, the musical timbre.

Theoretical implications of developing from carers to auxiliary therapists and principal attachment objects

The novelty of the model described lay in the way the carers participated in psychodynamic group music therapy: they were not present as escorts or in their carer role but rather in order to fulfil the patients' need for principal attachment figures, present in as large a part of their lives as possible. Yet the patients received psychodynamic group music therapy of no less intensity than in any other model, such as one including a single co-therapist. In fact, psychodynamic group music therapy was the groundwork that made possible the evolution of the complete model. It provided an incentive, a stimulation, a binding force, a reassurance of the dynamic interrelatedness of all members evidenced through the medium of sound/music. It was in this context that affective behaviour made its initial appearance, followed by the formation of affective bonds.

Through becoming the patients' principal objects of attachment, through psychodynamic group music therapy itself and through the free-discussion group meetings, the carers also gradually became auxiliary therapists in what might be called an apprenticeship model. This was another aspect of the model's novelty. (A similar methodology has since been applied to other groups and to parents becoming auxiliary music therapists in the music therapy work with their children.) Thus, Ms Antouna knew how close she should be in order to help Sarah realise her first walk. Ms Demetriou knew how to strike the right balance by encouraging, rather than forcing, Pamina during her first xylophone playing. The carers' balance between support, encouragement and faith in the patients' abilities without violation was amazingly appropriate within the first 5 months of the group's life. Their abilities to improvise music followed a similar route. While in the session of 15 July 1994 their participation consisted of some soft cymbal touches or brief drum phrases, which served as accompaniments to my techniques, in the session of 6 October 1997 their contribution in the creation of music therapy techniques consisted of sustained symmetrical and independent melodic and rhythmical parts. Their contribution entailed a very attentive listening to another four or five players, while at the same time focusing on Pamina's music and how to support it in the best possible way.

In the free-discussion group meeting on 6 October 1997, Ms Kazakaiou said that Pamina's mouth repertoire, interpolated amidst her synthesiser playing, was her way of communicating to Ms Kazakaiou and the group the following: 'Remember, this is how I started years ago and this is what I can do *now.*' This summarises the carers' evolution too.

References

Agrotou, A. (1993) 'Spontaneous Ritualized Play in Music Therapy: A Technical and Theoretical Analysis.' In T. Wigram and M. Heal (eds) *Music Therapy in Health and Education.* London: Jessica Kingsley Publishers.

Agrotou, A. (1994) 'Isolation and the multi-handicapped patient: an analysis of the music therapist–patient affects and processes.' *The Arts in Psychotherapy 21,* 5, 359–365.

Agrotou, A. (1998) 'Psychodynamic Group Music Therapy with Profoundly Learning Disabled Residents and Their Carers: Developing a Theory and Practice for the Realisation of Therapeutic Aims for Residents and the Acquirement of Therapist's Skills by Carers.' PhD thesis, University of Sheffield. Available at http://ethos.bl.uk/OrderDetails.do?uin=uk.bl.ethos.575159, accessed on 2 October 2015.

Alvarez, A. (1992) *Live Company.* London: Routledge.

Bowlby, J. (1988) *A Secure Base: Clinical Applications of Attachment Theory.* London: Routledge.

Foulkes, S.H. (1975) *Group Analytic Psychotherapy: Method and Principles.* London: Maresfield Library.

Foulkes, S.H. (1990a) 'Group Dynamic Processes and Group Analysis.' In E. Foulkes (ed) *Selected Papers of S.H. Foulkes: Psychoanalysis and Group Analysis.* London: Karnac Books. (Original work published in 1968.)

Foulkes, S.H. (1990b) 'The Group as Matrix of the Individual's Mental Life.' In E. Foulkes (ed) *Selected Papers of S.H. Foulkes: Psychoanalysis and Group Analysis.* London: Karnac Books. (Original work published in 1973.)

Ganzarain, R. (1989) *Object Relations Group Psychotherapy: The Group as an Object, a Tool, and a Training Base.* Madison, CT: International Universities Press.

Klein, M. (ed) (1988a) 'A Contribution to the Psychogenesis of Manic-Depressive States.' In *Love, Guilt and Reparation and Other Works, 1921–1945.* London: Virago Press. (Original work published in 1935.)

Klein, M. (ed) (1988b) 'Notes on Some Schizoid Mechanisms.' In *Envy and Gratitude and Other Works, 1946–1963.* London: Virago Press. (Original work published in 1946.)

Klein, M. (ed) (1988c) 'Some Theoretical Conclusions Regarding the Emotional Life of the Infant.' In *Envy and Gratitude and Other Works, 1946–1963.* London: Virago Press. (Original work published in 1952.)

Sinason, V. (1986) 'Secondary mental handicap and its relation to trauma.' *Psychoanalytic Psychotherapy 2,* 2, 131–154.

Sinason, V. (1992) *Mental Handicap and the Human Condition: New Approaches from the Tavistock.* London: Free Association Books.

Sinason, V. (1997) 'Gender-Linked Issues in Psychotherapy with Abused and Learning Disabled Female Patients.' In J. Raphael-Leff and R.J. Perelberg (eds) *Female Experience: Three Generations of British Women Psychoanalysts on Work with Women.* London: Routledge.

Tustin, F. (1986) *Autistic Barriers in Neurotic Patients.* London: Karnac Books.

Tustin, F. (1990) *The Protective Shell in Children and Adults.* London: Karnac Books.

Chapter 9

Supporting the Unplanned Journey

Music Therapy as a Developmental Resource with People with Profound and Multiple Learning Disabilities and Their Carers and Staff

Tessa Watson

Introduction

Tuesday, 10 a.m.

'Hi Tessa,' calls Cath, one of the care staff, as I walk into the centre. 'We'll see you at 10 – we'll make sure everyone is ready to start. I wonder what will happen in the group today.'

Half an hour later, there are 10 of us in the therapy room. There is much music – from voices, Soundbeam,[1] percussion, cello, violin, cymbal and ocean drum. One person is rocking rhythmically and playing the Soundbeam as she does so. That's Ranjit. She stops every now and then to check that she is making the sound, and to see what will happen to the therapists' music in response to her pause. Then she looks up, makes eye contact and shouts, and starts to play again. Pat, the member of care staff sitting next to her, rocks with her from time to time, echoing her movements and energy, using an intensive interaction approach. Mandy is sitting more quietly, watchful, finding the group hard today, on the edge of distress. Fran, another member of care staff, sits quietly with her, waiting, aware that Mandy's contact with the group is fragile and still growing. She gently offers opportunities for interaction by presenting instruments, guided by the music therapist. Another person in the room is scat singing – loudly, confidently. That's John. He's the soloist, and he knows he's leading the group at that moment. He hears the response from others to his sounds, and continues to sing. The music therapists draw all the music into a group sound with their musical responses.

This is a music therapy and sensory interaction group for people with profound and multiple learning disabilities (developed by Minna

---

1   Soundbeam is an electronic instrument with an onboard sampler that uses sensor technology to translate body movement into digitally generated sound. See www. soundbeam.co.uk for more information; also see Magee and Burland (2009).

Harman and Tessa Watson) (Lovell *et al.* 2014). This chapter tells the story and thinking behind this group, which supported not only service users but also their carers.

Music therapists working with people with learning disability tend to use varied and creative practice, reflecting the continuum of need presented by people who may have mild, moderate, severe or profound and multiple learning disabilities. Karkou and Sanderson (2006) suggest that 'due to the wide diversity of needs of this client group, a wide diversity of therapeutic models is followed' (p.101). When I began work as a music therapist in 1990, music therapy was beginning to grapple seriously with the idea of working with colleagues and carers. Music therapists were beginning to explore different ways of engaging with carers in and out of the clinical space. As thinking and practice have developed, work with carers and colleagues is delivered on a needs-led basis: Aigen's ideal of a 'situationally determined approach' is helpful here (2005). Asking the question 'How will it help the person in therapy if I also engage and work in some way with their parent or carer?' has led to my practice taking various different avenues (Watson 2007). In my current clinical work I engage with carers in different ways: in clinical sessions, through the provision of training for family and paid carers, and through support groups for family carers. The group described in this chapter engages with carers specifically in order to develop their own working practice.

Music therapy and sensory interaction group

The music therapy and sensory interaction group that I will describe was developed over many years of clinical experience and discussion with other music therapists (Watson 2011, 2014) and uses pre-composed and improvised music as well as physiotherapy exercises and intensive interaction approaches (Nind and Hewett 2001). Music technology, such as Soundbeam, and acoustic instruments are used. The group is run by two therapists, with support from one or more members of care staff. Trainees (music therapists and other disciplines) may also work and learn in the group. This group is designed to be an environment where healthy relationships can be established and grown, and thought about, frequently through a framework of theoretical constructs such as containment and attachment.

This provides a developmental environment for service users, carers, trainees and therapists.

Beginnings

We begin the group in the same way every week. As we bring the instruments into the room and set the group up, we listen to the same CD. This provides a musical boundary into the session; it announces, 'We're here, we will soon be starting.' This sound boundary is very important for this group, who may not be able to understand words.

The idea of boundaries was understood by Bick (1968) as follows:

> …in its most primitive form the parts of the personality are felt to have no binding force amongst themselves and must therefore be held together in a way that is experienced by them passively, by the skin functioning as a boundary. (p.55)

She understands the experience of the very young baby to be unintegrated and potentially terrifying. We, too, have thought about this vulnerability and possible experience of lack of integration for our group members. We think of the way in which they use sensory experiences to provide themselves with boundaries of self and others, self and the world. We have carefully planned and shaped the session to allow for a process moving from initial engagement, active involvement and then to an ending, and we think of the musical medium as having the function of a boundary. In writing this chapter, I was struck by the importance of the flow of the group – the serious work that contributed to planning the timing and order of the different sections and the transitions between them. This part of the chapter follows the same shape and journey.

Greeting and moving

In this part of the session, we sing a greeting song to each member of the group. We encourage the group members to indicate to us their wish or readiness to be sung to, and we wait for these signals to show us where to focus our attention. Group members might call out or shout, move or gesture, look or wake up. We consider these actions to be intentional communications to the group. In this way we show right at the beginning of the session that we will be led by the

group members. We encourage care staff to help us read the group and
see the signals. This immediately helps us to work together; it allows
care staff to bring their detailed knowledge of the people in the group
to the session, and we learn about their communication repertoire and
use our music to create connections. At this point we are modelling
waiting; sometimes we wait for several minutes. Modelling that waiting
as acceptable and valuable is important work in this clinical area, as
people with profound and multiple learning disabilities can take time
to initiate their responses.

The therapist who is leading the session moves, with guitar, to
sit close to the person who has indicated they want to be sung to. A
member of care staff also comes to sit close. All staff in the session
sing, with harmony where possible, providing a thick musical texture.
We use a well-known English folk tune with altered harmonies and
words, which staff feel confident to sing. The song is altered in the
moment to match and respond to the communication style of each
person, and here we show that all kinds of communications are valued
(e.g. humming, groaning, rocking, roaring, laughing, shouting). We
think here about reverie, holding each person in mind, and about
containment:

> ...the state of mind in which it is possible for the mother unconsciously
> to be in touch with the baby's evacuations or communications of
> pain, and of his expressions of pleasure, to receive them, to be able
> to engage with and savour them if calm and loving, or to modulate
> them if distressed and hating, and to hand them back to him in
> recognizable and now tolerable form. (Alvarez 1992, p.36)

Here we are also informed by other theory. Alvarez (1992) writes of
the 'undrawn' child, suggesting that the 'maternal object needs...to
be seen as pulling the child, drawing the child, attracting the child
or interesting the child' (p.77). Part of this initial engagement in the
session can involve us attracting and drawing the child into the musical
world – being more engaging than the person's own self-stimulatory
or sensory world.

Fonagy (2001) writes that, in order to be helpful to the child,
the mother's reflection in containment needs to 'consist of a subtle
combination of mirroring and the communication of a contrasting
affect' (p.171). He suggests that this contrasting affect conveys that
difficult feelings are manageable, and writes that if caregivers fail

to respond to their infant's distress or reflect back distress only, opportunities are lost for the infant to build internalised representations that help him to regulate his affective states. Although we are providing a different relationship, this idea has been useful. Music therapists' clinical improvisation has this capacity to combine a mirroring and contrasting affect. For example, the therapist might respond to a raw or wild vocal sound with her voice, and use guitar chords to punctuate, but also provide a sense of warmth with the type of chord. Excited rhythmic rocking and calling, possibly tipping into anxious sounds, can be met by percussive guitar techniques with a calmer vocal response. Using the ability of music to say two things at once allows us to provide active containment of emotional states, in a way that feels safe for service users and observing carers.

After the song has been sung once, the member of care staff invites the person to begin moving and stretching, as the therapist continues to sing and echo the movements and sounds that they are making. The other therapists in the group sing too and respond to the vocal sounds and movements of others, drawing the group together. The member of care staff uses physiotherapy exercises specifically designed for each person. This physical contact is always offered gently and withdrawn if the person does not wish to engage. As members become familiar with the group, they appear to anticipate this part of the session and engage in it eagerly.

Thinking about embodiment and working with touch is important for those working with people with profound and multiple learning disabilities; it is an area about which little has been written, and perhaps we underestimate it. Touch is present in all early attachment relationships. It is hard to know how to use touch therapeutically with adults; indeed, some places of work have 'no touch' policies. Hewett (2007), one of the architects of intensive interaction, has written usefully about physicality, touch and 'empathic handling', and their importance in life for people with profound and multiple learning disabilities. Bringing touch into the group has been helpful for care staff who may feel that physical contact is important but who are concerned about its appropriate use in their work. Using touch and movement in the early stages of the group has helped to find an acceptable way to begin the group with a physical experience of being connected to others. This may be particularly important for this group of people, some of whom are in 'sensation dominated states' (Tustin 1981).

Music (2011), writing about attachment, suggests that sensory autistic-like self-stimulating behaviours, such as rocking, nodding and teeth grinding, can result from 'very depriving early experiences' (p.53). Tustin also thought of these behaviours as strategies to shut out the living world and to protect and give comfort in the face of powerful and intense experiences. We are using touch here, however, to show possibilities: those of making contact with another and of using objects (to make sounds and music). This part of the session has proved essential, providing, as Fearn and O'Connor (2008, p.56) write, 'double feedback' for the group through both music and movement. By assisting the people in the group with stretching and moving in this context, we aim for them to achieve greater awareness and control of their bodies. They also physically rehearse movements and actions that will help them to use the group more fully as it unfolds. After each person has been sung to, the group often continues their singing together. This idea came from the group, who have often continued to vocalise after the 'hello' songs have finished – as though they are continuing to make contact with each other. The therapists sing with this and encourage the connections to grow.

This opening section provides specifically tailored individual musical and physical attention. It aims to draw each member of the group into active engagement as far as is possible, making a link between their material (musical or physical) and the rest of the group. It promotes a process of awareness of self and others, and brings awareness to different ways of communicating. In this part of the group we are providing a space into which communications can come, be heard and be responded to sensitively.

Thoughts about time, silence and waiting

This greeting, moving and singing section of the group takes up to 30 minutes. There seems to be real importance in waiting here, accepting and valuing silence, and taking this part of the group slowly, helping each person to 'wake up' to the possibilities in the room and to prepare for the improvisation ahead. It can be hard for care staff to wait and sit in silence with us; it's much easier to jump in and do something, make something happen. However, 'the silence out of which music comes is fundamental' (Sutton 2007, p.170). Timing and pace are important in this group. Interactive gestures are carefully offered, and time is given to take in what is happening. This group of people may need time to process experiences and respond, and waiting is important. If we cannot judge, through sensitive observation, the right moment to interact, our contact may feel intrusive, or even violent. It is important that we do not force our reality onto the group. Engaging carers in this slow-paced work can provide a useful tool for their work in varied situations.

Improvising

The group now moves from individual contact into group play. It takes a little time to help the group members find instruments before they settle down to play. In earlier sessions, a CD of pre-recorded music was used at this point, to keep a musical thread or container alive and active. As the group has developed, however, we have felt that they can maintain interest and alertness during the break between greeting and improvisation. They wait for the instruments, able to stay engaged rather than become hidden again. We may consider that they are able to internalise something about the group which holds them through the transition between sections.

In this part of the group there is free improvisatory group music play with the instruments and vocalisations. Stern (2001) writes that 'playing can only occur in a setting where there is a feeling of ease, of security, of not having to be vigilant, being free of pressing other needs' (p.145). The opening sections help to create a sense of containment and healthy engagement, in order that the group can playfully explore.

A range of usual music therapy percussion instruments is available, and also a Soundbeam. We use two devices with this technology. First is the Soundbeam itself. This is a little like a microphone in shape, but it emits an ultrasonic beam. When the beam is broken by movement, it creates a run of notes. There are two beams available. Second, there are four switches, which can easily be pushed or squeezed to create a note. The beams and switches can be programmed to a large number of different sounds.

It has been liberating for the group to work with Soundbeam. Group members who could not or would not hold instruments, and were therefore limited mainly to the use of voice, have been able to take a fuller part in the group through the use of Soundbeam. This has developed their independence in the group. The physical actions involved in playing Soundbeam also help group members to understand more about cause and effect, and the impact that they might be able to have in the group. Thus, individual members have been able to experience influencing the group, changing the music. This has allowed reciprocity to develop in our attachment relationships. Opportunities for reciprocal, interactive contact are particularly important for people with profound disabilities as they cannot often independently seek and maintain attachments with peers.

The improvisation is led by the service users. The therapists support the sounds, music, movements and other contributions that emerge in the improvisation. The quality of the group music comes from these contributions; the therapists elaborate and develop the particular qualities of sounds and movements that the group bring, and weave these qualities into a group dialogue, linking the group members together. The music holds diverse feeling experiences. Some of these experiences are obvious – for example, David roaring in anger, banging and rocking his chair, but held by the music, and eventually processing this rage; or Sarah weeping as she sings, experiencing some deep sadness, supported by the music and by the member of care staff who holds her hand. At times, the music therapists have needed to give reassurance to care staff that they, and the music, can hold these strong feelings, that it is not necessary to take other action (e.g. getting a drink, removing someone, stopping the group). This indicates the powerful nature of the feelings that are brought to the session, and the importance of the music in matching, containing and processing them. The music allows the experiences of the service users to be witnessed safely and acknowledged as real and valid.

How the group ends

The ending of the group is carefully planned. There are two stages:

1. Pre-composed music is used at this point, introducing a wide variety of styles and genres of music to the group. The playing of pre-composed CDs is a way of maintaining the attachment with music while the instruments are slowly removed and put away.

2. New music is introduced and the responses of the group are observed. Ideas are taken back into the next session in our improvisation. The music played here is diverse: Bach solo violin suites, John Tavener, opera by Verdi and others, Stevie Wonder, Nitin Sawhney and world music – from Bollywood through to English folk songs and South African styles.

As the music plays and the instruments are slowly put away, the music therapists also talk with the group about what has happened in the session, about the music and the interaction. They comment on what they have noticed, on new developments and choices, or a return to favourite instruments and sounds, and on connections between group members. This helps care staff to be aware of developments and changes, and to see that things that they do in the group are noticed and valued. It also models a respectful and inclusive way of talking about the people using the group.

It has been challenging to articulate the value of this group for users and carers within the current economic climate, which focuses largely on quantifiable outcomes that can be counted or seen. Painful realities can be hard to consider. Supporting and developing emotional resilience, skills and capacity for both service users and the workforce is hard to measure (particularly in a service-user population who cannot self-report). Blaustein and Kinniburgh (2010) write of the importance of providing supportive, not punitive, cultures, suggesting that work cultures should:

…accept that providers – like our clients – are people with built-in human emotions and danger-response systems. By building appropriate, boundaried forums for staff support, we reduce the likelihood that these emotions and responses will play out in our work with clients. Consider professional supports such as supervision, clinical or staffing meetings, and training. Pay attention to forums that are process oriented as well as task oriented… Building safe forums in which staff members can explore their own responses and actions – both positive and negative – is crucial to using these experiences as building blocks for future successes. (p.63)

Containment: Parental and staff experiences

A parent describes the experience of having a disabled child:

> The fact of my son's disability suddenly comes to the forefront of my mind and I'm wondering what he would have been like, wondering what he would have been like if he had been typical, what our lives as parents would have been like, and what our relationship with him would have been like? As he gets older and is no longer a child, I feel increasing sadness. (Bruce and Schultz, p.66)

This part of the chapter considers the experiences of parents and carers, and the importance of music therapists having a role in their support. In recent history, parents of some of the adults with whom we now work were given little support, or were encouraged to put their young children in institutions (in the 1960s and 1970s) and forget about them, with devastating impact on attachment and future relationships (Nickson 2005). While services have changed dramatically in the way they support families, parents of children and adults with learning disabilities may still experience high levels of parental stress and grief, as they enter a world that 'plunges children, young people and their families into a confusing and previously unknown world' (Royal College of Nursing 2013, p.3). Emmanuel (2004) suggests that 'feelings of grief and anger in parents, when faced with a damaged baby, are seldom processed. The unbearable fact of damage cannot be thought about and thereby contained' (p.59). There may be great challenges to parents in managing and processing their own feelings, and providing containment for their disabled child or adult.

Non-finite grief

Hooper (undated), mother and music therapist, states:

> Being the parent of a child who doesn't fit can have an unexpected consequence: you don't fit either. As other mums celebrated their babies' milestones, I waited and, eventually, I realised I was waiting alone. I didn't know, until it happened to me, how lonely that place could be. (p.1)

Babb (2007), the mother of a learning-disabled woman, describes her hopes and dreams being continually shattered, and writes:

The sense of loss and isolation over the years has often felt too huge to bear...this grief carries multiple and successive losses throughout the life of a learning disabled person. Jayne was never going to have a job, leave home or have a family...[it was like]...being on a battlefield: constantly fighting for funding and for appropriate resources for Jayne's best qualities of life has been a lifelong struggle. The impact on my own health and the strain on family relationships were overwhelming, and all that one is trying to do is provide the best for one's child. (p.17)

Bruce and Schultz (2001) also write about these ideas of non-finite grief and disenfranchised grief in relation to disability, noting that these have 'a haunting and inescapable quality' (p.8). These are losses that aren't recognised by others and can't be publicly mourned. Jónsdóttir (2008) writes compellingly about the way in which music therapy has been used to explore themes such as these in a carers' support group.

Facing the damage together: Why reflection is important

These themes of self-judgement, stress and grief are also relevant for staff, though rarely considered in the literature. A colleague recently recounted an experience of being with a service user with profound and multiple learning disabilities and his paid carer in the community as part of a therapeutic assessment. She described the unwelcome attention, rejection and horror they encountered (alongside more positive responses), and noted how she struggled to contain and manage this experience for herself. She felt powerless, sad and guilty, and found it hard to reflect. Many parents and carers report this kind of unwelcome and stressful attention (Beadle-Brown *et al.* 2013). If carers do not have mechanisms to contain and manage their own feelings, it will be hard for them to contain the feelings given to them by service users. Parents and carers are frequently very resilient because of these experiences, and this resilience is important to nurture and develop.

Supporting carers is a government priority (Department of Health 2012). The context for our work – the modern health and care landscape – is changing, and there are new priorities such as prevention, well-being, service-user involvement and new frameworks for commissioning services (Department of Health 2012). These changes require music therapists to engage, educate and work with many partners, and to reflect further on the discourse they use to describe and situate their work (see Barrington 2008, pp.203–213). Working with others is now a central part of the role of music therapists and can be rewarding and enjoyable (Twyford and Watson 2008). In the UK, the care staff who work with people with learning disabilities are frequently committed and caring. But they are also unqualified and poorly paid. They may have had little formal training about disabilities. Music therapists spend significant time in their training carefully considering the way in which their work affects them, in order that they can sustain a long career in their work with very disabled or ill people. Care staff are rarely presented with this encouragement or perspective. Both music therapists and care staff have supervision as part of the governance and development of their work. For care staff this tends to be procedure focused, rather than process focused, with little support given to think about the kinds of relationships that they are developing in their work with service users, and about how these relationships might affect them as staff. Joint supervision for music therapists and care staff was not possible within this working environment; instead, the music therapists played a partly supervisory role in their support of care staff, hoping to encourage reflection on the experience of care staff, in the service of raising standards to the service users.

Work with people with profound and multiple learning disabilities is rewarding and challenging. It can bring difficult feelings. Going back to the idea of containment, Waddell (1998) states: 'The good mother is not the one who denies her hatred and aggressive feelings but the one who knows about them and is able to tolerate them in herself' (p.41). Knowing about, tolerating and naming feelings that group members and carers might have – difficult feelings such as anger, aggression, sadness and so forth – has helped these feelings to be contained and processed within this setting.

Supporting staff to work with self-awareness

Bowlby (2005) discusses attachment in both childhood and adulthood, writing that attachments change throughout life. Children with profound and multiple learning disabilities become adults, but they do not develop their attachments into romantic relationships, and then become parents (Bowlby 2005; Howe 2011). Instead, they may be stuck at a particular place in their development and in their attachment relationships. This can be painful for staff, who may be of a similar age to the service users, and who must manage the disjunction between the person's age and their development. They may resort to managing the pain of this by treating people as though they were still young children. Simpson (2004) notes this:

> ...infancy and childhood are being held on to like a saving grace or blessing, with even a promise of immortality, the price of which is the handicap itself... The cost, however, of time standing still is that development cannot occur. (p.80)

Gently reframing the way in which staff think about service users can allow more authentic relationships to develop.

Linington (2009), a psychotherapist, writes about his experience of his own baby being born, and how he had to interrogate his horror that his child might be born with a learning disability. He writes: 'Surely, after all my years of contact with people with learning disabilities and my advocacy for their rights as human beings, it should really make no difference whether my son had a learning disability or not' (p.55). This is important writing and thinking; if we block our own responses to the work, such as guilt, relief or shame, we may not be open to feelings brought to us by our clients. In the same way, if we can help staff to name and acknowledge their feelings about their work and their clients, they may be able to work differently. This seems to be particularly important when there are no words, or limited words. We can become wordless ourselves in a parallel process, stuck and unable to progress or to have ideas. The current health care climate focuses on positive outcomes and it is hard to consider painful realities. How does our work and our feelings about our work interact with policy and strategic thinking? Roman (2016) writes thoughtfully about the idea of internal and external pressures, and the way in which they might impact on our work and thinking in music therapy.

Holding a space to reflect and process

We have been able to offer a parallel process for staff. For example, through the work of the group we contain staff difficulties and anxiety about being with people with such profound disabilities, and help transference to be processed. Agrotou (1999) refers to this idea in her moving video (also discussed in Chapter 8) when she talks about 'bringing carers and residents into a parallel process of change'. Once some of this processing has been done in the group, it is easier for staff to slow their pace down and wait for the communications of the service user.

The care staff working in this group value it as a place where people with profound disabilities develop strong, trusting relationships and communicate through music. Care staff witness group members bringing their own ideas, playing independently, expressing their individual personalities and influencing the group. But as well as witnessing this, staff are encouraged to adopt the attitudes and approaches they see the therapists using, to develop their own relationships with group members. The therapists actively model useful ways of being with, and communicating with, the group, challenging staff and discussing their approaches with them. This experiential learning is supported through formal training in intensive interaction and supervision or consultations to staff in partnership with multidisciplinary team colleagues.

Conclusion

The parallel process provided for staff is as important as the group itself (Morrissey and Tribe 2001). Care staff working with people with learning disabilities benefit from support to use their personal feelings as therapeutic tools in their work (Storey, Collis and Clegg 2012). By giving staff this support, stress and difficult feelings are contained in order that staff can work with more self-awareness (Wonnacott 2014). Gilbert and Evans (2000) describe this as the worker being able to feel their experiences 'unedited' (p.11). By working with and containing service users' emotional expression, the therapists in turn also contain staff pressures and anxieties. This allows projections and transference to be processed and behaviour to be more thoughtfully understood, and gives space for more creative thinking and acting with service users. Staff can then find their own ways to create opportunities for the development of new attachments, skills and abilities.

Emmanuel (2004) wrote a chapter about psychotherapeutic work with adults with learning disabilities with the title 'Facing the Damage Together'. I have been struck by this phrase and the fact that the group presented in that chapter involved a number of staff. Usually there are two music therapists, one member of care staff and often one or two students. Perhaps we have been facing the damage together.

Perhaps we have needed the support of each other to work directly with painful and difficult projections, to be able to contain these projections and begin to see the potential and development in the group. Music therapists also learn in this environment – from the care staff who work closely with the service users and know them well, from colleagues who may contribute a specialist perspective, and from the service users themselves.

In this music therapy and sensory interaction group, music therapists perform healthy, containing, attachment relationships in music therapy. The music therapists reframe the way in which staff can think about service users, and model facilitative relating. This reframing encourages more authentic relationships and new creativity to develop within these relationships. Bartram (2013) writes of her work in psychotherapy with parents as helping them 'to develop their capacity to observe the child perhaps previously unobserved' (p.175), and this resonates with our aim to provide carers with an environment where emotions are contained and where a creative space can be made for observation and reflection about the personal qualities of people in new and evolving ways.

References

Agrotou, A. (1999) *Sounds and Meaning: Group Music Therapy with People with Profound Learning Difficulties and Their Carers* (video). Nicosia: Agrotou.

Aigen, K. (2005) *Music-Centred Music Therapy*. Gilsum, NH: Barcelona Publishers.

Alvarez, A. (1992) *Live Company*. London: Routledge.

Babb, C. (2007) 'Living with shattered dreams: a parent's perspective of living with learning disability.' *Learning Disability Practice 10*, 5, 14–18.

Barrington, A. (2008) 'Collaboration: The Bigger Picture.' In K. Twyford and T. Watson (eds) *Integrated Team Working: Music Therapy as Part of Transdisciplinary and Collaborative Approaches*. London: Jessica Kingsley Publishers.

Bartram, P. (2013) 'Melancholia, mourning, love: transforming the melancholic response to disability through psychotherapy.' *British Journal of Psychotherapy 29*, 2, 168–181.

Beadle-Brown, J., Guest, C., Richardson, L., Malovic, A., Bradshaw, J. and Himmerich, J. (2013) *Living in Fear: Better Outcomes for People with Learning Disabilities and Autism: Executive Summary*. Canterbury: Tizard Centre, University of Kent.

Bick, E. (1968) 'The experience of the skin in early object relations.' *International Journal of Psychoanalysis 49*, 484–486.

Blaustein, M.E. and Kinniburgh, K.M. (2010) *Treating Traumatic Stress in Children and Adolescents: How to Foster Resilience Through Attachment, Self-Regulation, and Competency*. New York, NY: Guilford Press.

Bowlby, J. (2005) *The Making and Breaking of Affectional Bonds*. London: Routledge. (Original work published in 1979.)

Bruce, E.J. and Schultz, C.L. (2001) *Nonfinite Loss and Grief: A Psycho Educational Approach*. London: Jessica Kingsley Publishers.

Emmanuel, L. (2004) 'Facing the Damage Together: Some Reflections Arising from the Treatment in Psychotherapy of a Severely Mentally Handicapped Child.' In D. Simpson and L. Miller (eds) *Unexpected Gains: Psychotherapy with People with Learning Disabilities*. London: Karnac Books.

Fearn, M.C. and O'Connor, R. (2008) 'Collaborative Working at the Cheyne Day Centre, London.' In K. Twyford and T. Watson (eds) *Integrated Team Working: Music Therapy as Part of Transdisciplinary and Collaborative Approaches*. London: Jessica Kingsley Publishers.

Fonagy, P. (2001) *Attachment Theory and Psycho-Analysis*. New York, NY: Other Press.

Gilbert, M.C. and Evans, K. (2000) *Psychotherapy Supervision: An Integrative Rational Approach to Psychotherapy Supervision*. Buckingham: Open University Press.

Hewett, D. (2007) 'Do touch: physical contact and people who have severe, profound and multiple learning disabilities.' *Support for Learning 22*, 3, 116–123.

Hooper, J. (undated) 'The loneliness of parents.' In *Special Educational Needs*. Available at https://senmagazine.co.uk/articles/articles/senarticles/the-loneliness-of-parents, accessed on 30 December 2015.

Howe, D. (2011) *Attachment Across the Lifecourse: A Brief Introduction*. London: Palgrave Macmillan.

Jónsdóttir, V. (2008) 'Music Therapy and Early Intervention from a Caring Perspective.' In G. Trondalen and E. Ruud (eds) *Perspektiver På Musikk og Helse 30 År med Norsk Musikkterapi* [Perspectives on Music and Health: 30 Years of Norwegian Music Therapy]. Oslo: NMH-publikasjoner.

Karkou, V. and Sanderson, P. (2006) *Arts Therapies: A Research-Based Map of the Field*. London: Elsevier Churchill Livingstone.

Linington, M. (2009) 'Enduring horror: psychotherapy with monsters.' *Attachment 3*, 1, 53–70.

Lovell, E., Goodridge, E., Harman, M. and Watson, T. (2014) 'Facing the Damage Together: Innovative Work with Carers in Music Therapy Services for People with Learning Disabilities.' In G. Tsiris, C. Warner and G. Watts (eds) *Book of Abstracts – Counterpoints: Music Therapy Practice in the 21st Century*. London: British Association for Music Therapy.

Magee, W.L. and Burland, K. (2009) 'An exploratory study of the use of electronic music technologies in clinical music therapy.' *Nordic Journal of Music Therapy 17*, 2, 124–141.

Morrissey, J. and Tribe, R. (2001) 'Parallel process in supervision.' *Counselling Psychology Quarterly 14*, 2, 103–110.

Music, G. (2011) *Nurturing Natures: Attachment and Children's Emotional, Social and Brain Development*. Hove: Psychology Press.

Nickson, B. (2005) 'Never Take No for an Answer.' In S. Rolph, D. Atkinson, M. Nind, J. Welshman *et al.* (eds) *Witnesses to Change: Families, Learning Difficulties and History*. Kidderminster: British Institute of Learning Disabilities.

Nind, M. and Hewett, D. (2001) *A Practical Guide to Intensive Interaction*. Kidderminster: British Institute of Learning Disabilities.

Roman, T. (2016) '"Were they better today?" Valuing a client's individual therapeutic process within an institution's expectation of positive progress and predictable outcomes.' *British Journal of Music Therapy 30*, 1, 13–21.

Royal College of Nursing (2013) *Breaking Bad News: Supporting Parents When They Are Told of Their Child's Diagnosis*. London: Royal College of Nursing.

Simpson, D. (2004) 'Learning Disability as a Refuge from Knowledge.' In D. Simpson and L. Miller (eds) *Unexpected Gains: Psychotherapy with People with Learning Disabilities.* London: Karnac Books.

Stern, D.N. (2001) 'Face-to-Face Play.' In J. Jaffe, B. Beebe, S. Feldenstein, S.C. Crown and M.D. Jasnow (eds) *Rhythms of Dialogue in Infancy: Coordinated Timing in Development. Monographs of the Society for Research in Child Development* (Vol. 66). Ann Arbor, MI: Society for Research in Child Development.

Storey, J., Collis, M.-A. and Clegg, J. (2012) 'A psychodynamic interpretation of staff accounts of working with people who have learning disabilities and complex needs.' *British Journal of Learning Disabilities 40,* 229–235.

Sutton, J. (2007) 'The Air Between Two Hands.' In N. Losseff and J. Doctor (eds) *Silence, Music, Silent Music.* Abingdon: Routledge.

Tustin, F. (1981) *Autistic States in Children.* London: Routledge.

Twyford, K. and Watson, T. (2008) *Integrated Team Working: Music Therapy as Part of Transdisciplinary and Collaborative Approaches.* London: Jessica Kingsley Publishers.

UK Department of Health (2012) *Caring for Our Future: Reforming Care and Support.* London: UK Department of Health.

Waddell, M. (1998) *Inside Lives.* London: Duckworth and Company.

Watson, T. (2007) *Music Therapy with Adults with Learning Disabilities.* London: Routledge.

Watson, T. (2011) *It Is a Joy to Be Hidden but a Disaster Not to Be Found.* Paper given to the Scottish Music Therapy Trust, Edinburgh, 25 June 2013.

Watson, T. (2014) 'The World Is Alive! Music Therapy with Adults with Learning Disabilities.' In J. Edwards (ed) *The Oxford Handbook of Music Therapy.* Oxford: Oxford University Press.

Wonnacott, J. (2014) *Developing and Supporting Effective Staff Supervision.* London: Pavilion Books.

Chapter 10

From Assistance to Co-Therapy
On the Role of the Co-Therapist in Nordoff Robbins Music Therapy

Jörg Fachner

Introduction

The objective of this chapter is to understand the characteristics of the role and actions of the co-therapist in Nordoff Robbins Music Therapy (NRMT) from the perspective of the music therapist (who may have worked as a co-therapist) and to contribute to an empirical profile of co-therapy in music therapy. In their book *Creative Music Therapy* Nordoff and Robbins (1977) point out that this specific music therapy form emerged from teamwork, with Nordoff as the musician and Robbins as the special education teacher working at the Sunfield children's homes.

Turry and Marcus (2005) describe how Nordoff and Robbins grew into teamwork by doing group and individual music therapy sessions in which the roles of the team members are either to be "'primary therapists" playing their primary instruments – or "co-therapists" – "on the floor" with the clients' (p.56). Robbins, interviewed in their article, pointed out the importance of 'co-creative' teamwork, and that the division between primary therapist and co-therapist, between leading and assisting in the therapy process, shifts between the team members, especially when working in groups (see Nordoff and Robbins 1977; Turry and Marcus 2005, p.56). To achieve this ideal equilibrium of co-creativity, students in training should not focus on the difference between leading and assisting but on the difference between being the musician and being the person "'on the floor" with the client' (Turry and Marcus 2005, p.56). However, how far this works in practice seems to depend on the level of experience and how good a team is at working together. The two therapists may have completely different perceptions and opinions about what is needed next and may disagree with each other. Nowikas (1993) explored team relations in NRMT and studied the dynamics of both team members, pointing to the importance of joint supervision in order to facilitate communication between team members. Both people need to talk and get to know each other to develop and recognise their specific team identity. 'This new awareness has the potential to accelerate the team's and the client's growth processes in music therapy' (p.39).

The present volume explores the role of assistants and collaborators in music therapy settings and how working with them is for the benefit of the clients. This chapter differs from the others in that a Nordoff Robbins co-therapist is most likely a trained music therapist who is 'on the floor the with the client' and only meets the client in the therapy context. My focus will be on the role of the co-therapist in NRMT, although the role differences between co-therapist and therapist cannot be defined as fixed or static:

> It is difficult if not impossible to define such an intuitive, musical, improvisational process as Nordoff Robbins music therapy in terms of fixed or static roles. This is particularly true of the role of the co-therapist, which evolved from the work's inception and continues to evolve today. (Turry and Marcus 2005, p.67)

Clive Robbins was at the very beginning assisting the musician in playing with the clients, but by finding himself part of a team he then developed into being a co-therapist and in this way established a triadic system for music therapy purposes.

> The first situation was that Paul Nordoff played for my class, and then he had the idea: 'We should use a drum.' So we got a small jazz drum – we call it a jazz drum – it was something, perhaps you would buy a young person of 13, 14. A single drum and a cymbal. And Paul said: 'Let's have the children beat the drum and see what they do.' (Fachner 1994, p.191)

However, being asked in an interview whether the work of a co-therapist would be possible without prior experience, Robbins answered:

> You have to know about music and you also have to have a feeling for the child. So therefore you need to have experience. And you need to know: 'What is the right thing to do with the child?' When to give

the child space and when to focus the child. You have to know this from experience, either as a therapist, as a co-therapist, because you have done it for some time…a co-therapist might dance with the child…takes care of the situation and he mediates between the child and the therapist. (Fachner 1994, pp.192–194)

Co-therapists in other therapy settings

There is almost no music therapy literature addressing and exploring the specific situation and perspectives of co-therapists. Davies and Richards (1998) discuss their experience and the specific dynamics of working as co-therapists in group settings. A positive finding was that stress is reduced by working with a professional peer, the attention of two minds 'bringing different sensitivities and perspectives' (p.56). Transference and counter-transference issues then have a double structure, that is, maternal and paternal family roles enter the relationship processes and might serve as a positive new model. Fearn and O'Connor (2003) demonstrate that working as a team over 10 years resulted in significant improvements to the therapy given to children with special needs aged between 2 and 18 years, and also to the support offered to their parents. The various topics these authors cover include the development of a co-therapy assessment procedure, group psychodynamic music therapy for children with special needs, sessions for children and their parents, the significance of counter-transference and the importance of supervision.

A few psychotherapy papers discuss co-therapy (Geyer 1981; Neuert 1989; Roller and Nelson 1993; Lonergan 1995; Stone 1995), addressing mainly the role of co-therapy in psychotherapy groups. Schwabe (1983), in his short comments on co-therapy, points out the basic financial problem involved in using co-therapists: 'It is no luxury, as some still believe, to have two therapists in psychotherapy groups but a necessity and improves therapy effects' (p.143). In practice, it is quite rare that an institution has more than two music therapists, and even rarer that they work according to the same therapy approach and can or might cooperate as a team. In most cases the co-therapists are employees of the same institution but working in other professional fields, for example as physiotherapists (compare Mutthesius 1990, pp.48–49; Davies and Richards 1998; Fearn and O'Connor 2003). The Nordoff Robbins model of co-therapy is usually only made possible, therefore, through a deliberate choice to employ two therapists with the intention of offering this type of therapy.

Methodology of a research study investigating the role of the co-therapist

In 1993 I interviewed six therapists from NRMT training centres in Witten/Herdecke (three), London (one) and New York (two) about their experiences and views on the role of the co-therapist (see Fachner 1994). These semi-structured interviews provided the database to which a qualitative analysis was applied to reconstruct the role of the co-therapist. The interviews addressed preselected issues and were presented in the results section accordingly, but were also open to spontaneously emerging additional issues. The aim was to permit interview partners to present the issues under discussion according to their personal views and wishes. For example, one central topic that I had for the interviews, to which the interview responses differed considerably between the representatives of the three NR centres, was the issue of 'hand-over-hand' assistance from the co-therapist in order to enable the client to learn to play (Fachner 1994, pp.156–158). One argument made for directing body movements onto instruments was the idea of making the 'music child' emerge – to enable musical experiences and communication by sensing the child's impulse and reading the intention to play from movement gestures, while possibly touching the client and executing the intended playing with hand-over-hand assistance. By contrast, there was agreement, in response to the question of whether a co-therapist needs to be a music therapist, that music therapy teamwork was more efficient if the co-therapist is a music therapist.

The responses were structured according to similarities and then categorised. As many of the original statements as possible were used in the text of the original study (Fachner 1994). An analysis of the characteristics of a co-therapist derived from these interviews was published in German in 1997. An English version, published online in 2007 but no longer available, has been incorporated into the summary which follows. This does not contain verbatim responses, but some individual words and phrases used by respondents are included in quotation marks. Where respondents made similar points in differing language, this diversity of expression has been preserved where the resulting nuances of meaning enrich the account. It was not thought appropriate to employ Grounded Theory, as the object was not to uncover a supposed unitary theory of NRMT. The approach adopted conveys the richness and unity in diversity of the collection of interview responses, rather than attempting to distil the content to a single essence or set of principles.

Results

Scope of the role of co-therapist

Responsibility for the physical environment

In NRMT co-therapists are most active in group music therapy sessions with mentally and physically handicapped children, where they take the lead. A co-therapist is responsible for the set-up of the therapy room and for ensuring safety in the therapy context (protection from sharp edges and possibly harmful objects, and so forth). He adjusts the setting with a view to the patient's needs and to specific therapeutic intentions and experience, and creates visual attractions for a child, positioning instruments as required. He must listen attentively to the music and anticipate practical procedures and movement directions and the 'flow' of therapy, being able, for example, to hold up a cymbal at the right place and exactly the right moment, to adjust the height of the drum and so on. The way he handles the instruments should be playful and convey this impression to the child.

Mediating between therapist, child and music

A co-therapist is part of the same musical process as therapist and child, and therefore part of the same temporal continuum together with therapist and child or any other person present (in both a temporal and a local sense). He furthers the relationship between therapist and child, and assists the process of relating between music and child. He helps the child to do what he or she wants to do and 'to get into the music'. He is not, however, a mere helper, but generally supports a child's 'positive actions' and efforts to expand the limits of his or her expressivity. He backs children in their intentions to act and must also be able to perceive the therapist's intentions. If the therapist clearly 'demands' a structure with his music, then the co-therapist can help the child to achieve this structure. Co-therapists amplify and channel;

they intensify the relation between music, therapist and child, and they guide and direct the energy flow between therapist and child. They convey a basic emotional experience.

The basic attitude of the co-therapist

(Attitude in this context means a categorical perspective that determines the knowledge of something, the general evaluation of and approach to something, and also the pertinent forms of action and behaviour.) The basic attitude of the co-therapist is characterised by openness in perception and awareness, and by an unbiased view of the child. The co-therapist should not be guided excessively by other opinions, such as those of physicians, psychologists, educationalists, non-music therapists and so forth, as to the ability or lack of ability of a child. Music is a very specific form of stimulation and not to be compared to other stimulating forms and contexts. Like the therapist, the co-therapist does not start a session with a predefined plan but develops and realises his intention in the situational relation with the child.

During sessions, the co-therapist has to be alert and must, for example, be present at the right moment to provide physical help. As a kind of 'catalyst of art' he is the projection of both therapist and child. The co-therapist is the servant of both child and music in a facilitating capacity, with the intention of being helpful, humane and supportive. His hope is that the patient achieves some personal benefit; he does not determine or structure the objective but facilitates what may be achieved. He develops his personal style from experience. He may follow his human instincts and the free flow of his ideas, including musical ideas.

Potential problems regarding the balance
between process and action

A co-therapist should always try to maintain a general overview of the therapy situation. His perspective on the session differs from that of the therapist. He is in eye and ear contact with the child and with events in the therapy room, and is alert to the music. Most important is ear contact. In terms of practical interventions, he may again and again need to offer drum sticks and collect those the child has dropped or thrown away in order to keep the child's musical activities within the musical flow. If the child plays on drums, the co-therapist should convey the impression that drumming is just as important and helpful as medicine.

The co-therapist knows that in the first session he must wait for, and be attentive to, the child. Sometimes he must do nothing but simply observe. If the child is active, the co-therapist may withdraw from the process. But his passive presence may also be disturbing, and then he may not know what to do. Often he must get used to being an active part of therapy, which may include having physical contact with the child, but this may bring too much 'power' to the therapy. He must continually ask himself whether what he does facilitates something or prevents something, and why he wants the child to behave in a specific manner. The co-therapist may help a child to find a musical structure, but there is also the risk of playing too much himself, instead of letting the child play, thus preventing developments.

The relational quality of therapy

In a creative arts therapy approach, such as NRMT, the art of music is the therapeutic agent, so that music is at the centre of the human relationships involved; however, as a part of a relational structure that comprises four elements – child, therapist, co-therapist and music – the co-therapist has a specific kind of relationship with each of the other three elements.

Relationship with the child

The co-therapist meets the child before they get to the therapy room. While bringing the child from the waiting area to the therapy room, he gets an impression of the child's mood and behaviour towards objects or persons 'outside therapy'. He learns from his encounters and experience with this child and thus is ultimately able to build a different and more sensitive relation to the child than the therapist, and to perceive things which might elude the therapist at the piano. He may, for example, detect the smallest physical movements and interact with the child accordingly.

The co-therapist guides a child's concentrated attention if the child is active but unstructured in his or her perception. He often takes on the additional function of an instrumental teacher and supports the child's efforts to realise forms of musical performance. He may initiate songs, which are known to help the perception of such concepts of form, and may thus acquaint the child, through music, with the experience of form and ordered patterns in action-related communication.

Non-verbal signals

A co-therapist may observe and signal something to the child or therapist, just as musicians in an ensemble observe and nod to each other. He conveys and communicates through symbolic body movements; this is part of the relational basis of therapy. His movements form a symbolic imitation background for possible intentions of the child to act (e.g. showing how to drum with movements in the air).

Relations and changes in the team of therapists

The co-therapist develops his relation to the therapist as his work with the child proceeds and he should build up an inner connection with the therapist over long periods of teamwork. This was the case with Nordoff and Robbins in their intensive and perfectly coordinated therapy approach. From the perspective of professional development, it is good for a co-therapist to cooperate with a therapist of a comparable level of experience, development and training, if they want to grow together as a true team. In this way, he has a better chance to develop an understanding of the therapist's work and to become better and better in the course of a prolonged team-forming process. An overly personal and intensive relation to a therapist may, of course, impair the co-therapist's perception of what the therapist does, but in general we may say that therapy profits from good relations between co-therapist and therapist.

In sessions, the co-therapist becomes almost an additional arm of the therapist; he gives to the patient what the therapist is unable to give. He may, however, find it difficult not to disturb the therapist with his own activities. Therapists must therefore clarify in situational contexts when they expect action from co-therapists and when not.

Co-therapists as well as therapists need supervision. Supervision can clarify and resolve differences of opinion or recurrent basic misunderstandings about the therapeutic activities of both therapists. The term co-therapist itself should not be misinterpreted as implying that the co-therapist is the inferior therapist. In reality the co-therapist may be the one who realises that the music the therapist is playing may not be quite appropriate. He need not necessarily stick to his role as co-therapist throughout a session but should be free to use the piano as well, if he believes this to be necessary.

Teamwork between therapists appears to have developed differently in different cultures. According to an American colleague, co-therapists in the United States are more active compared with those in Witten/ Herdecke. In New York, therapists and co-therapists frequently change roles in order to achieve a wider range of perspectives.

Verbal and non-verbal signals between therapist and co-therapist

A co-therapist's perspective on the music therapy session differs from that of the music therapist. He provides impulses for the therapist, is closer to the child and in a position to perceive even the smallest responses. His gestures and facial expressions show the therapist which musical activities are the child's and which are his own. He should communicate with the therapist mainly by gestures and eye contact, and verbally only if absolutely necessary, for example if they are not acting in harmony.

Relation to music

Relation to music is determined by the mental flow of music, its implied inter-subjectivity, inner laws and specific initiatory qualities. A co-therapist's music-related activities make him part of the inter-subjectivity of music that emerges from the subjective soul of the improvising interpreter but is based on the inter-subjective reality of music as a form of sound and time.

The co-therapist experiences, and is part of, the same mental flow that follows the inner laws of musical language; he is part of a very real existence in the moment that is without material reality but has musical form. He is one element in a process, in a mental world of music. This enables him to be associated mentally with others in the same room through the emerging music.

A co-therapist should be able to anticipate promises and development possibilities in the music that emerges during sessions. He must always be alert to surprising developments and observant in order to react to musical laws in an appropriate way. He is able to *feel* when someone is going to develop musical activities; this cannot be grasped by mere observation. He cannot achieve anything if the music does not 'carry along' or 'stimulate'; he can only act in relation to music. A co-therapist perceives the therapy mainly on the basis of what he hears.

Co-therapist as music therapist

The co-therapist must be able to follow the musical development in his mind and to think like a music therapist; he must understand the musical processes taking place and possess the required knowledge and experience of musical form. He must place himself at the disposal of the musical development and separate his personal expectations from those emerging in the music. In all this he must develop an intuitive understanding of the child and perceive the moment when a child really wants to make music.

Forms of acting

The co-therapist is the 'servant' of the patient and the music in a facilitating capacity. He acts musically, but the form of his musical expression is different – he has no instrument. In a way, he plays 'on and through' the patient, or allows the patient to make music with himself as the medium. He 'plays the child' like an instrument but in accordance with the child's intentions. As a musician he may have long intervals of not intervening and may enter the musical development only in moments where something must be facilitated.

Patterns and indicators of activity

A co-therapist must be able to enter the child's mood and, on the basis of the child's perception, assess any limitations arising from pathology; this ability to put himself in the position of another individual allows him to assess the other person's willingness or unwillingness to make music. He must first enter the child's mood, create an inner distance from what he has perceived, and then use the results as a basis for his support or guidance. He observes the child's movements, motor intentions and directions, and thus detects intended activities. He knows 'what the child wants'. He can feel this in the child's limbs as an impulse involving the entire body, and through touch he senses the child's action-related presence or absence. In guiding the child's hand he feels not only muscle movements but also senses and anticipates the direction and intention of the movement. In a typical interaction, he will not analyse the physical frequencies and sound production of speech activity, but he *will* listen to what is intended, to the meaning. Two persons starting simultaneously after having assessed special conditions, with the same motor intention but different gait tempi, may still be expected to arrive at the same time. Translated to music therapy, this means that a jointly played rhythmical phrase will follow the laws of music and resolve into a simultaneous ending and a final beat.

A co-therapist finds confirmation of his therapeutic activities in the applied findings about the signifying function of body language and non-verbal communication, and above all from previous events in sessions, the development of the child and his or her growing musical abilities. He therefore knows about the physical abilities, or lack of abilities, of the child and is able to assess the activities in evidence in relation to the child's impairment. Hugs and touches by the child are signals of the child's need for protection, comfort, affection and love. Nevertheless, the co-therapist should provide as little assistance and physical contact as necessary, since the child is expected to produce the musical activity. The intention to act and the individual experience of musical activity should be realised in the purest possible form.

Problem areas of the co-therapist's physical activities

A co-therapist guides the child's musical intentions. He senses the impulse to act, helps to realise this impulse and directs the playful impulse to the drum, for example. A supportive touch and guidance of body parts relevant to action, for example the child's arm, promote and facilitate music-related activity. The physical activity of the co-therapist may become problematic for himself, because he must sense that single and decisive musical impulse and must find a mode in which physical contact remains agreeable. He must be able to sense whether his touch is unwelcome or whether the impulse to act is related to music. The co-therapist will basically perform interventions that are intended to release, not to restrict. So he has to find a balance between the impulse to act that he offers himself and the child's impulse he has to guide; this happens in a continuous giving and withdrawing on his part. The success of 'hand-over-hand' guidance may lead him to an accepting perspective of his physical intervention; the measure for this is always the individual case, the child. He may also apply knowledge from physiotherapy and transfer it to music, and sometimes even, in contrast with physiotherapy interventions, achieve a similar success through music-related cues. He may, for example, hold up the cymbals rhythmically and thus lead spontaneous reflexes into a musical metre and simultaneously train a stretching movement when he varies the distance to the drum.

Co-therapy by non-musicians or non-music therapists

Clive Robbins was trained as a special education teacher, and he did not play the piano often in therapy sessions during his partnership with Paul Nordoff. A recurring question in this context is whether the co-therapist in NRMT must necessarily be a trained musician or music therapist. An analysis of the answers to this question revealed that there is no need for the co-therapist to be a musician or music therapist; if he is not, however, the balance in the teamwork changes. He should still be acquainted with musical processes. Every individual with the ability to observe and follow the music and its characteristics closely has the potential to become a co-therapist. Not being trained as a musician, he may cooperate even better, and his cooperation may be just as intuitive as co-therapy provided by a music therapist.

The co-therapist works in an independent therapy realm; his work demands specific skills that not everybody possesses. Co-therapists in NRMT integrate within their person the potential of physiotherapy, drama therapy (in miming activities) and speech therapy. In institutions with only one music therapist, physiotherapists, ergotherapists, other therapists or medical staff employed in a hospital frequently assume the role of the co-therapist. In direct patient contact, physiotherapists may offer the right support at the right moment owing to their knowledge of physical impairments, provided they are sufficiently open to the music.

Summary

In group music therapy, the co-therapist is in charge in most cases. He works mainly with physically and mentally handicapped children. He arranges a therapy setting in accordance with the therapy situation and clients' personal needs. He anticipates requirements as regards instruments and equipment and also possible hazards. He mediates between therapist, child and music, and is an integral part of the entire process. He is a kind of 'catalyst of art', acting as the extended arm of therapist and child. Ideally his basic attitude is to be helpful, facilitating and open to the situation, alert and personal at the same time. His relation to the child is defined by physical nearness, which gives him a different perception and perspective compared with the therapist. In the therapy process he has to find an adequate procedural balance between active intervention and passive observation (i.e. letting things develop). He may also give non-verbal cues to the child.

A good team of therapists ideally starts on an identical level of development and experience, and gradually develops an implicit understanding of each partner's intentions. This inner connection grown out of joint experience and intimate knowledge of each other turns a co-therapist into a therapist's 'third arm'. As Turry and Marcus (2005) put it:

> Having been a therapist, the co-therapist can live in the musical process of the primary therapist and create music along with the primary therapist when it is called for as well as refraining from activity when this is deemed necessary. (p.58)

But this situation is not without potential conflict. Exchange of information between therapist and co-therapist is mostly non-verbal. The relation to music (therapy) is based on the inter-subjectively perceivable flow of music and its development. The inner laws of music and its temporal and acoustical structures may be anticipated in its expectations and almost inevitable developmental steps. In this way, music initiates an impulse to act in order to realise inherent objectives. A co-therapist does not necessarily have to be a musician, but he must be able to follow the musical development and must know about musical processes. He should possess the required knowledge and experience of musical forms, should be at the service of music and be able to separate personal expectations from actual musical events in therapy. It is the art of co-therapy to intervene and withdraw continuously, and thus to develop a feeling for the individual child, to sense whether and what a child really wants to play and which contact might be disagreeable to the child. This may require a fine balance between a therapist's offered patterns of action and guidance by the child.

References

Davies, A. and Richards, E. (1998) 'Music therapy in acute psychiatry: our experience of working as co-therapist with a group for patients from two neighbouring wards.' *British Journal of Music Therapy 12, 2,* 53–59.

Fachner, J. (1994) *Die kunsttherapeutisch orientierte Nordoff Robbins Musiktherapie in Witten/ Herdecke.* [Art Therapeutic Orientation in Nordof–Robbins Music Therapy]. Thesis available at https://drive.google.com/open?id=0B7nPwcLtlzGYNGg3YXFRU3ZBSVk, accessed on 4 October 2016.

Fearn, M.-C. and O'Connor, R. (2003) 'The whole is greater than the sum of its parts: experiences of co-working as music therapists.' *British Journal of Music Therapy 17, 2,* 67–75.

Geyer, M. (1981) 'Zum Problem der Co-Therapie in dynamischen Gesprächspsycho-therapiegruppen' [On the Problem of Co-Therapy in Dynamic Verbal Therapy Groups]. In J. Ott (ed) *Theoretische Probleme der Gruppenpsychotherapie.* Leipzig: Barth Verlag.

Lonergan, E.C. (1995) 'The dynamics of the co-therapy relationship: a symposium – discussion.' *Group 19, 2,* 100–107.

Mutthesius, D. (1990) *Musiktherapie im klinischen Bereich: eine Untersuchung über Arbeitsbedingungen und Methodik* [Music Therapy in the Clinical Setting: An Investigation of Working Conditions and Methodology]. Frankfurt: Verlag E. Bochinsky.

Neuert, C. (1989) 'Aspekte der Co-Therapie in analytischen und musiktherapeutischen Gruppen.' [Aspects of Co-Therapy in Analytic and Music Therapy Groups]. Unpublished diploma dissertation, Institut für Musiktherapie, Fachhochschule, Heidelberg.

Nordoff, P. and Robbins, C. (1977) *Creative Music Therapy: Individualized Treatment for the Handicapped Child.* New York, NY: John Day Co.

Nowikas, S. (1993) 'A Qualitative Investigation of Teamwork in Nordoff Robbins Music Therapy.' Unpublished MA thesis, New York University, New York, NY.

Roller, B. and Nelson, V. (1993) *Die Kunst der Co-Therapie* [The Art of Co-therapy]. Köln: Edition Humanistische Psychologie.

Schwabe, C. (1983) *Aktive Gruppenmusiktherapie für erwachsene Patienten* [Active Group Music Therapy for Adult Patients]. Stuttgart: Fischer.

Stone, W.N. (1995) 'The dynamics of the co-therapy relationship: a symposium – discussion.' *Group 19, 2,* 117–119.

Turry, A. and Marcus, D. (2005) 'Teamwork: therapist and co-therapist in the Nordoff Robbins approach to music therapy.' *Music Therapy Perspectives 23, 1,* 53–69.

Chapter 11

Music and Attuned Movement Therapy

How the Facilitator Mediates Between Client and Therapist

John Strange, Mary-Clare Fearn and Rebecca O'Connor

The challenge of communicating with the profoundly disabled child

Human communication depends on more than words. Body language is equally important. As well as augmenting, qualifying and occasionally contradicting verbal expression, body language conveys rich meaning non-verbally. Impairment or absence of verbal language constitutes a significant disability, but if body language remains intact, much communication is possible. If, however, body language is also impaired, either distorted by physical disability, making it hard to interpret, or even suppressed so that others are unaware of it, how can communication survive? A child's emotional well-being and developmental progress depend on meaningful human contact as well as on the more tangible essentials of food, warmth and shelter. If communication is impaired, her carers must seek ways to convey their love, respect, interest and hope, whatever the obstacles. They must also strive to support whatever communication she can offer in return, and understand and respond to that communication. (In this chapter female pronouns will be used for the child, except when writing about 'Tom', to redress the historical dominance of male pronouns.)

When communicating with profoundly disabled children, a music therapist must detect, interpret and respond to the child's communication, however restricted. This was the challenge facing Mary-Clare and Rebecca, joint Head IV music therapists at the Cheyne Child Development Service (CCDS), Chelsea and Westminster

Hospital, in the early 1990s. The children accessing the service with the most profound neurological damage had extremely limited control of their bodies. Deprived of the ability to explore their human and physical environment by movement and touch, some were also unable to do so by sight. Having never experienced themselves as able to influence other people or their environment, they might never realise this was possible. In the most extreme cases, the process by which the normal infant learns to differentiate one sensory modality from another and her body from her environment, to form attachments to significant carers, to signal her needs and wishes, and to recognise feelings as her own, had barely begun. There was an urgent need, therefore, to find a way of facilitating this process by offering the children these developmental opportunities in a form they could access. The solution, which came to be known as Music and Attuned Movement Therapy (MAMT) (Fearn and O'Connor 2008), was developed by Mary-Clare and Rebecca in partnership with the multidisciplinary team and with the children's families.

The development of Music and Attuned Movement Therapy

Mary-Clare and Rebecca (Fearn, O'Connor and Ledden 2005) write that the constant distress of one little boy disabled in this way triggered the development of MAMT. Tom (not his real name) was blind, with little recognisable bodily movement, and almost constantly distressed. His breathing was the expression of his troubled being which both his teacher and Rebecca, his music therapist, working independently, first felt able to connect with, the former by resting her hand on his chest to share its movement, the latter by playing the flute in time with his breaths. Breathing patterns are closely related to the child's state of arousal, which at the earliest stage of development can only be regulated with the help of the mother or other carer. By following Tom's breathing, teacher and music therapist were each able to help him regulate his distress, to show empathy and to gain a first foothold in his world.

When they decided to work with Tom in partnership, the communication they offered him became multimodal. Tom and the teacher communicated through shared movement, Tom and the music therapist through a cross-modal interplay of sound and movement as the therapist breathed through the flute to mirror Tom's breathing. This is an instance of what Stern (1985) describes as 'affect attunement' – the synchronisation of feelings between mother and infant, achieved not by simply mirroring the infant's sound, movement or facial expression but by reflecting it back in a contrasting modality.

At the start of joint working, the aim was that Tom should 'realise that he was not alone and that there was something about himself that could be shared' (Fearn *et al.* 2005, p.25). The therapist's musical reflection and the teacher's physical reflection of Tom's sounds and movements complemented each other, the whole making an impact greater than the sum of the parts. As his distress abated, he became able to relax and listen to the music, vary or briefly stop his breathing, initiate small movements, smile and vocalise. He was motivated in these advances by discovering that what he did was noticed and responded to. It was clear that, despite Tom's profound disability, two-way communication was occurring.

The role of the 'movement facilitator'

MAMT brings together familiar concepts and practices in a new way. Working with affect attunement is common in psychodynamically informed music therapy (Pavlicevic 1997; Trondalen and Skårderud 2007; Edwards 2011; Davies 2015; Levinge 2015). Similarly, the presence of assistants or collaborators is common to a range of approaches. The unique feature of MAMT is the way a 'movement facilitator' conveys affect attunement by supporting the child's movement, self-experience and self-expression, and linking the therapist's musical communication with the child's communication through movement. This distinguishes MAMT both from other approaches using affect attunement and from those in which an adult other than the music therapist engages physically with the client, such as 'Music and Movement' (see Chapter 12).

Tom's therapy became the prototype for work with several similar children, in which the music therapist (either Mary-Clare or Rebecca) would be joined by a variety of professionals, and sometimes by family members, in the role of movement facilitator. After consultation with the physiotherapy department to ascertain which movements a child might be able to make (and which movements should be avoided), the movement facilitator's first task is to remain relaxed and vigilant, waiting to sense any incipient movement which the child is only able to make with her assistance. As well as providing the right amount of physical assistance to facilitate the movement, she may sometimes signal to the music therapist what she senses is about to happen, enabling the latter to accompany the movement musically as it occurs.

Mary-Clare and Rebecca also incorporated MAMT into group work, providing each child in the group with a movement facilitator to develop her breathing patterns and intention to move (Fearn *et al.* 2005, p.31). The aim of working in groups was to foster the children's awareness of themselves in relationship with their peers. Greater emphasis was placed on vocal communication not requiring physical contact, together with the use of structured activities to develop shared attention and joint participation.

The need for a clear theoretical framework

MAMT has a robust theoretical underpinning which gives practitioners the confidence to sustain their model of working even when uncertain what, if anything, is happening for the child. The music therapist shapes musical parameters into 'dynamic forms' to attune to a child. The facilitator, on the other hand, attunes to the child through touch and movement, bodily channels of communication which form the basis of dance movement therapy, a discipline based on 'an essential belief that one's movement expression reflects one's psychic state' since 'it is through the body that we can express and get in touch with deep feelings...' (Bannerman-Haig 1999, p.155). If a person's bodily responses are distorted or suppressed, this process is likely to be much more difficult. To the extent that feelings are experienced through one's own bodily responses, what the body can and cannot do may influence what can and cannot be felt. This is why it is important to facilitate movement. In MAMT, as in dance movement therapy, the significance of the child's movements lies in what they express. The facilitator and the music therapist interpret and respond to that expression, conveying empathy and offering the child the experience of communicating and developing awareness of her feelings by sensing them in her body.

Sensing 'movement intention'

How does the facilitator 'sense' the movement she should facilitate? The word 'sense' is usefully elastic, stretching across a wide spectrum of meaning, including an intuitive awareness gained by attending to counter-transference feelings, a practised interpretation of barely detectable signs of an intention to move, or a direct sensing by touch of a specific 'intention to move'. The physiotherapist with whom Mary-Clare and Rebecca discussed the children and their therapy, while aware of the particular difficulty of accurately discerning 'intention to move' in the child with cerebral palsy, agreed that such discernment could be achieved in MAMT with sufficient familiarity with the child. Accepting that such discernment is attainable without fully understanding the process is not to deny the value of empirical understanding. Relying solely on intuition invites sceptics to dismiss the facilitator's special skill as fantasy and discourages systematic investigation in order to refine it.

A child's intention to move may be thwarted in three main ways: failure of muscles to contract, failure of opposing muscles to relax or failure to translate the intention (perhaps registered by mirror neurons and evident in subliminal physical changes) into actually initiating and carrying through the movement. In all cases, a child can benefit from the right amount of physical assistance (generally the minimum necessary), given at the right time, *to make the right movement* – the movement that feels right to the child when she makes it, even if she is not aware of having intended it.

It is important to recognise when a movement facilitator is actually needed, rather than assuming that her presence will always confer an advantage. If a child has even a modest ability to move independently and purposefully, assistance may be counterproductive and increase her dependency. If the child is to use her movement to explore the environment, express herself and communicate, spontaneity is key. For this reason, children should normally be given the minimum necessary physical support and guidance. Directed exercise programmes and passive stretching regimes to music (see Chapter 12) are a quite distinct intervention, used when the main obstacle to movement is spasticity and fixed deformity, necessitating much more proactive and forceful physical intervention than in MAMT.

One movement facilitator's experience

The environment

Tracy joined the Cheyne Centre in 1988 and became the senior nursery nurse responsible for a group of six preschool children, some as young as 2 years old, with a range of disabilities associated with cerebral palsy. The group pursued a nurturing, play-based, developmental approach, and Tracy helped to develop a sensory curriculum not unlike those still offered to children with complex disabilities. She remained at the Centre for two extended periods spanning about 15 years. Gradually, the proportion of children with profound disabilities rose, as the more able children were increasingly included in mainstream playgroups and schools.

Working with the music therapists

Tracy grew familiar with the children and skilled in meeting their needs for several years before Rebecca and, later, Mary-Clare were appointed. When MAMT was introduced, Tracy and other movement facilitators worked with both the therapists to support individual children whom they already knew very well. They realised from the training sessions given by the music therapists that MAMT was a good fit with their 'way of being with children, not to do things for them, but to be present with them, to support them, to give them opportunities to have an effect on things…giving them experiences that they may not have had'. Mutual respect and a shared agenda developed between the therapists and the nursery nurses and others acting as facilitators. By contrast, the focus on developmental milestones by psychologists and other professionals involved with the children on an occasional basis struck Tracy and her colleagues as less useful to the children and their parents.

Reviewing sessions

Tracy also worked with Alice (see below) in partnership in turn with Mary-Clare, Rebecca and the therapist who succeeded them, thus providing an invaluable experience of continuity for Alice and a knowledge resource for the therapists taking over the work, while expanding her own intuitive grasp of Alice's needs and capabilities.

Sessions were always followed with discussion, in which therapist and facilitator would exchange sometimes contrasting views of what had occurred. What the music therapist had experienced in the musical interaction occasionally differed from what the facilitator had 'felt' (both physically and intuitively) was happening. When Mary-Clare asked, 'How did Alice *feel?*', Tracy acted as 'a voice for Alice'. By sharing their different perspectives, they reached a fuller understanding. The therapists occasionally even suggested that the most crucial part of the therapy was this debriefing afterwards. Tracy came to realise that 'by actually saying something you're realising something for the first time'.

Maintaining therapeutic boundaries

Professionals unfamiliar with psychodynamic theory seldom appreciate the concept of therapeutic boundaries, and may see a music therapy service as making unrealistic demands for special treatment. The establishment of a therapeutic environment or frame depends on the maintenance of boundaries. The therapeutic space must be protected from intrusion, and the instruments, which may acquire the status of transitional objects, from unexpected disappearance on unauthorised 'loan'. This jealous guarding of essential elements of the therapy might seem high-handed to other staff, but the music therapists always took in good part the gentle ridicule coming their way in the early days. The advantage of secure boundaries soon became evident as movement facilitators experienced the safe therapeutic space thus created. Parents wishing to view MAMT sessions were asked to arrange this in advance with the team. All families appreciated what MAMT offered their children. Alice's family were 'very realistic about Alice and what she needed and what sort of environment they wanted her to be in'.

The web of relationships in MAMT

Even if we disregard the relationships with the Centre and the family which have a bearing on what happens and consider only the internal dynamic of the therapy room, the picture is still a complex one. The key process of attunement is evident in three two-way relationships: between the therapist's music and the child's movements and vocal sounds (and through these her feelings); between the child's intention to move (and thus her feelings) and the support of the facilitator; and between the therapist's musical (and feeling) response to the child and the facilitator's physical (and feeling) response. Tracy was naturally most conscious of the second of these three aspects of attunement. She described it as an emotional 'stripping away – getting to the heart of the matter'. Despite sadness at the children's limitations, she was surprised to find herself able to understand their communications. The closeness of the facilitator–child relationship in MAMT may explain why Tracy was unaware of the therapist's music influencing her own behaviour, but she conceded that experiencing movement patterns in which she supported the child being reflected by the therapist's music may have given her confidence.

Clinical examples from therapy with Alice

Tracy wondered whether in the early years she had done too much for the children by encouraging 'big fluid movements'. By the time she worked with a little girl named Alice, she had become less intrusive and directive. (Note that in the musical transcriptions in this chapter, words in italics convey information about the role of the movement facilitator above the top line, and information about the child's visible behaviour occurs below it. The upper musical stave shows the child's vocalisations, and the lower the therapist's music, both sung and played.)

CASE STUDY: DEVELOPING AWARENESS OF SELF AND OTHER

Alice, aged about 3 years, has recently been released from a splint, fitted in order to align and protect her hip joints following corrective surgery. When her legs were first freed she appeared unaware of them, but now she is starting to rediscover them. Her only independent leg movement appears to be an occasional contraction of the right hip and knee joint. When this occurs abruptly it seems like an involuntary spasm, but when it occurs more slowly it appears deliberate. Tracy develops this movement into a series of more controlled contractions and extensions. Alice cooperates with these contractions and extensions but also exerts some control herself, in bar 9 by relaxing more fully and promptly so that the movement can accelerate, and then in bar 10 by resisting the movement, which is reflected by a pause in Mary-Clare's music. These leg movements alternate with spells of rolling between supine and left side-lying positions. The rolling appears to rely mostly on Tracy, which is how she remembers it, but at one point (indicated by a question mark) Alice may have initiated the roll herself. Rolling onto her left side, by changing the orientation of her hip and knee relative to gravity, may have been the trigger for her leg movements.

To develop Alice's awareness of the two contrasting types of movement, Mary-Clare accompanies them with contrasting music. For the rolling she plays chromatic *melismas* in free tempo, descending as Alice rolls onto her side and ascending as she rolls onto her back. For the leg movements she plays shorter rhythmic, but still flexible, phrases in a higher register, without the sliding effect of chromaticism. The music is attuned, in its pitch contours, dynamic variations and phrasing, to the contrasting qualities of the movements and thus to Alice's experience of how those movements feel, and how she feels when making them. Her pleasure shows in her facial expressions and, after the section we have notated, in increasing vocalisations. Mary-Clare does not imitate these vocalisations closely but takes care to leave space in her music to hear and respond to them.

Mary-Clare's music follows the lead provided by Alice's movement yet remains musically logical and satisfying. It is unified by using only two themes, for rolling and leg movement respectively, each developed flexibly through 'continuous variation'. Such aesthetic values might seem irrelevant in music created for extra-musical ends, until we remember that Alice needs to feel that her movements have purpose and 'make sense', and that they are graceful and appreciated by others.

When watching this first video clip of their work together (Figure 11.1), Mary-Clare said she hoped Alice had enjoyed her relationship with the music and 'didn't notice me' helping her to move.

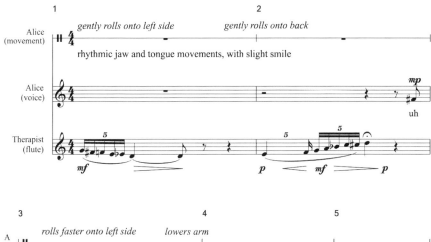

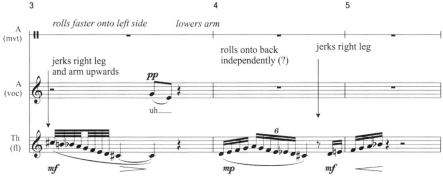

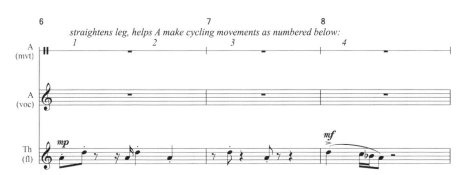

Figure 11.1 Mary-Clare's flute reflects Alice's assisted rolling and leg movements

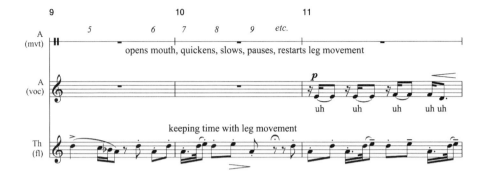

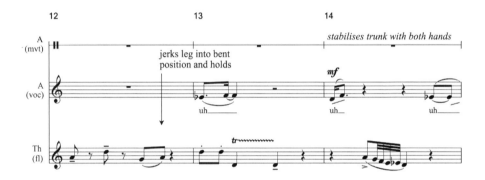

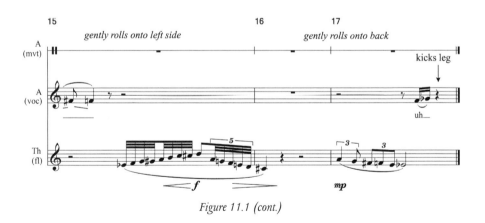

Figure 11.1 (cont.)

CASE STUDY CONTINUED

Alice lies with her head on Mary-Clare's lap. Tracy has just helped her roll onto her back. She supports Alice as she raises and slowly lowers her right arm. After a pause her left arm jerks, and Tracy helps her to raise it. Alice vocalises more strongly. After another pause, Tracy seems to be prompting Alice to raise her left arm again, waiting for a signal that she is ready to raise it more strongly, at which point Alice vocalises again, sharply bending her left and then her right knee. When her legs relax, Tracy supports both arms without raising them, then slowly raises her right arm in a circular movement. Alice shows pleasure by opening her mouth wide and moving her tongue and jaw.

Mary-Clare's music is more rhythmic than in the first example, and forms varied extended arching phrases to accompany Alice's more decisive arm movements, breaking up into more tentative rhythmic fragments suggestive of anticipation during the pauses in activity. After the section transcribed in Figure 11.2, further assisted arm movements are accompanied by quite passionate flute phrases and strong vocalisation from Alice.

Figure 11.2 Alice's vocalisations show her enjoyment of assisted arm movements

Figure 11.2 (cont.)

CASE STUDY CONTINUED

Several years later, Alice has grown considerably. Tracy kneels, facing Mary-Clare, stabilising Alice's hips with her knees. Alice is long-sitting, and her legs appear rather stiff, the knees flexing slightly at times. Beside her is a sounding bowl, a stringed instrument designed for therapeutic use by Tobias Kaye. In the excerpt transcribed, her right hand occasionally comes very near the strings but does not touch them, and Tracy accepts that she is not yet ready to do so. Alice, like many children with cerebral palsy, has lost some of her earlier flexibility, but with Tracy's help she is not only able to make smooth, graceful arm movements, but also to rotate, flex and extend her trunk. Her first significant vocalisation occurs not during her own movement, as in the previous example, but as a response to a high, staccato rhythmic flute figure Mary-Clare has played in response to Alice's movements. At the end of the section transcribed (Figure 11.3), her short vocal phrases and those of the flute form an intimate dialogue.

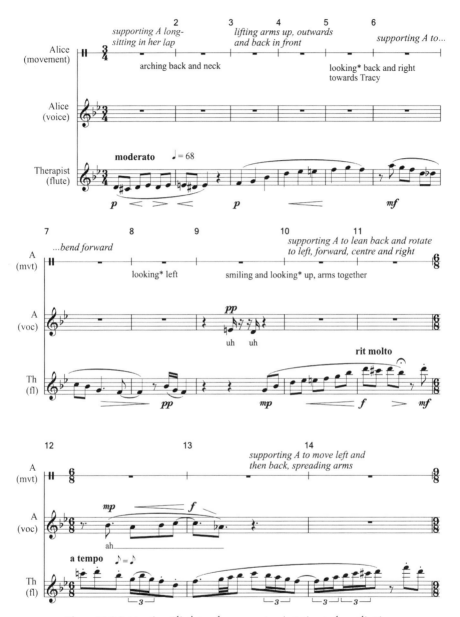

Figure 11.3 Supporting Alice's trunk movement, orientation and vocalisation (see below for an explanation of the asterisks)

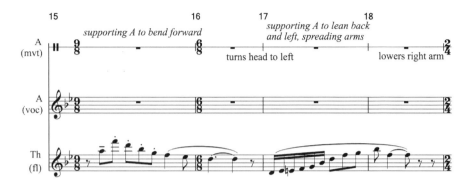

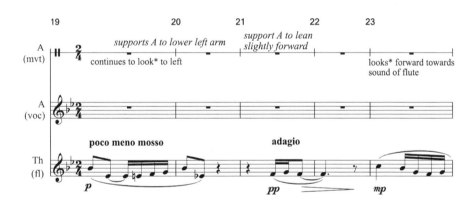

Figure 11.3 (cont.)

The foregoing description contains both prosaic details and interpretations in the language of feeling. What is the status of these interpretations? It is John, observing the video extract, who experiences Alice's movement as 'graceful' and her vocalisation first as an 'emotional response' and as part of an 'intimate dialogue'. He has never met Alice, although he has worked with many children of whom she reminds him. In such work, one must allow oneself to respond emotionally to what the child seems to be experiencing and expressing. This counter-transference experience is reflected upon in reviewing the session, sometimes in supervision, but more immediately it provides the feeling basis for the therapist's musical response. We answer feeling with feeling, not with analysis. Counter-transference feelings that therapists find themselves expressing in their music may only become evident in retrospect, when analysing the session. Streeter (1999) illustrates how studying the musical counter-transference may reveal how a therapist–client relationship has become 'stuck', and thus how to free the emotional blockage. The fact that an observer or listener with no personal relationship with Alice can experience counter-transference feelings shows how the child's feelings are embodied in actual music and body language.

In Figure 11.3 Alice, though blind, is repeatedly described as 'looking' (see the asterisks). Initially inadvertent, this factually inaccurate account of Alice's behaviour has not been corrected because the orienting response usually associated with vision is still present. Turning the head towards a sound source both enhances the aural experience and helps to locate the sound source in space. Furthermore, the experience of being 'looked' at by a person we know is blind evokes much the same emotional response as if they were sighted. Alice's 'looking' is thus an aspect of her body language to which Mary-Clare and Tracy were most probably responding.

CASE STUDY CONTINUED

A few weeks later, Tracy has decided to allow Alice to focus on the sounding bowl, supporting her head so that she can rotate it between a position where her nose almost touches the strings and a turn to the left towards Mary-Clare's face. She also supports slight left arm movements, perhaps hoping Alice will sound the strings herself. Mary-Clare plucks a simple phrase on the sounding bowl and then pauses. Alice turns her head towards the instrument, and Mary-Clare uses her breath alone to create a melodic phrase in a pitched whisper. When Alice vocalises a gentle falling figure at bar 13, Mary-Clare develops its pitches into a sung staccato phrase. Alice's vocalisations grow in length and expressiveness, and an intimate vocal dialogue develops. This takes priority over any further playing for the remainder of the excerpt. The pitches both participants sing relate to the pentatonic tuning of the sounding bowl, and from close Alice may have heard the strings resonating in sympathy, although this is not clear from the recording (Figure 11.4).

Figure 11.4 Alice's fascination with the sounding bowl: developing vocal dialogue

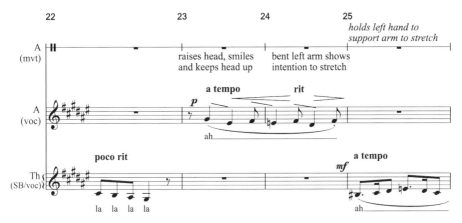

Figure 11.4 (cont.)

Interpersonal dynamics in the three-fold relationship in MAMT

The relationship between child, movement facilitator and music therapist is complex and perhaps unique to MAMT. Oedipal theory suggests that each member of such a trio may feel shut out of the relationship between the other two. However, Mary-Clare, Rebecca and Tracy have not found such a dynamic of jealousy in MAMT. For the child, both adults are attachment figures. They understand her and give her their undivided attention. She experiences the therapist's music and the facilitator's touch attuning to her feelings, giving her both security and a sense of agency. She does not perceive the attunement between the adults as an intimate relationship from which she is excluded. The facilitator's prime concern is to attune to the child, so the therapist's music, by attuning to her and the child's shared movement, confirms and supports her attunement to the child rather than challenging or competing with it. As she also hopes to help the child develop a relationship with the music, when her physical support becomes less necessary over time, this is viewed as an achievement, rather than as being sidelined. For the music therapist, the focus is always the child, and her music primarily relates to the child's movements and what they express. The facilitator supports this process by interpreting and realising the child's intentions to move. Thus, the music therapist can reflect and attune to the child, rather than struggling to evoke a response as she might when working single-handed.

The child's vocalisations do not require the facilitator's support in the same way as her movements. Music therapists are sometimes able to elicit vocal sounds and establish dialogue where others have had little success. However, most of Alice's vocalisations appear to be her feeling response to the facilitator's reassuring and empowering support, the movements that support allows her to make and the music attuned to those movements from the therapist. These vocal sounds are the most powerful way in which the child communicates how she feels about the whole experience.

MAMT in rehabilitation

The context

Rebecca currently works at the National Rehabilitation Hospital (NRH) in Dublin which has a small paediatric family-centred rehabilitation programme. This unit is the national medical service for children and adolescents up to 18 years old requiring intensive rehabilitation because of traumatic and non-traumatic brain injury, stroke, traumatic and non-traumatic spinal cord injury, neurological disorders, limb absence and other musculoskeletal and neuromuscular disorders. Referrals are received from across the Republic of Ireland.

Rehabilitation and adjustment for the family and child to their acquired disability may be both medical and emotional. As children learn to master tasks and manage disabilities, they require support, praise and guidance. At the NRH the interdisciplinary paediatric programme brings together staff with relevant experience and expertise in child neurological rehabilitation. The team works together in partnership with the child and their family to help the individual young person become as independent and confident as possible to achieve their full rehabilitation potential.

Children with an acquired disability at the NRH present different challenges from the children previously described at the Cheyne Child Development Service (CCDS). However, MAMT has a key role in their rehabilitation. Around 90% of music therapy at the NRH is interdisciplinary, with up to five professionals present in the session working with the child at any given point. Sessions usually take place in the music therapy room, where the music acts as the 'glue' enabling several therapists to access the child from their own professional perspective while working towards joint therapy rehabilitation goals. In this setting MAMT can flourish and showcase its unique benefits. As a medium for interdisciplinary members to observe and treat children, it optimises the team's understanding of the children's needs from the perspective of each discipline while maintaining a child-centred approach to therapy and rehabilitation.

Differences in the MAMT approach in rehabilitation

In a rehabilitation context the core collaboration of music therapist and movement facilitator remains, but beyond that there are significant differences. The movement facilitator may be another senior clinician, which was not normally the case at the CCDS, and the role may rotate among clinicians from different disciplines involved with the child. (Such rotation would not be effective in work with children like Tom and Alice, who require the prolonged support of a single movement facilitator as they slowly develop awareness of self and other.)

In this rehabilitation context, where children have greater understanding, self-awareness and ego strength, there is some relaxation of the requirement for the therapist's music to be attuned. A child with low muscle tone may need music to be upbeat and lively rather than simply attuned to their physical state, and a child with increased tone may need music to be more relaxed and calming to facilitate optimum participation. Sekeles (1996) and Perry (1998) make similar claims for music's role in regulating arousal. The music supports the movement facilitator in promoting effective patterns of movement and inhibiting undesirable movement responses or patterns.

At the NRH, team members not acting as a movement facilitator in a particular session nevertheless attend as observers. This greatly enriches the multidisciplinary review of sessions, since all have either participated or observed and each person has a first-hand perspective on the session. Those not actively involved offer observations on the session which may be both more detailed and more objective than the recollections of the active participants, at the same time enhancing their own understanding for when they next act as movement facilitator. The knowledge gained also informs their uni-disciplinary work with the child at other times.

The attendance of the whole therapy team also enhances the development of MAMT in general because the music therapist is able to draw on the discipline-specific advice of each team member. The speech and language therapist may point out subtleties in the pragmatics of the movement dialogue between child and facilitator or the musical dialogue between child and music therapist. The neuropsychologist may advise on the implications of the child's cognitive and executive functioning, and the physiotherapist and occupational therapist may help to remove barriers linked to handling, positioning, support and sensory integration.

In the following brief account of work with a girl named Seren, we incorporate the perspectives of physiotherapy and occupational therapy along with some thoughts expressed by her father concerning the ways in which MAMT has helped Seren.

Seren developed normally until shortly after her first birthday, when she started having seizures. Following a prolonged seizure, she was admitted to intensive care with a subdural haemorrhage. For several days doctors were unsure whether she would survive, but the acute bleeding resolved without the need for surgery. Previously a lively child, Seren was now profoundly physically disabled, with little vision and a cognitive impairment.

Once out of immediate danger, Seren was placed on the waiting list for the NRH on account of her initial history of normal development. For 9 months before admission, she received community-based treatment at the Central Rehabilitation Clinic in Dublin. This did not include music therapy, but Seren's reviving interest in music and sound was evident from her responsiveness to musical toys. The clinic used these toys to motivate particular movements needed for her physical rehabilitation.

Seren's treatment at the NRH totalled 3 months either side of her second birthday. She had already steadily regained strength and movement, but normalisation of her movement patterns was often hampered by the exaggerated extensor response which would interrupt many of her exercises. The team decided to modify the continuous musical attunement typical of the original MAMT model, as Seren's physiotherapist explains below.

Staff explained to Seren's parents that their approach aimed to facilitate recovery of the functional abilities and intellectual understanding which had been laid down in her brain prior to the neurological trauma. This was an approach which her father, Gareth, a loving parent and also a musician, had instinctively followed from the start by continuing the same playful routines and playing the same recorded music which Seren had enjoyed before her illness. The wisdom of this approach was confirmed by recordings, made at her bedside on his mobile phone, showing the first glimmers of her former smiles. Previously unfamiliar with music therapy, Gareth is in no doubt that MAMT has helped and enriched Seren's rehabilitation pathway.

A physiotherapist's perspective

Mairead Navin is a physiotherapist in the paediatric unit. She found working with music therapy a great adjunct to her intervention and mentioned three aspects of the MAMT approach which resemble ingredients of contemporary physiotherapy approaches to this patient group. The first aspect was the use of vocal patterns of often non-verbal rhythm and intonation with which the physiotherapist encourages, and in effect attunes to, the movement she facilitates for the child. The second aspect was the emphasis on facilitating coordinated movement *patterns*, in accordance with the Bobath model of physiotherapy. The third aspect was the use of biofeedback by reflecting back the child's movements in some other modality in order to increase her awareness and ability to monitor them. In relation to Seren's music therapy, Mairead was impressed by the way excursions to and from the tonic key as 'home' provided feedback on Seren's expanding explorations from a stable base.

Following neurological damage, some children can acquire abnormal movement patterns which hinder rehabilitation. Mairead explained that, to avoid reinforcing these patterns, there may need to be either a break in the music or an abrupt change to non-attuned music to distract the child from the undesirable movement pattern; however, this abandonment of attunement and empathy should last only as long as it is necessary.

Mairead was used to using both recorded and live music to support physiotherapy, yet had found that as a movement facilitator in MAMT she was often not aware of the therapist's music. Alice's movement facilitator Tracy had said the same, and the explanation may be the facilitator's intense focus on the child and the way that attuned music blends into the overall experience rather than demanding attention. Both Mairead and the occupational therapist described the therapist's music as following rather than leading.

An occupational therapist's perspective

Senior occupational therapist Michael Brogan had experienced music therapy when working with visually impaired children, and since joining the NRH team he had become a strong believer in MAMT. When working as movement facilitator he was aware of the music and felt that, for a child such as Seren with acquired visual, physical and cognitive impairment, the music's main function was to motivate active re-engagement with her environment, from which she had become rather detached. He found the child-led stance of MAMT similar to Intensive Interaction (Nind and Hewett 1994) and Sensory Integration Therapy (Ayres 1974). Musical structure, as distinct from the attunement function of the music, had developed Seren's understanding and anticipation, contributing to the interdisciplinary effort to reduce the frequency of the extensor movement patterns which had formerly made her handling so difficult. MAMT had contributed to Seren's active engagement in meaningful interactions and her ability to play in and explore her environment. Seren's parents were supported in carrying over key therapeutic strategies observed in MAMT sessions to the home environment, in accordance with the NRH's whole approach to family-centred rehabilitation.

Conclusion: The future of MAMT

As more infants with the profoundest disabilities survive, there are likely to be many children like Alice who would benefit from MAMT. We hope that approaches similar to those at the CCDS, and more recently at the NRH, will continue to be used where clinically indicated. We invite anyone who has followed a path of discovery similar to that of Mary-Clare and Rebecca to compare their experiences with ours, and we hope that those working with children with similar disabilities who have not tried this form of team working will be inspired to do so.

As the maturing music therapy profession moves from a phase of diversification to one of consolidation and sharing best practice, it should be remembered that although MAMT is a specialised approach developed for a particular group of clients, a music therapist wishing to practise it requires the same broad generic training undergone by all UK music therapists. The specialised skills of therapist and facilitator are developed and refined through joint practice and reflection. MAMT does not therefore co-opt additional theoretical concepts and special knowledge or require a further qualification, as does guided imagery and music or neurologic music therapy.

Mary-Clare and Rebecca write (Fearn *et al.* 2005, p.32): 'Over the years we have learnt that unless children experience affect attunement at an early pre-verbal level and develop awareness of a subjective self, they are unable to learn how to communicate effectively.' Few people now would challenge this statement, derived from the insights of

Stern (1985). While there are many ways for a child to experience affect attunement, MAMT has been found specially effective for two groups of children: those with profound disabilities, including an impaired ability to use movement to experience and express themselves and develop communication relationships with others, and also those who need motivation, support and guidance from a well-integrated multidisciplinary team in order to regain functionality lost through acquired neurological impairment.

References

Ayres, A.J. (1974) *The Development of Sensory Integrative Theory and Practice: A Collection of the Works of A. Jean Ayres.* Dubuque, IA: Kendall/Hunt.

Bannerman-Haig, S. (1999) 'Dance Movement Therapy: A Case Study.' In A. Cattanach (ed) *Process in the Arts Therapies.* London: Jessica Kingsley Publishers.

Davies, A. (2015) 'Early Years: Experiences with Others.' In A. Davies, E. Richards and N. Barwick. *Group Music Therapy: A Group Analytic Approach.* London: Routledge.

Edwards, J. (ed) (2011) *Music Therapy and Parent–Infant Bonding.* Oxford: Oxford University Press.

Fearn, M.-C. and O'Connor, R. (2008) 'Collaborative Working at the Cheyne Day Centre, London.' In K. Twyford and T. Watson (eds) *Integrated Team Working: Music Therapy as Part of Transdisciplinary and Collaborative Approaches.* London: Jessica Kingsley Publishers.

Fearn, M.-C., O'Connor, R. and Ledden, T. (2005) 'Music and Attuned Movement Therapy: A Therapeutic Approach Developed at the Cheyne Day Centre, London.' In *Changes: Exploring Clinical, Professional and Global Perspectives.* Proceedings of the British Society for Music Therapy and Association of Professional Music Therapists Annual Conference (pp.65–73), London, 13–14 February 2005.

Levinge, A. (2015) *The Music of Being: Music Therapy, Winnicott and the School of Object Relations.* London: Jessica Kingsley Publishers.

Nind, M. and Hewett, D. (1994) *Access to Communication: Developing the Basics of Communication with People with Severe Learning Difficulties Through Intensive Interaction.* London: David Fulton Publishers.

Pavlicevic, M. (1997) *Music Therapy in Context: Music, Meaning and Relationship.* London: Jessica Kingsley Publishers.

Perry, M.R. (1998) 'How Improvisation-Based Music Therapy Can Regulate Arousal to Facilitate the Communication Development of Children with Multiple Disabilities.' In R.R. Pratt and D.E. Grocke (eds) *Music Medicine 3: Music Medicine and Music Therapy – Expanding Horizons.* Victoria: University of Melbourne.

Sekeles, C. (1996) *Music, Motion and Emotion: The Developmental-Integrative Model in Music Therapy.* Gilsum, NH: Barcelona Publishers.

Stern, D. (1985) *The Interpersonal World of the Infant.* London: Karnac Books.

Streeter, E. (1999) 'Definition and Use of the Musical Transference Relationship.' In T. Wigram and J. De Backer (eds) *Clinical Applications of Music Therapy in Psychiatry.* London: Jessica Kingsley Publishers.

Trondalen, G. and Skårderud, F. (2007) 'Playing with affects…and the importance of "affect attunement".' *Nordic Journal of Music Therapy 16,* 2, 100–111.

Chapter 12

'Music and Movement'

Integrated Music Therapy and Physiotherapy
for People with Severe Physical Disabilities
at Risk of Developing Fixed Deformities

John Strange and Lyn Weekes[1]

A serendipitous meeting

Shortly after her appointment in the 1970s as Head Physiotherapist at a large UK National Health Service hospital for people with learning disabilities, Lyn Weekes met various key members of staff, one of whom was eventually to achieve worldwide recognition as a music therapy clinician, researcher, educator and ambassador. Her introduction to Tony Wigram was extremely informal. She recalls him casually leaning against a wall. 'What's music therapy?' she asked, having never heard of it. Tony simply responded, 'Come with me!' Lyn followed Tony onto an adult ward where he was immediately 'mobbed', as he approached the piano, by a group of patients chanting 'Tony, Tony, music man!' in a striking show of enthusiasm. Tony encouraged one man to join in on a drum and, finding the man's fingers clenched, he started to massage his hand in an attempt to release them. 'Not like that!' protested Lyn, explaining that the shoulder must be relaxed before the arm, and the arm before the hand and fingers.

As music therapy was a relatively recently developing profession, it is no surprise that Lyn had not previously encountered it. Physiotherapy was more securely established, but Tony, although aware of its importance, had not yet fully grasped the basic principle, that both exercise regimes and treatments involving manipulation, to

---

1   Physiotherapist Lyn Weekes is joined as co-author by John Strange, who was fortunate to have participated in 'Music and Movement' as a music therapy student under the supervision of the late Tony Wigram.

be both safe and effective, should work outwards from the body's core to its extremities. The practical instruction just described was the start of a fruitful inter-professional partnership. Soon Lyn and Tony were developing an approach which they entitled 'Music and Movement', involving a programme of assisted movement patterns, supported by music, for groups of severely physically disabled patients. Older British readers may recall that 'Music and Movement' was also the title of a weekly BBC Schools Radio programme, which had little in common with the approach developed at Harperbury beyond a general recognition of the multifaceted relationship between music and bodily movement, which the programme exploited for developmental and educational ends.

This method of working was presented by Lyn and Tony with video illustrations at the World Congress of Music Therapy in Paris in 1983, and by Tony at the Nordic Congress in Bergen in 2003. It was described in the *British Journal of Music Therapy* (Wigram and Weekes 1985) and in *Receptive Methods in Music Therapy* (Grocke and Wigram 2007). This last account is the most readily available and detailed treatment of the topic, and should be required reading for music therapists considering adopting the approach. It should also be noted that the close collaboration of a physiotherapist is essential in order to set up a programme of 'Music and Movement'. The present chapter aims to raise awareness of the potential of this approach, rather than providing a step-by-step guide, and to explore the various relationships between music therapist, physiotherapist, helpers and clients which it entails.

Placing 'Music and Movement' in context

Meadows (2002) surveys several independently developed therapeutic programmes which utilise music in support of movement. There are various differences between the programmes he describes, but also common elements. All programmes draw on the expertise of the music therapist and also, at least at the planning stage, of the physiotherapist. All programmes have the physical and associated psychological well-being of the client as their primary aim and concern. Differences between approaches concern the amount of structure versus freedom, the nature and role of the music, the overall design of the programme and the decision as to who directs the actual sessions. Meadows discusses only those approaches described in the literature for use with children, but the majority of Lyn and Tony's clients were in fact adults, and there seems no reason why the other approaches Meadows describes should not also be used with adults when clinically appropriate. While early intervention to address many pathologies leading to disability may reduce the need for treatment in later life, the adult with a profound intellectual and physical impairment continues to be at risk of deterioration. Programmes such as 'Music and Movement' therefore remain relevant and even increase in value as physical growth and the process of ageing render the person vulnerable to developing fixed deformities.

'Music and Movement' pre-dated most other music therapy and physiotherapy collaborations surveyed by Meadows. In the early 1970s, when Tony and Lyn first developed the method, Tony would probably have been aware of Nordoff and Robbins' *Therapy in Music for Handicapped Children*, a pioneer publication which discusses the needs of children with physical disabilities and how music therapy can meet them, but does not explore the benefits of inter-professional collaboration with physiotherapy (Nordoff and Robbins 2004). Tony welcomed the fresh horizons opened up by such a partnership. It was his and Lyn's willingness to learn from each other which made their model of 'Music and Movement' possible.

The patients

The movement needs of the adult patients with whom Lyn and Tony worked were very similar to those of the children with severe and profound multiple disabilities considered in Meadows' (2002) review. He explains that these children's condition makes it 'difficult to engage them in any kind of movement, even though movement is essential to their well-being'. They may display 'increased or decreased muscle tone, loss of range of movement, and loss of ability to coordinate movements. As a result…some children may have little or no independent movement, and show no apparent awareness of their body.' Additionally, they may 'find touch or physical movement painful and/or stressful. As these children are often handled extensively by adults, they can develop a resistance, sometimes even an animosity, to being moved' (p.17). In all the 'Music and Movement' approaches Meadows describes, the focus of sessions is on some aspect of the children's physical development and/or well-being, and a high ratio of staff to children, approaching one to one, is usual. When 'Music and Movement' was developed by Lyn and Tony, the adult helpers included: physiotherapists; physiotherapy aides and nursing staff; placement students of physiotherapy, nursing, music therapy and other relevant professions; and also volunteers.

The role of the physiotherapist

The effectiveness of the 'Music and Movement' programme at Harperbury sprang in the first instance from the series of exercises, carefully graded according to the best clinical and research evidence, selected and codified by Lyn Weekes. Movement experiences that were physically helpful for the patients were presented in a sequence that allowed the general relaxing or stimulating effect of each exercise, together with more specific effects on particular muscle groups, to carry over positively into the next, as illustrated by the sequence presented by Grocke and Wigram (2007, p.244).

All the movements, when executed passively, involve stretching of muscle groups and mobilisation of joints, as the helpers work to gently overcome the stiffness and resistance of the patients. Some of the movements can subsequently be performed independently by a few patients, but it is not seen as a failure if this cannot be achieved. While it is not uncommon for physiotherapists to use repeated small rhythmic movements with this client population as a form of massage to induce relaxation of a muscle group prior to more vigorous stretching, the use in 'Music and Movement' of rhythmically repeated movement throughout was quite innovative.

Having planned the movement programme, Lyn explained and demonstrated the hands-on handling techniques to the helpers who were to use them, monitored their performance and the progress of the patients, and regularly reviewed the programme, discussing with the team the differing needs of individual patients and the ways in which these could be met by varying the movements. A co-training programme was introduced, through which members of the music therapy and physiotherapy departments built up their knowledge and understanding of each other's discipline, and the helpers from outside those disciplines were initiated into some fundamental principles of both. Many helpers developed a sound understanding of the practical techniques used in 'Music and Movement' and of the aims and objectives and theoretical basis of this specialised intervention. Today they would be referred to as 'physiotherapy technicians'.

The role of the music therapist

As a music therapy trainee, John Strange had a clinical placement at Harperbury in 1985. As well as learning much about the client group from the experience of hands-on work as a helper in 'Music and Movement', he was able to observe the musical expertise Tony Wigram brought to the sessions. Tony was adept at playing both popular and classical music by ear and was also a versatile and inspiring improviser. This enabled him to provide appropriate music for each of the series of movement activities which Lyn had devised.

In his last and most detailed exposition of the rationale for the choice of music to support the various movement routines (Grocke and Wigram 2007, p.238), Tony relates musical elements to specific brain areas and functions. Foremost among these elements, tempo and rhythm, stimulate a thalamic reflex which tends to entrain movements to the tempo of the music. The music must therefore be at a tempo and contain a rhythm which will support, rather than conflict with, the intended movement. Next in importance come melody and harmony, which are principally processed in the temporal lobe, encouraging reminiscence, association and anticipation. These elements should be such as to encourage, sustain and develop the client's interest and awareness so that the client will be able to follow the form of the music and find it predictable. Finally, the style and timbre of the music should be adjusted according to whether the aim of the music is principally to relax or to stimulate.

Many familiar pieces of music suitable to address these general aims and the specific requirements of each movement are provided (Grocke and Wigram 2007, pp.242–254), and the therapist using improvisation is advised to 'construct it in a musical form that will provide a rhythmic base, a structure in melody and phrases, and predictability', characteristics that the less experienced improviser is liable to sacrifice in the pursuit of spontaneity. Tony writes from intimate experience of how various musical characteristics should be varied to meet the complex needs of individual clients and of the group as a whole, but neither he nor other writers on approaches to physiotherapy with music say much about how the music also affects the helpers, although there can be no doubt that he was acutely sensitive to their needs and reactions also. As well as structuring and sequencing the movements which the helpers assist the patients to perform, the music conveys mood and regulates the intensity of the helpers' movements. Since the patients simultaneously experience both the music and its translation into movement by the helpers, it is important for the helpers and the music to be coordinated. On a more mundane level, as the helpers' task entails considerable expenditure of energy for 30 to 50 minutes, the support of the music helps to combat fatigue and to engender enthusiasm for the work.

The role of the helpers

Although the helpers are guided and directed by the music therapist running the session, their role is not to follow the instructions mechanically. Each helper is in intimate contact with an individual patient, and must also be guided by that patient's responses and not simply 'go through the motions' or imitate what other helpers are doing. Several of the tempi recommended (Grocke and Wigram 2007, pp.242–254) are designed to be interpreted according to the individual patient's needs, by allowing a movement to be performed at half or even a quarter speed without losing the rhythmic relation to the music. Only the helper can decide what speed suits the individual patient. Figure 12.1 illustrates a simple application of this principle.

Bend   and stretch,   bend   and stretch,   bend   and   stretch and bend   and stretch
Bend   and bend,   stretch   and stretch,   bend   and   bend_ and stretch   and stretch
Bend   and bend,   bend   and bend,   stretch   and   stretch and stretch   and stretch

*Figure 12.1 Quick, medium and slow execution of
a leg exercise to the melody of 'Edelweiss'*

The 'how' of the helper's work is at least as important as the 'what'. A gentle but firm touch inspires confidence. Constant awareness and adaptation to the patient's response conveys empathy and avoids triggering resistance. However difficult a particular movement, the patient's emotional as well as physical comfort must always take precedence over any imagined 'ideal' execution of the movement.

The helpers also have an important role in monitoring and evaluation. They alone can provide the feedback the music therapist needs in order to refine his musical support. Feedback need not wait until after the session, as helpers can silently signal when an exercise is going well, and when patients are getting tired, enabling the music therapist to decide when it is time to wind down an exercise and move on to the next. If an exercise is proving difficult for a patient, the helper may alert the music therapist to the problem, thereby enabling him to make some helpful adjustment in his musical support. Helpers can also provide detailed feedback on each patient's progress to the physiotherapy team by filling in standard weekly reporting forms placed on the floor beside them after each exercise, and by participating in team discussions after the session.

Conclusion – A hybrid intervention with a key role for assistants

Various models of interdisciplinary collaboration have become more widespread in recent years (Twyford and Watson 2008). The collaboration between music therapy and physiotherapy seen in 'Music and Movement' led to a hybrid intervention. The aims were ultimately those of physiotherapy, in their focus on maintaining and extending flexibility and range of movement, but the means were modifications of both physiotherapeutic and music-therapeutic techniques. The reach and scope of both professions in the clinical setting was extended by the collaboration, and others have used the method, notably Helen Odell-Miller in her first clinical post, at the Ida Darwin Hospital in Cambridge. Since the early 1990s, however, great improvements in early intervention have meant that fewer learning-disabled people develop fixed deformities. Remaining sufferers in schools are likely to be integrated into mainstream education and adults are no longer segregated into large learning-disability hospitals but living in the community. Large groups of people with fixed deformities are thus now a rarity in Britain, and 'Music and Movement' in its original large-group format can only be offered if it is practicable to gather a group together for that express purpose.

In addition to the collaboration between the physiotherapist and music therapist, it is the indispensable contribution of the hands-on assistants, and their sensitive use of touch to facilitate movement, which lies at the core of this model. This is similar to the role of the facilitator in Music and Attuned Movement Therapy, as described in Chapter 11. Touch is a sensory modality furnishing each individual person with information about both his or her body and its environment, but even more importantly it is a key component in communication between individuals and thus vital to human well-being.

In 'Music and Movement' an enrichment of human relationships by touch is experienced not only by the clients, but also by the helpers, as they form more intimate bonds with the clients and develop a fuller understanding of their needs and reactions. These mutual benefits are likely to generalise to contacts between client and helper in other situations. Such generalisation of modes of interaction developed in music therapy is a feature of many of the other assistant–client relationships described in this book.

References

Grocke, D. and Wigram, T. (2007) *Receptive Methods in Music Therapy: Techniques and Clinical Applications for Music Therapy Clinicians, Educators and Students.* London: Jessica Kingsley Publishers.

Meadows, A. (2002) 'Approaches to Music and Movement for Children with Severe and Profound Multiple Disabilities.' *Australian Journal of Music Therapy 13,* 17–27.

Nordoff, P. and Robbins, C. (2004) *Therapy in Music for Handicapped Children.* Gilsum, NH: Barcelona Publishers. (Original work published in 1971.)

Twyford, K. and Watson, T. (eds) (2008) *Integrated Team Working: Music Therapy as Part of Transdisciplinary and Collaborative Approaches.* London: Jessica Kingsley Publishers.

Wigram, A. and Weekes, L. (1985) 'A specific approach to overcoming motor dysfunction: children and adolescents with severe mental and physical handicap using Music and Movement.' *British Journal of Music Therapy 16,* 1, 2–12.

Chapter 13

Improvised Music to Support Client–Assistant Interaction

The Perceptions of Music Therapists[1]

John Strange

The case for process research

Outcome research into improvisational music therapy poses a particular challenge. Hooper *et al.* (2008) point out that normal clinical practice is liable to be distorted by the requirements of experimental investigation. A special difficulty is the requirement of replicability, since improvised music, by definition, cannot be replicated. However, there are other reasons for turning instead to process research. At a research conference in the early 1980s, Dr (now Professor) Eric Clarke expressed the hope that the profession might move on from simply *demonstrating* to actually *explaining* music therapy's effectiveness. One of the reasons that even 'extensive and convincing' evidence for music therapy's effectiveness fails to persuade everyone (Gold and Wigram 2012, p.165) may be the scarcity of comprehensible and plausible accounts of *how* it works. It is clearly easier to believe an intervention is effective if we have a credible explanation of the mechanisms involved. This is a question for process research, in which we look at what actually happens in the clinical setting. Every case is unique, but case series can reveal suggestive trends.

Chapter 1 explores how learning support assistants (LSAs) experienced triadic support of interaction by improvisation (TSII). It is noted in that chapter that LSAs made few references to the influence upon themselves of the therapist's improvised music. The present chapter takes a closer look at the music and its therapeutic

---

1   This chapter is a further exploration of the clinical work described in Chapter 1, which should preferably be read first.

intention and effect, on the LSAs as well as the teenagers with whom they worked.

Investigating triadic support of interaction by improvisation

Bruscia (1987) catalogued a variety of distinct models of clinical improvisation. General theories about improvisation have been proposed by Aigen (2005), Garred (2006), Pavlicevic (1997) and Smeijsters (2005). Darnley-Smith (2013) has examined the ontological status of the music improvised in therapy. Lee (1992) used a detailed examination of individual cases to investigate the role of clinical improvisation in the therapeutic process. De Backer and Sutton (2014) have assembled a wide range of case studies illustrating aspects of how music functions in therapy, and many others have explored how particular effects might relate to particular musical features, often with reference to writings by Daniel Stern, culminating in *Forms of Vitality* (Stern 2010).

In TSII the therapist's active intervention is almost entirely musical. His improvisation is given a particularly high profile by his relative abstinence from social forms of intervention. But TSII neither originated from a general theory nor sought to construct one. The data gathered from my music therapy research collaborators (Strange 2014) were spontaneous continuous responses to purposively selected video clips and subsequent reflections, which were then collated with musical transcriptions. The object was to investigate how my improvised music had influenced the client–assistant interaction.

In considering how to relate the therapist's judgements of clinical effects to the transcriptions, I was clear that the process should not start with musical analysis. Ruud (2010, p.84) asks, '…what do we look for? Thematic unity, tempo changes, texture, patterns of dialogue, changes in complexity, melodic or thematic characteristics?' By leaving the question unanswered, Ruud implies that analysing music into its separate components may be problematic. Furthermore, while it is of the utmost importance what the music means to the client, 'To what extent can we expect a correspondence between the music heard or notated and the experience as it occurred in the client?' (p.85).

Discovering the clients' experiences of and reactions to the music improvised in therapy would reduce this uncertainty, but directly researching such experiences is seldom feasible. Lee's (1992) subjects were highly articulate and motivated to share and explore the music's meaning and significance. Many music therapy clients, however, would be unable to assist in this way, or might experience it as an intrusion into their therapy. Often the only ethical and practical way of exploring how music in therapy 'works' for clients, especially if they are non-verbal, is for others to observe the therapeutic process and infer the clients' experiences from their behaviour. The music therapist collaborators in this part of my research considered the behaviour and inferred the internal processes of not only the students but also the LSAs interacting with them.

A theoretical model of the triadic relationship

Following Ruud (2010) I was reluctant to analyse *music* into its elements – melody, harmony, rhythm and so on. Instead I decided to analyse the *therapy process* into distinct components. I sensed that in episodes of TSII my improvised music had been addressed simultaneously to each of the interacting partners, with reference to both their observable behaviour and their inferred internal processes. As regards observable behaviour, musical or non-musical, my music had sometimes attempted to influence it directly, by contagion or entrainment, and sometimes indirectly, by suggesting to either partner a possible style of interaction with the other which she or he could then consciously or unconsciously imitate. As regards the mental processes of the interacting partners – their perceptions, understandings and feelings – my music had also addressed these both directly and indirectly. The direct channel of influence was emotional, resembling the way film music stimulates emotions, often unconsciously, in cinema audiences, in order to influence their perceptions and interpretations of events on the screen (Cohen 2010, p.885). The indirect channel targeted more cognitive processes, alerting one partner to something in the other's behaviour and communication which might otherwise have been missed, so as to enhance empathy and understanding.

I found this range of possibilities neatly mirrored by Stern's (1998) classification of different models of mother–infant psychotherapy. Stern uses the term 'representation' to denote the internal model which mother and infant build of their relationship as they accumulate many experiences of being together and store them in implicit procedural memory. The concept is similar to Bowlby's 'internal working model' (Bowlby 1973, p.203) except that Stern's primary focus as a clinician is on the manifestation of representations in the here and now of the therapy setting, rather than on how such representations provide a blueprint which is then transferred to many other relationships. Thus, when Stern refers to behaviours as 'enactments' of representations, he is thinking primarily of the present unfolding of the mother–infant relationship, rather than its future role in forming the infant's attachment style.

Stern (1998) surveys a range of different schools of parent–infant psychotherapy, first distinguishing those which target representations from those which target enactments, then subdividing each group into those which select the mother as the 'port of entry' and those which select the infant. Substituting assistant for mother and student for infant, I present these possibilities in Table 13.1 as four 'scenarios' which I asked the three music therapists to consider in relation to the examples of TSII. The task I set was to assess the influence of the music in each scenario in terms of the degree of support or challenge it provided. By this I meant that they should decide whether my playing was intended to support and sustain an existing behaviour or representation, or to change or modify it, and how strongly. This distinction caused some initial confusion among the music therapists, who rightly pointed out that a therapist should never withdraw support. We therefore agreed that 'challenge' was shorthand for 'support and challenge'.

Table 13.1 Scenarios to consider when investigating TSII (classification derived from Stern 1998)

	Infant/client (student)	Mother/LSA
Enactment/ behaviour	SCENARIO 1	SCENARIO 3
Representation	SCENARIO 2	SCENARIO 4

TSII: triadic support of interaction by improvisation;
LSA: learning support assistant.

A similar distinction between support and challenge is implicit in Bruscia's list (1987, p.533) of 64 clinical techniques in improvisational music therapy. Figure 13.1 shows how techniques from the list which are common in work with learning-disabled clients may be divided into two rows, the upper row targeting behaviour and the lower row mental processes (a broader concept than representations), and into two columns, the left column for techniques supporting the status quo and the right for techniques challenging it. (Note that this division bears no relation to that in Table 13.1.)

Clinical intention / Client function	To support, encourage, reinforce, sustain, affirm	To develop, modify, challenge, change
Musical or other observable behaviour	Techniques of empathy Imitating, synchronising, incorporating, pacing, exaggerating Structuring techniques Rhythmic grounding, tonal centring Techniques of elicitation Making spaces, extending, completing Procedural techniques Receding	Structuring techniques Shaping Techniques of elicitation Repeating, modelling Redirection techniques Introducing change, differentiating, intervening
Internal processes	Techniques of empathy Reflecting Techniques of intimacy Soliloquys Emotional exploration techniques Holding, doubling	Redirection techniques Intensifying, calming Emotional exploration techniques Making transitions, integrating

Figure 13.1 Selected clinical techniques classified by target and intention (adapted from Bruscia 1987)

A novel continuous response method

Therapy is a dynamic process. Though it is possible to study an extended passage of music therapy as a whole, this is not how clients (or therapists) experience music improvised in therapy, which is both created and first experienced from moment to moment. Its effects are therefore most appropriately studied by a continuous response method, allowing the observer to get closer to the likely experience of the participants. Schubert (2010) discusses various continuous response methods for use in music listening, many involving the use of sophisticated software and computer interfaces. Responding to video is, however, a special case, requiring a response device that can be operated by touch alone so as not to distract from the video being assessed. I therefore designed and constructed a dial (Figure 13.2) on which each therapist could move a pointer as the video played, having first become familiar by touch with the position of the seven segments. (Originally segment 0 was white, segments A to C light to dark blue, and segments X to Z light to dark pink.) As the therapist moved the pointer, a video camera re-recorded the video clip together with the therapist's pointer movements (Figure 13.3).

Response scale for the effect of improvised keyboard music on:

1. The student's behaviour   2. The student's representation
3. The LSA's behaviour   4. The LSA's representation

Moving the pointer
0 is neutral
A, B and C are progressively stronger supporting/reinforcing effects
X, Y and Z are progressively stronger modifying/challenging effects

Always keep the pointer within a segment, not on a boundary

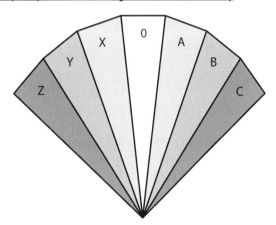

Figure 13.2 Dial for registering continuous responses to music therapy video clips (LSA: learning support assistant)

Figure 13.3 A therapist responding to a video clip with the continuous response device

Each therapist's responses were then transcribed onto musical transcriptions which I had prepared previously, on 12 strips above the music of the clips so that they could be viewed synoptically by the therapists. As colour was integral to this display, no illustration is given here, but the whole design can be viewed online (Strange 2014, Vol.3: Supplement, pp.2–50). Each therapist assessed the clinical situation solely from what she or he saw and heard in the video clips, without the benefit of background information, and registered continuous responses on the dial (illustrated in Figures 13.2 and 13.3) for each of the four scenarios in turn (see Table 13.1).

High inter-rater agreement was not to be expected. When I digitised the results, by time-sampling at 5-second intervals, none of a series of statistical analyses revealed significant levels of agreement between therapists in respect of any scenario. It became clear that no definitive conclusions as to the influence of the music at any point could be drawn by combining the responses of the three therapists. That, however, had not been the purpose of the exercise. My intention was always to feed back to the three therapists their own and their colleagues' responses, collated with musical transcriptions which they had not seen when making those responses, so that their interpretations could be compared and discussed.

In the absence of significant inter-rater agreement, it was interesting to discover a degree of *intra*-rater agreement between *scenarios*. One therapist in particular, and the other two to a lesser extent, had for much of the time made similar judgements from moment to moment in respect of two or more scenarios. These relationships, for the therapist in whose responses they were strongest, are represented by the thickness of the lines in Figure 13.4. The thicker the line, the stronger the correlation between judgements in respect of the pair of scenarios it links. The statistical calculations are explained in the thesis (Strange 2014, pp.152–154).

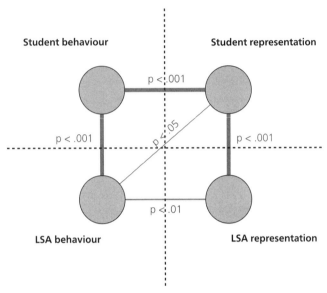

Figure 13.4 Agreement (χ^2) between therapist 3's responses with respect to pairs of scenarios (LSA: learning support assistant)

Panel discussion

As there were few moments in the clips showing clear agreement between all three therapists' responses, I focused instead on moments where one therapist had made a pronounced pointer movement which *contrasted* with the judgements of the others. On the synoptic response sheets which I sent to the therapists I marked a number of such moments in their own response records as 'decision points', asking them to select four they would be prepared to explain and defend when we later met as a panel. I removed one from each therapist's selection to achieve a more balanced coverage of the four scenarios. This left nine decision points (three per therapist) for the panel to discuss. Each therapist opened the discussion of her or his own decision points. Relevant parts of the video clips were played again as many times as the panel requested. The discussion was transcribed and significant comments on the influence of my improvised music at particular points were added to the musical score.

The discussions of two of the nine points will now be summarised. In each case, a description of the clip will be given, followed by quotations and paraphrases from the therapists' comments and an excerpt from a page of the transcribed score, with the actual decision point discussed shown by an *arrow*. It will be seen that although there is some evidence of mutual influence between therapists' views as a result of the discussion, they often focus on distinct salient points. It appeared that they were not disagreeing with each other so much as trying to offer additional and complementary insights.

CASE STUDY: FACILITATING VOLUNTARY MOVEMENT IN A CLIENT WITH LIMITED MOTOR CONTROL

'Shaun', who had extreme hypotonia and was only able to make very small, weak, voluntary arm movements, sat reclining in his wheelchair with his left arm hanging limply. His right forearm was supported by 'Gina' so that his fingers could tap the bongos she held above his lap. A second LSA brought a stick so that Shaun could get a clearer sound from the bongos, because his hand was too floppy to make much impact. Shaun smiled as he received the stick, straightened his arm and managed to grip it. Gina supported his elbow and his grip so that he could beat the bongos. He only played briefly and intermittently because Gina only supported a few beats at a time, periodically stopping to give him the chance to make the movement independently. Although this did not happen, Gina's comments in her interview strongly suggest that she sensed changes in Shaun's muscle tone, indicating incipient movements, which determined whether she prompted or just supported and waited.

After a slow and steady section of my improvised music, during most of which Shaun stopped beating, two other more physically able students started to play more quickly. I picked up their new tempo and sang repeatedly: 'They're telling you it's faster now.' Gina controlled Shaun's arm so that he could have the experience of playing with his friends in this faster tempo, which he could not have done independently. He smiled and opened his mouth wide with pleasure. When the original tempo returned, he played almost independently for a few bars, then stopped soon after the start of some loud accents played by another student. After an interval during which Gina allowed Shaun to listen without prompting him to play, I slowed down and then resumed the earlier steady tempo, at which point she supported him to play steadily again. When she stopped, Shaun did not play any more. All three LSAs in the room agreed that he had been very excited during the quick passage (Figure 13.5).

1 I think it's because previous to that it was unclear whether the child or the assistant was moving, whether they were supporting or not, and from that it became clear that it was the child

2 That phrase comes to a close and then you kind of start up again and she picks the drum up at the same time is the start of the new phrase so I think you were kind of encouraging her to start again

3 Just before that there's a triplet, that it's almost as if Shaun's getting faster at that point, and you respond by getting faster

Decision point where therapist 1 judged that there was strong support for student behaviour

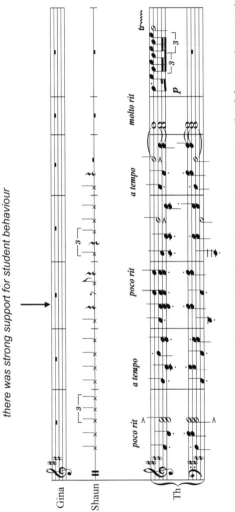

Figure 13.5 Therapist 1's decision point: Music supporting student behaviour (scenario 1)

Therapist 1, when considering this excerpt in terms of scenario 1 (student behaviour), had chosen to discuss the decision point near the end of the clip, where she or he had suddenly indicated, using the pointer, that she or he felt that my music had provided strong musical support for Shaun's behaviour. Although there was no marked change in the music at that point, she or he explained that it was then that it had become clear that Shaun was moving independently and not simply having his arm controlled by Gina. She or he seemed to have based this judgement on observation of the student–LSA interaction rather than on any feature of the music, while apparently accepting that the music had some unspecified influence.

After a second viewing of the extract, therapist 2 cited the smooth transition between two musical phrases but now viewed this as influencing Gina to resume, rather than Shaun, thus straying from the intended focus on scenario 1. Therapist 3 felt my return to a steady pace after slowing down was supportive of Shaun because he himself had introduced the quicker beat (notated as a triplet in the slower tempo) and I had immediately taken it up. The numbers before the comments indicate which therapist was speaking. (On the score, Gina's stave was included in the transcription to carry her occasional comments to Shaun, but there are none in this example.)

CASE STUDY: CREATIVE MUSIC-MAKING UNDER THE PROUD GAZE OF A MOTHER FIGURE

'Aprille' held an ocean drum flat on her lap and hit it vigorously in short bursts with her left hand. She then stopped and looked at 'Lucy', her LSA. When I sang her name, she picked up the drum and tipped it from side to side and backwards and forwards, watching the beads moving. The movement involved her whole body and was mirrored by Lucy. After a pause, apparently daydreaming, she started to tip the drum more vigorously from side to side. She then shook it briefly, stopped and looked at Lucy, swayed and, seeing Lucy swaying in response, resumed playing. She then held the drum upright on her lap and tapped it with her fingers. She reached out for Lucy's arm, and when Lucy declined to take the drum, she stood up and held the drum near her face. Lucy gently turned her round and Aprille deliberately dropped the drum as she was eased, somewhat unwillingly, back onto her chair. Lucy's musical contribution had been limited to imitating a dotted rhythm I introduced to help establish the quicker tempo which Aprille had introduced. Her empathic swaying and her steady gaze, only occasionally returned by Aprille, and the calm way in which she deflected the drum when it threatened to hit her head, constituted a truly 'motherly' presence, helping Aprille to explore the instrument with a creativity not previously seen in a whole year of therapy (Figure 13.6).

1 It's sort of an emotional support

2 If I was John I'd really want that to to continue, so would kind of facilitate that in any way
I could...I think the *legato* matched the movement very well

3 I think the *legato*...and the long notes, which is *poco allargando*...it matches her movement, which is supportive, but I think it also directs her awareness to her own body movement... you're not just matching but changing how she sees you and herself... 'starting up the mu——sic' is such a big change in how you're singing...you're more smooth....more gentle than she is able to be physically...you're giving her that experience of being, you know, sort of steady

Decision point where therapist 3 judged that the music challenged the student's representation

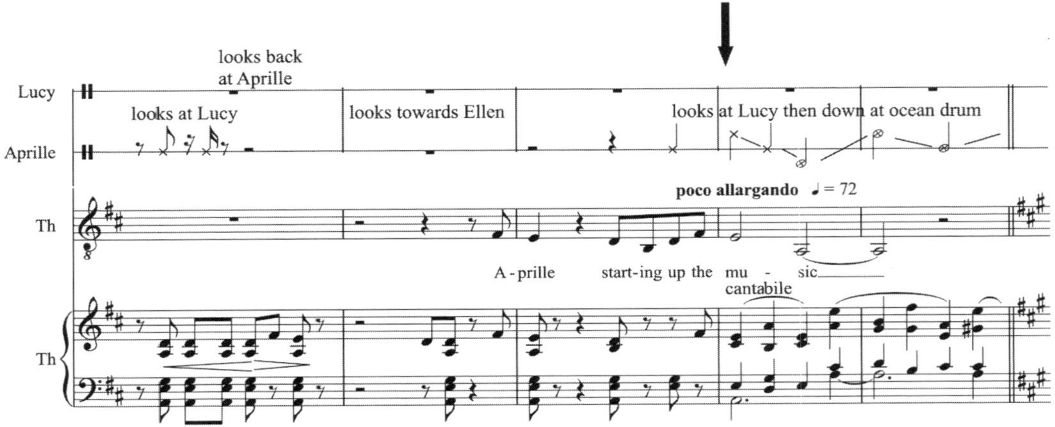

Figure 13.6 Therapist 3's decision point: Music challenging student representation (scenario 2)

Therapist 3, when considering this excerpt in terms of scenario 2 (student representation), had chosen a decision point several seconds after Aprille started to tip the ocean drum (see Figure 13.6). At this point she or he had moved the pointer to indicate that the music challenged Aprille's representation, whereas therapists 1 and 2 had felt the music was purely supportive. Therapist 3 explained that although the music matched Aprille's body movements, by making her aware of them it had enhanced her self-awareness, hence challenging an aspect of her representation. Therapist 2 had indicated that the music was supportive because she or he identified with my (presumed) wish for Aprille to continue her playing, although she found it harder to pinpoint musical features. Therapist 1 cited the *allargando*, and therapist 3 re-emphasised the importance of the long notes on the first syllable of '*mu*-sic' and a little later spoke of the music as becoming 'smooth', 'warm', 'gentle' and 'flowing', thus offering Aprille an experience which contrasted with her physical gaucheness. Therapist 1 said this created a kind of 'emotional support', and therapist 2 commented that the words I sang acknowledged that Aprille, who 'did not have many opportunities to be autonomous', was controlling the music, which was 'quite a big thing'.

Musical features which therapists associated with influences on student–LSA interaction

The therapists had been happy to think out loud and offer tentative ideas for consideration and elaboration by colleagues. They made fewer musical references than might be expected, though more than the LSAs. Although aware that the influence of the improvised music was the topic of the investigation, it seems they often found it hard to pinpoint the 'active ingredient'. Their first concern, as clinicians rather than musicologists, was the client and the assistant rather than the music. They then proceeded from the perception of moments of special therapeutic significance to the discussion of aspects of the music, both momentary and more extended, which they associated with that influence. Wishing to avoid prejudging what might prove relevant, I had given the therapists no checklists of musical features to consider. Aggregating their responses to all the clips, the musical features most often cited concerned tempo (five mentions) followed by phrasing and articulation (three mentions each), rhythm and timing (two mentions each) and texture (one mention). There were also some vaguely implied references: two to harmony, one to dynamic contrast and one to texture. Nothing was said about melodic line, modulation or absolute dynamic level. The therapists' greater interest in temporally based, rather than pitch-based, musical elements may be explained in terms of Stern's (2010) concept of 'forms of vitality' which posits a universal human responsiveness to the dynamic aspects of experience, including musical experience. The related concept of 'affect attunement' (Stern 1985), according to which empathy is communicated by a parent through the cross-modal mirroring of the infant's (or the client's) responses in another modality, which nevertheless preserves their temporal contour, has been found useful by many music therapists (e.g. Trondalen and Skårderud 2007). The concepts of forms of vitality and affect attunement provide a ready source of metaphor to bridge the conceptual gap between features of the music and the feelings and actions of people in therapy. Temporally based features of music can be discussed metaphorically without technical musical terminology, whereas harmony, counterpoint, modulation or even melody are harder to describe without such terminology. The music therapists may also have focused on temporally based musical elements because they believed that the students and LSAs would have perceived these elements in the same way as they themselves, whereas appreciating harmony and modulation would require more analytic listening and greater prior experience of the sort of music in which these features are important.

The value of the project

The panel discussion provided a rich variety of subjective judgements, often ideographic and sometimes contradictory. This does not mean that the phenomena discussed were trivial or illusory. What happens in therapy is often 'over-determined' in the sense that two or more independent influences, any one of which might account for what happens, operate simultaneously. The therapists seemed in no doubt of the clinical relevance of detailed features of the improvised music.

Qualitative evaluation plays an important role in terms of public and even professional perception. The reputation for effectiveness of an entire music therapy model like Creative Music Therapy still, after half a century, owes more to expertly presented case material, clinical opinion and user satisfaction than to the smaller body of quantitative research which has shown it to be effective. The research experience also helped me and my music therapist collaborators to listen and watch attentively and to think creatively about musical aspects of our practice, just as supervisee and supervisor often learn from each other by discussing video. The discovery of a musical 'recipe book' for producing specific clinical effects, had it proved possible, would have been of more dubious value. It is, however, possible to provide some general guidance about how to work musically in TSII.

What is distinctive about the improvised music used in TSII?

The distinctive features of TSII are the whole-hearted involvement of non-professional assistants as interaction partners and the use of improvised music to develop their skills and actively support them in that role, rather than the nature of the improvised music. Existing skills of clinical improvisation are adapted to new purposes rather than radically changed. Descriptions of all the musical skills required may be found in publications such as Wigram (2004) and Nordoff, Robbins and Marcus (2007), but in TSII the therapist abstains from those techniques which might encourage a social interaction between client and therapist rather than between client and assistant. A greater physical distance should normally be maintained between the therapist and the client–assistant dyad than between the client and the assistant. This strategy exploits the fact that the communicative effect of music attenuates much less with distance than does that of body language, gaze and facial expression. In my case, I sat at some distance behind a keyboard, but there is no reason why another harmonic instrument such as guitar or harp, or an expressive melody instrument such as clarinet or cello, played at a certain distance, should not be equally effective.

In scenarios 1 and 2 where music is used to influence the client, the therapist wishes his music to be heard and responded to without drawing attention to itself or to him. He may use 'frameworking' (Wigram 2004, p.118) to ground, guide and stimulate the client's music, or indeed any other communicative behaviour exhibited by the client. 'Empathy' and 'reflection' (p.89) may be used to unobtrusively support the client's representation of his relationship with the assistant, either allowing it to evolve spontaneously or subtly challenging it to change. 'Seductive' (p.142), 'limbo' (p.144) and 'overlap' (p.154) transitions are effective techniques to encourage change without disrupting the client–assistant interaction by too abrupt and ear-catching contrasts in the music. Such subtle, non-intrusive 'arm's length' techniques are often used in therapy involving only client and therapist, but there they are usually a prelude to a more personal dialogue with the therapist when the client is ready for it, which is not the aim in TSII. The client offered TSII may, of course, spontaneously decide to interact with the therapist rather than the assistant. This could be a positive development, suggesting that the assistant's support is becoming less necessary.

In scenarios 3 and 4 where music is used to influence the assistant, frameworking and empathic improvisation and reflection may again be used, but there is less need to avoid marked and even attention-grabbing contrasts, since a strong cue may be needed to prompt the LSA to make a change in her music or behaviour, and she is less likely than the client to find this disturbing. However, although the therapist's music may suggest how it might be helpful for the assistant to behave towards the client or to think about their relationship, he should still stay in the background socially. The aim is for the assistant to focus her actions, thoughts and feelings on the client, as well as to become more aware of how she herself, rather than the therapist, is interacting with the client.

The improvised music always potentially influences both client and assistant, since both hear it, whether or not they consciously attend to it. The therapist must never lose sight of this dual influence and become insensitive to the effect his music may have on one partner while he is targeting the other. This dual influence may indeed be deliberately exploited in specific ways. For example, the music may stimulate, support and guide both sides of an actual client–assistant interaction, musical or other, as it is occurring. The music may have superficial and underlying characteristics with differing levels of complexity, allowing the client to respond to an aspect of the simple surface level, for example a repeating melodic figure, whereas the assistant might respond to something more complex which lies beneath, such as varying harmonisation. The music may even combine contrasting or conflicting elements reflecting contrasts or conflicts between the behaviours and representations of client and assistant. The object here is to acknowledge and contain both, facilitate a reconciliation or compromise, or reveal an unsuspected affinity. In all cases, however, musical and other communicative behaviours initiated by the assistant should be given a higher profile and allowed more autonomy than in work where the assistant's role is to support the relationship between client and therapist.

TSII is a procedure, not a model (Bruscia 1987, p.16), and was only developed for use intermittently at appropriate points in a session of group therapy. It originated in work with clients whose limited communication skills severely restricted their ability to interact creatively with assistants and especially with communication-impaired peers, and who benefited developmentally from a group setting where they could observe and be observed by peers while sharing some more structured and directed activities with them at other points in the session.

Conclusion

TSII is most clearly indicated for clients at a developmental stage where the fostering of interaction within a secure attachment relationship is a priority, and when the assistant, rather than the therapist, is felt to be the appropriate person with whom to develop that interaction and relationship. Thus, it might be appropriate for work with mothers and infants, as well as people in advanced stages of dementia and their carers. In an individual therapy setting, rather than the group setting in which TSII evolved, the approach could be used, if clinically indicated, continuously rather than intermittently. Work in such individual settings could more easily be presented so as to document client progress, in contrast to the present study's focus on the music and the therapy process.

References

Aigen, K. (2005) *Music Centered Music Therapy*. Gilsum, NH: Barcelona Publishers.

Bowlby, J. (1973) *Separation*. London: Tavistock Press.

Bruscia, K.E. (1987) *Improvisational Models of Music Therapy*. Springfield, IL: Charles C. Thomas.

Cohen, A.J. (2010) 'Music as a Source of Emotion in Film.' In P.N. Juslin and J.A. Sloboda (eds) *Music and Emotion: Theory, Research, Applications*. New York, NY: Oxford University Press.

Darnley-Smith, R.M.R. (2013) 'What is the Music of Music Therapy? An Enquiry into the Aesthetics of Clinical Improvisation.' PhD, University of Durham. Available at http://etheses.dur.ac.uk/6975, accessed on 1 February 2015.

De Backer, J. and Sutton, J. (eds) (2014) *The Music in Music Therapy: Psychodynamic Music Therapy in Europe*. London: Jessica Kingsley Publishers.

Garred, R. (2006) *Music in Therapy: A Dialogical Perspective.* Gilsum, NH: Barcelona Publishers.

Gold, C. and Wigram, T. (2012) 'The Religion of Evidence-Based Practice: Helpful or Harmful to Health and Wellbeing?' In R. MacDonald, G. Kreutz and L. Mitchell (eds) *Music, Health and Wellbeing.* Oxford: Oxford University Press.

Hooper, J., Wigram, T., Carson, D. and Lindsay, B. (2008) 'A review of the music and intellectual disability literature (1943–2006). Part Two: Experimental writing.' *Music Therapy Perspectives 26,* 2, 80–96.

Lee, C.A. (1992) 'The Analysis of Therapeutic Improvisatory Music with People Living with the Virus HIV and AIDS.' PhD, The City University, London. Available at http://openaccess.city.ac.uk/7549, accessed on 1 February 2015.

Nordoff, P., Robbins, C. and Marcus, D. (2007) *Creative Music Therapy: A Guide to Fostering Clinical Musicianship* (2nd ed.). Gilsum, NH: Barcelona Publishers.

Pavlicevic, M. (1997) *Music Therapy in Context: Music, Meaning and Relationship.* London: Jessica Kingsley Publishers.

Ruud, E. (2010) *Music Therapy: A Perspective from the Humanities.* Gilsum, NH: Barcelona Publishers.

Schubert, E. (2010) 'Continuous Self-Report Methods.' In P. Juslin and J. Sloboda (eds) *Music and Emotion: Theory, Research, Applications.* New York, NY: Oxford University Press.

Smeijsters, H. (2005) *Sounding the Self: Analogy in Improvisational Music Therapy.* Gilsum, NH: Barcelona Publishers.

Stern, D.N. (1985) *The Interpersonal World of the Infant.* London: Karnac.

Stern, D.N. (1998) *The Motherhood Constellation: A Unified View of Parent-Infant Psychotherapy.* London: Karnac.

Stern, D.N. (2010) *Forms of Vitality: Exploring Dynamic Experience in Psychology and the Arts.* London: Karnac.

Strange, J. (2014) 'Improvised Music to Support Interaction Between Profoundly Learning-Disabled Teenagers and Their Learning Support Assistants.' PhD thesis, Anglia Ruskin University, Cambridge. Available at http://hdl.handle.net/10540/314588, accessed on 30 April 2016.

Trondalen, G. and Skårderud, F. (2007) 'Playing with affects and the importance of "affect attunement".' *Nordic Journal of Music Therapy 16,* 2, 100–111.

Wigram, T. (2004) *Improvisation: Methods and Techniques for Music Therapy Clinicians, Educators and Students.* London: Jessica Kingsley Publishers.

Chapter 14

Who Knows Me Best?

Exploring the Collaborative Roles of
Transient Practitioners and Constant
Practitioners in Music Therapy

Sarah Hadley

A time to build bridges

The 30 years I have worked as a music therapist in the UK National Health Service (NHS) have seen great change both within my profession and also in the never-ending reforms within the NHS as an organisation, imposed by successive governments. Out of this continual state of flux I have had the pleasure of witnessing and being part of an evolving relationship between the music therapy profession and the NHS, and have welcomed the increasing respect and value placed on the clinical impact of music therapy. The development of the clinical gravitas attributed to our profession is crucial given that the NHS now operates in a highly competitive tendering arena. In order to ensure the safest, most impactful and most cost-effective use of resources, integrated care pathways and cross-agency working between education, health and social care have been formalised in Education, Health and Care Plans (The Children and Families Act 2014). In order to manage the challenge of reduced resources and to ensure the best quality of service delivery within our local community, statutory sector organisations are highly reliant on collaborative working partnerships with the third sector.

Music therapy lends itself beautifully to building bridges across these sectors through collaborative strategic partnerships with other service providers and collaborative clinical partnerships with their practitioners. Within the NHS, music therapy helpfully bridges the divide between 'psyche' health (by working closely with the psychological teams within Child and Adolescent Mental Health

Services) and 'soma' health (by working closely with the functional therapies such as speech and language therapy, physiotherapy or occupational therapy). There are exciting opportunities to embed music therapy practice in joint working within and beyond the therapy room. Collaborative working is a strategic and clinical imperative, and music therapists are well positioned to deliver on this imperative.

Impactful music therapy depends on collaborative teamwork

As a clinician I believe music therapy practice is at its optimum effectiveness when embedded within a collaborating team (central to which is the client's family) all focusing on the client, in order for me to gain knowledge from every possible perspective and to really get to know about my client. This collaborative focus on the client allows me to construct a therapeutic relationship based on an informed, multifaceted understanding of my client across a range of external relationships with those around them. This makes the therapeutic containment process more robust, provides an informed benchmark for the perceived strengths and needs of my client, and establishes trust in my working relationships with the important people in my client's life. Once I have gained an understanding of my client from those who have known them over a period of time, I am better positioned to contribute a music therapy perspective from the individual work shared between my client and myself. In this way we can all reach a united understanding of the client and work effectively together to meet their needs and achieve sustainable positive outcomes. So my work as a music therapist when thinking about my client hangs on this question: 'Who knows me best?'

The clinical scope of the Oxleas Music Therapy Service

The Oxleas Music Therapy Service comprises a community-based team of 15 music therapists, one Interactive Music Making specialist and one indispensable personal assistant. Children and young people with two distinct types and levels of need are served. First, professional music therapists work with:

…children and young people aged 0–19 years who are registered with a GP practice within the Royal Borough of Greenwich and who have a complex profile of psycho-social needs. This may include emotional difficulties, psychological difficulties, social difficulties, behavioural difficulties, communication difficulties, and/ or relationship difficulties. (Oxleas Music Therapy Service referral criteria, unpublished)

Second, the Interactive Music Making specialist delivers targeted provision for children under 5 years, referred because specific developmental difficulties are significantly impacting on their overall developmental progress (including emotional, social, behavioural, communication and relationship skills) but whose current needs are not of sufficient emotional complexity to place them in the first category. Importantly, this early-intervention role has served to prevent the children's needs from escalating to a level where music therapy would be needed.

The clinical work in the context of collaborative team working

Within the Oxleas Music Therapy Service we work with a vast variety of children and young people aged from 6 months to 19 years. While psychosocial presentation, as opposed to pathology, is our primary concern when accepting a referral, the clients with whom I personally have worked include children and young people with developmental delay, mild, moderate and severe learning disability, autistic spectrum disorder (ASD), specific learning disability, sensory impairment and emotional trauma (following abuse, domestic violence, or parent or sibling bereavement). I have provided early intervention for primary-aged children causing moderate levels of concern, and for children and young people who have suffered a sudden catastrophic neurological insult or accident, assessed children and young people to profile for diagnosis, and assisted in universal triage within children's centres. My own special clinical interests are the under-fives and children and young people with ASD.

At one time or another I have practised music therapy according to all of the collaborative team models described by Stember (1991). These models fall into a continuum from 'cross-disciplinary' (viewing one discipline from the perspective of another), through 'multidisciplinary' (co-working by different disciplines, each drawing on its own theoretical framework) and 'interdisciplinary' (different disciplines integrating and synthesising their respective knowledge and methods), to 'transdisciplinary', the most thoroughly integrated model, in which a unified intellectual framework is created in place of individual disciplinary perspectives.

The teams with whom I have worked have included teams with a specific function such as child development assessment and diagnosis; pathway teams such as the neurodevelopmental care pathway team; virtual teams such as the rapid response community rehabilitation team; a plethora of bespoke teams based on the 'Team Around the Child' model, to meet the child's changing needs at any point in time; and last but not least, the music therapy team itself.

In essence, the Oxleas Music Therapy Service, embedded within a range of teams, is working with an enormous diversity of children and young people who, for whatever reason, are all so vulnerable as to need specialist intervention to help them develop sufficient resilience to manage life's demands and access all of life's opportunities to their personal optimum.

Collaborative working between the 'transient practitioner' and the 'constant practitioner'

Music therapy provision is 'clinical' in being highly individualised. For me this means that the environment is consistent from week to week, without distraction or interruption, and the dynamic is tailored to the client from moment to moment. The treatment focuses on the client's internal world by first creating a meeting point of trust between client and therapist, based on the model of secure attachment. Client and therapist can then embark on a journey into the client's internal world. Through clinical musical improvisation this internal world is brought to life in the therapy room so that the therapist can experience with the client his or her internal emotional rollercoaster through the rich, attuned, flexible, responsive, non-judgemental and safe creative medium of shared improvised music-making. This is quite unlike daily life, and after a period of time, after careful preparation, sessions will come to a close. At this point 'the proof of the pudding is in the eating' and the enduring clinical effectiveness of the treatment is tested.

In this respect the music therapist is a 'transient practitioner' in the sense of being 'temporary' in the client's life, but certainly not in any of the behavioural senses of 'temporary', such as 'mutable, unstable, volatile, fly-by-night', listed in the *Oxford Thesaurus of English* (Waite 2009, p.901) – which are the very antithesis of the work of a music therapist. Consistency and 'being present' for the client are integral to the therapeutic process, but at the same time the music therapist must be transient in their presence during the client's life in the sense of 'brief, temporary, transitional, short-lived' in order to:

- support the client's transition from a place of vulnerability to a place of resilience

- facilitate the client in surviving healthy therapeutic closure, which is fundamental to the effective management of transitions and defines the success of treatment

- ensure that ongoing dependence on the therapist is avoided, since this would constitute a contraindication for the intervention as well as an indicator of poorly internalised integration of the client's therapeutic process.

It is important to be clear about the contrasting role played by 'constant practitioners'. They can include any number of people in the child's life, first and foremost the mother, father or anyone with parental responsibility and then, for example, the teacher, learning support assistant, community nurse or health care assistant. These key people are those with whom the child has contact on an ongoing basis, at least weekly if not daily. There will, of course, be planned breaks in some of these constant relationships (e.g. school holidays) as well as unplanned breaks (e.g. sickness), but these breaks can be repaired owing to the ongoing nature of the constant relationship, forming an important opportunity for practising resilience when managing the inevitable inconsistencies encountered as part of mainstream life. Many of the personal qualities required by the constant practitioner, such as being 'steadfast, resolute, determined, persevering, tenacious, unflagging, unshaken', closely correlate with those of music therapists. But the child's relationship with the constant practitioner is constant, in the sense of 'continual, abiding, around-the-clock, unceasing, unending' (Waite 2009, p.164).

In my role as a music therapist, I provide individual (as opposed to systemic) therapy for the client, who may well experience this exploration of their internal world and their manner of responding and managing their life experiences by a transient practitioner as intrusive and destabilising. Meanwhile, the constant practitioner holds an overarching, in-depth knowledge of the client, gathered over time and across many situations, which cannot be attained by meeting the client only once a week in a highly individualised clinical setting. As music therapy proceeds, the constant practitioner may see new aspects of the child's potential and needs. She or he can report back to the transient practitioner (music therapist) any changes witnessed at home, in the playground or in the classroom, information which will then inform the clinical direction of travel for the transient practitioner.

However, in my role as music therapy manager, the collaborative relationship between the transient practitioner and constant practitioner became formalised at practice level through a process of development driven by the needs of the children who came into my professional life. This led to the need for sharing some of the key principles of music therapy which could be applied in practice with both integrity and impact by a constant practitioner.

The Music Therapy Home Programme

This concept of the collaboration between the transient practitioner and the constant practitioner roles, and the importance of their collaborative working in music therapy, was taken to a new level in the mid 1990s when an unprecedented event occurred in the local community. Two separate clusters of babies were born with Down syndrome over a period of 18 months, amounting to 10 babies in total. The health visitors involved with the families noticed that the babies were particularly responsive to music. They contacted the Oxleas Music Therapy Service to see if we could do anything for these children. This was the trigger for me to develop a new approach which I termed the 'Music Therapy Home Programme'. Starting when the babies were 6 months old, the mothers or fathers came to work with me on a monthly basis. I would demonstrate some simple musical activities to stimulate and promote early responses within the following developmental domains extracted from the analysis by Sharma and Cockerill (2014):

• posture and large movements

• visual perception and fine motor skills

• speech, language and communication

• social behaviour and play

• self-care and independence.

These five areas of development were addressed through the use of creative musical structures, and used flexibly, responding to the child from moment to moment. I would provide the parents with a toolkit of simple techniques to stimulate a spontaneous response, reinforce that response and develop it interactively, following the pattern of affective attunement behaviour of the securely attached mother and infant, so brilliantly described in directly transferable musical terms by Stern (1998). The techniques I taught these constant practitioners are shown in Figure 14.1.

I video-recorded these sessions and the parents took their video home, with an activity sheet which we had developed during our session. The parents were loaned the necessary musical instruments (e.g. tambourine, cabassa, handheld wind chimes, tambour and two small drumsticks) and would then carry out the programme at home and return the following month to review and update the activities. To bring the newly conceived Music Therapy Home Programme to life, a case example is given here.

Stimulate

Create a musically interactive context using simple phrases from favourite nursery rhymes or made-up songs

Use a vocal and/or visual anacrusis when presenting an instrument (e.g. 'ready, steady and…Bom!' with the tambourine). 'Bom' is sung as your child places the beat on the tambourine

a

Provide a physical prompt at a minimal level for your child to then take over independently

Model an action and then provide space for your child to imitate you

response

Consider the placement of the instruments you are using, e.g. present the tambourine to each of your child's hands alternately to encourage bilateral motor skills, or slowly shake it across your child's field of vision from one side to the other to stimulate visual tracking

Reinforce

Directly imitate your child's response on the same instrument

a

Directly imitate your child's response but use another instrument (cross-modal) or use your voice or body percussion

response

Acknowledge and celebrate your child's response in words or singing (usually singing)

Develop

Develop turn-taking structures: you play one beat on the tambourine and then offer the tambourine to your child to play a beat and then repeat the sequence

Change the speed and/or volume of your voice slightly just for a moment and watch for your child's response

a

Extend the length of your child's reinforced response by using longer-sung musical phrases but make sure that your singing is in time with your child's movements and duration of attention (e.g. slow 'Twinkle' down and sing it phrase by phrase)

response

Re-engage your child when her or his attention is lost by using anticipation structures (see 'Stimulate a response') or turn-taking structures (see above)

Figure 14.1 Techniques taught to parents on the Music Therapy Home Programme

CASE STUDY: AUGMENTING EARLY-INTERACTION SKILLS

Leyla was 6 months old when her parents joined the Music Therapy Home Programme. I first demonstrated to Leyla's parents how early-interaction skills could be augmented and developmental responses stimulated through creative and spontaneous music-making. I encouraged Leyla to use her hands and her feet to play the tambourine, promoting body awareness and a physical sense of herself. The immediacy of the sound she made on the tambourine reinforced and highlighted her actions, giving her the experience of cause and effect. Indications of Leyla's awareness in the interaction were eye-contact, hand–eye coordination, repeated motor responses, listening, visual tracking, concentration and smiles.

I observed that Leyla had made the following developmental responses: lateralising (gaining a sense of right and left)

- alternating between using her hands and feet

- object permanence

- visual alertness connected to social responsiveness

- a sense of self and other within a social partnership.

From these observations we developed the following activity sheet for the parents to take home:

1. 'Are you ready to hide?' – peek-a-boo game using a see-through cloth

   a) Waft the cloth up to Leyla several times singing, 'Are you ready to hide?'

   b) Gently place a cloth on her head singing, 'Where is Leyla?'

   c) Wait and see if Leyla removes the cloth, and if she doesn't, do so for her.

   d) In either event, when the cloth is removed from her head, sing in celebration, 'There she is!'

2. 'Here comes the tambourine'

   a) Shake the tambourine gently up to Leyla's hand, whispering rhythmically, 'Here it comes, here it comes, here it comes and ready to…play!' On 'play!' you demonstrate a single beat on the tambourine.

   b) Repeat this, watching carefully where Leyla is visually focused and allowing time for her hand to come up to the tambourine.

   c) When Leyla plays, match the speed and volume of her playing with your voice (which, please remember, even if *you* don't like it, is the most wonderful sound for Leyla!) and celebrate.

    d)   Try presenting it to each side and wait for Leyla to reach out, and notice whether she begins to anticipate the sequence from side to side.

    e)   Present it to her hands and then her feet, and observe whether she begins to anticipate the sequence from hands to feet (physically prompt, if needed, to start her off).

3. 'Twinkle Twinkle Little Star with wind chimes'

    a)   Singing the song slowly, present the chimes from side to side watching for visual tracking, and raise the chimes just above Leyla's eye-line to encourage reaching up. Place them behind your back…'where oh where?'…then present her with the wind chimes…'here they are!' and repeat the sequence.

One important aspect of the Music Therapy Home Programme was that despite their wonderment at my highly specialised music therapy training, the parents discovered that my contribution could not compare with their own when stimulating and facilitating their child's responses themselves within the safe container of the secure parental attachment. This experience is summed up by a parent, 20 years later:

> In November 1994 I had a daughter with Down Syndrome and we got referred to music therapy and invited to come along to sessions when she was about 5 or 6 months old. My daughter needed more structured teaching, she needed more help and guidance, so to do fun things through nursery rhymes and music made it easier for us as well, but also you could see how beneficial it was. It definitely made a difference to our lives. (Payne 2014)

Music as Therapy International

My recruitment to the charity Music as Therapy International in 1999 provided the perfect opportunity to extend my work with constant practitioners, flex my skill-sharing abilities further and build on my experience with developing the Music Therapy Home Programme. Music as Therapy International tasked me with delivering a 6-week training programme to two teams of care staff in orphanages in Romania. The objective was for these teams to be able to run Music as Therapy sessions independently, to promote the children's emotional, physical, social and cognitive development.

    After my partner, Becca Sayers, and I had led the music sessions for 3 weeks, provided workshops to teach new techniques and introduced the staff to theories underpinning the work, we gradually handed over the sessions to our Romanian partners. Eventually, they were able to run the sessions entirely by themselves. Becca and I observed our fledgling colleagues in their new practice. Below are my notes evaluating the first 'Flying Solo' session of November 1999.

THE FIRST 'FLYING SOLO' SESSION

The staff took the groups from Leagen (orphanages) 1 and 2 without any assistance today and did a brilliant job...HOORAY! The room was prepared ahead of the children coming in and an unneeded chair in the circle was removed, bringing the group physically closer together. Careful consideration had been given to the musical activities, based on their previous observations of the sessions I led, and the leaders were clearly relating their chosen activities to the children's strengths and needs, which we have been discussing over the past 3 weeks. The session ran as follows:

- **'Hello' song**
  All of the three children were individually greeted in this song. A lovely welcome was given to J, who was new to the group, where M (who is very confident) was invited to sing the 'hello' song to her, which he did with great pleasure. L's reticence was well managed by the leader who sang the song using a *mezzo piano* dynamic, and when he offered his foot, rather than his hand, to play the tambourine, the leader accepted this and incorporated L's kicking of the tambourine immediately into the music-making using a direct vocal match of 'tschoo' each time L kicked the tambourine.

- **'Drum and Cymbal' song**
  Excellent introduction to this activity where M was asked to count the drumsticks ('batz') using the counting song, leaving space within the music of the phrase 'How many batz are here today?' for M to complete the key word 'batz' while handing the sticks out to the group. J was intrigued by these instruments and the leader responded by offering her the first turn to play a solo. The leader also noted that L was more nervous of the drum and so did not extend this play too much and quickly substituted the drum with the cymbal, which he began to confidently play. M enjoyed being stretched in this activity by playing a sequence of single beats on the drum and then the cymbal alternately. The exuberant quality of his play was well matched by the energy and enthusiasm of the leader's sung support.

- **'Old MacDonald Had a Farm'**
  The leader created a lovely development of this song by responding to, and extending, the children's spontaneous imaginative play as they made the animals 'talk' with one another. The closure of this activity was extremely sensitively managed by the leader as she encouraged the children to soothe their chosen animal into sleep,

put them in the bag and explained that none of the animals would cry as they were all together.

- **'Good-bye' song**
  Each child was sung to by the leader and given the opportunity to complete the end of the sung phrase by the leader, who effectively used the technique of making a *ritardando* and leaving a space on the final phrase. L managed to sing 'ciao' (bye) in a whispered voice, which was a thrilling moment for the leader (and me!).

The quality of the work undertaken by these constant practitioners at so many levels (e.g. developing social skills, confidence and supportive friendships as well as re-enacting safe separation through the symbolic play in the nursery rhyme 'Old MacDonald') is evident from my notes, which show that the children engaged confidently and purposefully in their music-making led by my Romanian colleague.

Working with my Romanian partners was an enriching and awe-inspiring experience which had a profound effect on my clinical thinking and affirmed my belief in the value of skill sharing with constant practitioners. It served as a spur for me to write up the skills and techniques that I had been imparting over several years, in the form of a practice guide for Interactive Music Making practitioners on using music as a developmental resource.

Interactive Music Making training and role development

The development of my practice guide came at an opportune time when the UK national priority for children took a specific focus on early identification and prevention, with a view to averting the escalation of children's needs to a critical level. This national driver precipitated a new referral trend for the Music Therapy Service, namely very young children with much less complex needs but whose life chances without intervention would be at risk. However, the music therapy referral criteria had been ratified in line with local requirements to target the most highly complex client cohorts which continued to be very present, so our focus of service delivery was no longer aligned with the focus of the new national agenda. The immediate impact of this significantly broader client base was a rapid increase in demand for music therapy which outstripped our physical capacity. It therefore became an imperative for the Music Therapy Service to explore role re-design and skill sharing, specifically to develop a workforce which could provide targeted intervention for the very young children who were being referred because of developmental, rather than emotional, needs. The practice guide provided the basis for me to develop with Alexia Quin, director of the charity Music as Therapy International, the university training module 'Interactive Music Making for Practice: Working with the Under Fives'. Thus, with the approval of the then Training and Education Committee of the UK Association of Professional Music Therapists, the role of Interactive Music Maker was born. In 2008 Interactive Music Making (IMM) was formally defined as a 'child-centred approach to music-making, which establishes positive relationships and fosters the child's individual potential' (S. Hadley and A. Quin, unpublished).

The IMM training course is a 12-week module including teaching, practical workshops, self-directed study and an 8-week practical assignment. Following this, students have the option of having their studies formally credit rated by the University of Greenwich upon production of a 2000-word assignment. The open nature of access to this course is beautifully summed up by one of our graduates, Margaret: 'You don't need to play instruments to go on the course and you don't need to be musical. You just need to have an interest in child development and an interest in supporting children' (Corcoran 2014).

The key ingredient of this training is a structured approach to teaching an attachment-based model of music-making. A striking aspect of the learning journey of our IMM students which the tutor team frequently encounters is that the students are not so much learning new skills but, rather, they are made aware of competencies which they are already intuitively using within their daily interactions with their children. As a result, the students' unconscious competency is raised to a conscious level and these competencies can then be used in a confident and considered way to meet the children's developmental needs with a clear understanding of the impact of their techniques within targeted IMM practice. Margaret again beautifully sums this up: 'Going on the course I thought "Oh! I do that!" *That's* why I do that and I never knew I was doing it for that reason' (Corcoran 2014).

Interactive goal-setting

As well as providing a toolkit of musical resources, both pre-composed and improvisational, we develop students' ability to identify and evaluate progress towards developmental goals set for the children in their IMM sessions. Table 14.1 shows the indicators used in setting the IMM baseline.

Table 14.1 Indicators assessed in setting the IMM baseline

Indicator	Characteristic(s)
General behaviour	Confidence, motivation, engaging in play, avoiding play
Attention	Concentration, listening, eye-contact, visual tracking, purposeful participation
Listening skills	Ability to listen and respond
Facial expressions	Range of emotions (happy, sad, serious, excited)
Body movements	Reaching out, hand–eye coordination, rocking, swaying, walking, jumping, dancing
Vocalising	Babble, vocal play, singing, verbalising, screaming, crying, intonation
Instrumental responses	Choice of instruments, fast or slow playing, loud or soft playing, random or ordered playing
Understanding of interaction	Imitating others' play, initiating play (being the leader), anticipating turn
Shared play	Turn-taking, sharing interest in others' play
Responsiveness to interaction	Channelling of energy, defence strategies
Expression of emotions	Capacity to spontaneously express range of emotions (e.g. joy, anger and so forth)

Having created developmental profiles of the children's strengths and needs, the students then identify and develop goals for the eight sessions they are required to deliver at their workplace as part of the training programme. At least one session is observed and assessed by an IMM tutor. The goals students set need to offer the children experiences of interaction, sharing, turn-taking, responsibility, spontaneity, achievement and emotional expression, and target the developmental goals of the children's confidence, attention and motivation, as well as the skills of initiation, anticipation, vocal response and communication.

The importance of secure attachment

The cornerstone of IMM is understanding what is required to create a secure attachment bond between practitioner and child, and how to facilitate this through shared music-making; in effect, the practitioner learns to replicate the secure mother–infant relationship using the non-verbal medium of music with a developmental focus. The importance of secure attachment is supported by research into many aspects of child development. Bowlby (2005) writes that attachment behaviour is of 'the greatest importance clinically' and that 'if [the attachment relationship] goes well, there is joy and a sense of security. If it is threatened, there is jealousy, anxiety, and anger. If broken, there is grief and depression.' The way music can replicate the secure mother–infant attachment is endorsed by the research of Trevarthen (2008), who writes: 'Infants are ready at birth to take turns in a "dialogue" of movements with a loving parent… When the expressive forms are examined in detail, infant and partner are found to be sharing a subtle "musicality" of communication.' The neurological benefits of secure attachment in achieving sustainable developmental outcomes are evidenced in the research of Schore (2000):

> The infant's early developing right hemisphere…is dominant for the human stress response…the [secure] attachment relationship facilitates the expansion of the child's coping capacities… This efficient right brain function is a resilience factor for optimal development over the later stages of the life cycle. (p.1)

Finally, the research of Geddes (2006) shows that only when the child has the ability to build secure attachments can they be fully engaged in learning tasks, since they have developed the capacity to:

- tolerate separation and have sufficient sense of autonomy

- face challenges and cope with uncertainty and not knowing

- be interested and take creative risks in exploration of the outside world

- trust the teacher to help when needed and to be able to tolerate 'not knowing' when learning new things.

The role of the Interactive Music Maker

Interactive Music Makers play an important part in the music therapy care pathway within our local community in Greenwich, where colleagues in children's centres and nurseries are implementing IMM sessions for their children. They are able to work with the children with whom the music therapists cannot, because the latter do not meet the Music Therapy Service referral thresholds. Interactive Music Makers are also trained to signpost children into the Music Therapy Service when they have persistent concerns about the child's development. All these referrals are channelled through the IMM specialist who is employed within the core Music Therapy Service. This advanced level of practice in IMM is also a transient practitioner role and is of crucial importance in the music therapy care pathway, providing a bridge between the constant practitioners and the transient practitioners. The IMM specialist usefully differentiates IMM from music therapy: 'Music therapy focuses on the emotional growth of the child, whereas Interactive Music Making has a specific developmental approach.'

The role of the IMM specialist is not further explored in this chapter, although Table 14.2 provides an overview of the scope of each of the roles within the music therapy care pathway.

Table 14.2 Comparison of roles

	Interactive Music Maker	Interactive Music Making specialist	Music therapist
Experience and training	Extensive experience of working with children as a constant practitioner	Extensive experience of working with children with additional needs	Clinical background of working with children as a transient practitioner
	Interactive Music Making for Practice (Greenwich University)	Experience in and currently working across two or more paediatric therapies (music therapy, occupational therapy, physiotherapy or speech and language therapy)	Masters degree in music therapy (university accredited)
		1 year's training in Interactive Music Making (externally moderated) and 1 year's supervised practice (internally moderated)	
Client group	Children under the age of 5 years who are at low risk or no risk of social exclusion (including learning, peer and family relationships, leisure and play)	Children under the age of 5 years who may be at risk of social exclusion (including learning, peer and family relationships, leisure and play) because of an identified additional need which impacts on their physical, cognitive, social and/or behavioural functioning	Children (0–19 years) who are at high risk or are actually experiencing social exclusion (including learning, peer and family relationships, leisure and play) because of an identified or unidentified additional need which impacts on their cognitive, social, behavioural and/or emotional functioning

	Interactive Music Maker	Interactive Music Making Specialist	Music Therapist
Outcomes and impact	Developmental goals set, adapted where necessary and evaluated within a secure attachment base	Developmental goals set, adapted where necessary and evaluated within a secure attachment base	Development of child's ego strength, resilience and capacity to make meaningful and sustainable relationships often with the need to remediate defensive attachment styles
	Signpost to IMM specialist in music therapy team	Skill sharing with parents and staff	Signpost to IMM specialist or IMM practitioner
		Signpost to music therapist	

Evaluation of IMM skill sharing

After the first cohort of students qualified in 2011, an independent researcher was commissioned by Music as Therapy International to test the impact of IMM training within the workplace. Our researcher conducted workshops and interviews with five of the seven IMM students and their managers to identify the progress of children who had attended sessions against five broad developmental areas:

> Past students were asked to provide examples of children they felt had made most progress through their involvement in Interactive Music Making; and managers were asked to reflect on outcomes for the children involved in IMM groups. It was interesting that social needs (e.g. engaging in a group, turn-taking, interacting with others) featured most strongly in managers' feedback, while IMM graduates' examples covered the full range of needs, focusing most strongly on progress made in language and communication. (A. Pinney, unpublished)

One example from each developmental area has been chosen to give a flavour of the results (A. Pinney, unpublished):

- Language and communication needs

> 'There was a boy with social and communication needs in one of my groups... He came out with his first word ever

and kept going from there! I was able to get him referred on to music therapy; music was clearly making an impact.' (Interactive Music Maker)

- Social needs

  'We've seen some clear progress, for example, in concentration and social interaction – in at least one area always. For one child who had high-end autistic spectrum and behavioural difficulties, this was the first time we found an intervention that really engaged him and to which his parents committed.' (Manager)

- Emotional needs

  'It's amazing to see shy children really getting into "ready, steady, go!" – saying "stop" in loud voices, enjoying themselves, having fun and learning at the same time.' (Interactive Music Maker)

- Physical needs

  'One child I worked with had cerebral palsy; he had a tightly clenched arm and hand. Over time, he relaxed with the music and started to reach out and use his hand to feel the chimes.' (Interactive Music Maker)

- Cognitive needs

  'There's one child we work with who has Down syndrome, who loves IMM – as soon as I get the instruments out, he immediately pays attention, comes and waits for me…it's an amazing tool.' (Interactive Music Maker)

The impact of the training on graduates' professional development was also explored from the perspective of the Interactive Music Makers' managers. Four themes emerged (A. Pinney, unpublished):

- More confidence

  'It has enabled her to work more flexibly: she was always a good planner, but she would struggle if things didn't go according to plan. This has improved her ability to adapt, accept the need for flexibility and be more confident about doing so.'

- New skills and techniques, with a sound theoretical base

    'The course gave her a deeper understanding of what she's doing, greater knowledge and understanding. Greater awareness of the power of music – how music interacts with children, and working with small groups of children and their parents.'

- A specialism and an enhanced role

    'It helped her to focus more and take a lead on activities in the Children's Centre, and it developed her role tremendously. It's such a confidence booster to have a specialism. She supports others' colleagues more now, delivering music-based play sessions and herself delivering small groups.'

- Planning and evaluating

    'It developed her understanding of how to structure the sessions she delivers. She can give clearer direction to people she works with, and she is clearer about what she wants to achieve.'

Figure 14.2 shows one of our Interactive Music Makers at work.

Figure 14.2 Interactive Music Making

The scope of safe and effective skill sharing

Given the significance of the constant practitioner's role, it has been important to explore what transferables can be safely and impactfully made out of the clinical music therapy setting into the generic setting. The Interactive Music Makers (who at the time of writing total 30 colleagues), who as constant practitioners work with the children day in and day out at children's centres and nurseries, are now a skilled workforce providing universal access to targeted music-making which focuses on achieving developmental outcomes through a secure attachment base. In this way we are delivering a responsive, effective and accessible early intervention and prevention service to our 'under fives', which links directly into the core Music Therapy Service through the bridging role of our IMM specialist.

This in turn allows the music therapists to focus on the highly complex children and young people. Music therapy is a highly specialist profession with powerful potential. It can be both incisive and intrusive in terms of the music therapist getting to know and understand their client at a profound and fundamental level – an inner self which may well have become hidden for a multitude of reasons. Nevertheless, the outcome and ongoing sustainability of the intervention is dependent on the 'constant practitioners' in the client's life. This is because inherent within this collaborative stance is a rich deepening of understanding about the client's internal world which can be shared between the transient practitioner and the constant practitioner. To this effect, once music therapy has done its work, the impact can be monitored and/or sustained by the securely attached constant practitioner.

Conclusion

In conclusion, I return to the title of this chapter, 'Who Knows Me Best?' This question is not a provocation into competition; rather, it is a trigger to consider the significance of a collaborative stance for pooling the resources of the transient (music therapist) practitioner with those of the constant (significant person) practitioner. What has to be shared by the two practitioner roles is that in both cases the practitioner–child relationship is founded on the basis of a secure attachment. This echoes what Winnicott (1971) is at pains to say: that the 'mother' role can be any person who acts in the role of 'carer' who bonds with the child.

Without the collaboration between the constant practitioner and the transient practitioner, as a clinician I would not be able to deliver the quality of practice in music therapy I aspire to deliver, nor as a service manager would I be able to deliver the reach of service I aspire to reach. I shall therefore always be grateful to the 10 babies and the two Romanian care teams who inspired and led me to develop the concept of the collaborative partnership between the constant practitioner and the transient practitioner, and to also conceive the practice of IMM.

References

Bowlby, J. (2005) *A Secure Base*. Oxford: Routledge. (Original work published in 1988.)

Corcoran, M. (2014) Quotation from *Interactive Music Making* (video). London: Music as Therapy International. Available at www.musicastherapy.org/what_we_do/uk_partnerships.html, accessed on 22 November 2015.

HMSO (2014) *The Children and Families Act*. London: HMSO.

Geddes, H. (2006) *Attachment in the Classroom*. Twickenham: Worth.

Payne, M. (2014) Quotation from *Interactive Music Making* (video). London: Music as Therapy International. Available at www.musicastherapy.org/what_we_do/uk_partnerships.html, accessed on 22 November 2015.

Schore, A.N. (2000) 'Attachment and the regulation of the right brain.' *Attachment and Human Development 2*, 1, 23–47.

Sharma, A. and Cockerill, H. (2014) *Mary Sheridan's From Birth to Five Years: Children's Developmental Progress* (4th ed.). London: Routledge.

Stember, M. (1991) 'Advancing the social sciences through the interdisciplinary exercise.' *The Social Science Journal 28*, 1, 1–14.

Stern, D. (1998) *The Interpersonal World of the Infant: A View from Psychoanalysis and Developmental Psychology*. London: Karnac Books. (Original work published in 1985.)

Trevarthen, C. (2008) 'The Musical art of infant conversation: Narrating in the time of sympathetic experience without rational interpretation, before words.' *Musicae Scientiae 12*, 1, suppl. 15.

Waite, M. (ed) (2009) *The Oxford Thesaurus of English* (3rd ed.). Oxford: Oxford University Press.

Winnicott, D.W. (1971) *Playing and Reality*. London: Tavistock Publications.

Chapter 15

An Inclusion Group for Primary School Pupils With and Without Profound Learning Disability

Motoko Hayata and John Strange

Inclusive education

An early landmark in the drive towards educational inclusion was the Salamanca Statement in which 92 national governments and 25 international organisations affirmed the right to education of all children, regardless of individual differences (UNESCO 1994). As 'part of a wider reform of education needed to improve its quality and relevance and promote higher levels of learning achievement by all learners' (p.21), the Statement focused in particular on how special educational needs could act as a barrier to educational entitlement, and described the changes required to remove that barrier.

In the UK and elsewhere, policies of *integration* have been largely replaced by *inclusion* in the vocabulary of both educationalists and politicians. Integration might be likened to Piaget's concept of *assimilation*, in which one fits new information about the world into an existing conceptual framework, whereas inclusion resembles Piaget's *accommodation*, whereby one expands and modifies one's existing conceptual framework to take account of new information. Educationalists' responses to the special child have shifted from assimilation to accommodation. Whereas in the early phases of integration pupils with special needs (the 'new information') were expected to adapt (assimilate) as far as possible to the curriculum and organisation (the 'conceptual framework') of the mainstream schools into which they were drafted, now schools are expected to adapt (accommodate) teaching methods to the needs of pupils with special needs by 'differentiating' learning experiences to the abilities and interests of each individual pupil. Earlier policies of integration sprang in large part from a medical model of disability, which assumed that there was something 'wrong' with the special child, whereas more recent inclusion policies espouse the social model of disability, which sees society's failure to accommodate as the source of the handicap experienced by those with special needs.

The advantages and disadvantages of educational inclusion, both to children with and without special educational needs and also to society as a whole, continue to be argued and can at times become something of a political football. Historically, the most consistent impetus for inclusive policies has come, as with many social reforms, not from above but from those who have found themselves disadvantaged and their advocates. Among parents of children with special needs, those favouring highly specialised segregated school provision have been outnumbered by those pressing for their children to be included in mainstream schools. Some parents of children without special needs have understandably feared their children's education will suffer from the inclusion of special children in classes. Another obstacle to inclusion has been the anxiety of teachers who lack the skills and training needed to teach children with special needs, especially those with severe difficulties, in the same class as abler children. Of the four nations of the UK, only Scotland requires all trainee teachers to receive specific instruction in special-needs teaching.

The clinical work described in this chapter took place early in the present century, in a school regarded at the time as a flagship example of the inclusive practice to which the local authority as a whole was unequivocally committed. We were thus able to work with teaching and support staff wholeheartedly behind inclusive policies, a situation very different from that of Elefant (2010a) whose music therapy group for children from special and mainstream schools in Ranaana, Israel, pioneered inclusive practice for 10 years in a community where the concept was unfamiliar and viewed with misgivings by parents of both special and mainstream children. Elefant (2010b) gives a vivid account of the development, expansion and wider societal impact of the project, illustrating how it changed the attitudes of parents and especially of the mainstream pupils involved. Her account, presented as a manifestation of community music therapy, focuses on the social benefits to both groups of children, their parents and the community. The work presented in the present chapter was more modest in scope, and our account deals only with the actual sessions rather than their wider influence.

We soon found that involving children with and without disabilities, together with teaching and support staff, in shared therapeutic activities and experiences with a recreational flavour, was a good way to develop the matrix of relationships between all four groups of participants as well as between individual group members.

The spur to develop this inclusive music therapy provision was the referral from the Child and Adolescent Mental Health Service of a child with profound and complex needs. We asked the school if we could set up individual music therapy for the child, but we were told that only group work could be considered. We identified two other children with comparable levels of disability from the same class, but we were then told that it was against school policy to segregate special children. We therefore asked for three children without special needs to be added to the group, thus creating what we called an 'inclusion group' of six. We felt this idea would have therapeutic benefits, broaden our practice and present new challenges. (The epithet 'inclusion' was preferred to 'inclusive', which would have applied to every grouping in the school, to emphasise that inclusion would be among the main aims of the group.)

John ran two such groups before Motoko took over responsibility for the two groups referred to in the case studies below, one for Key Stage 1 children (ages 5–7 years) and one for Key Stage 2 children (ages 8–11 years). Each group consisted of three children with special educational needs (SEN), three mainstream children as helpers for the SEN children, one special education teacher and two teaching assistants. Each week, the children as well as the teaching and support staff made the 400-metre journey on foot or in buggies from their school to the music therapy room where the sessions took place. SEN children attended sessions for 1 year, but mainstream children were changed by the school every term so as not to miss too many classes.

The assistants were the school's regular classroom assistants. All would have been receiving in-service training for their role and some may have undertaken courses leading to basic qualifications with a focus on the needs of the special child. In the music therapy groups, the assistants' role was not simply one of supporting the individual special needs child, the teacher or indeed the music therapist; instead, they were encouraged also to participate in activities themselves as group members, on an equal basis with both teachers and pupils. Not surprisingly, a few assistants found this rather awkward, especially at first.

Benefits of the inclusion groups

The way the groups were run had benefits for all group members. The teacher's statutory role of oversight remained and was actually facilitated by handing over the directing of the group's activities to the music therapist, as this left her more freedom to observe and reflect upon the interaction between group members, and particularly on individual pupils' developing participation. For the assistants, observation and reflection were similarly facilitated. The music therapist, by observing how the special needs children responded to the inclusive setting, discovered aspects of both their needs and their strengths which might not have been so evident from working with them individually, or in a group composed solely of children with special needs. Finally, the mainstream child 'helpers' gained a fuller appreciation of the children with special needs by sharing non-academic activities which encouraged creativity, rather than academic tasks, which often require such radical differentiation that mainstream and special children are hardly aware of being engaged in the same activity.

Describing the mainstream children as helpers does not mean that they were there simply to act as additional adults and valued for attributes such as their:

- ability to understand the activities presented to the group

- ability to understand and accept SEN children's disabilities

- willingness to help SEN children.

They were also valued for what they brought to the sessions as children, such as:

- playfulness

- imagination

- creativity.

CASE STUDY: JASON AND DAVID
(KEY STAGE 2 GROUP) – SUPPORT

Many of the mainstream children seen during the 3 years over which groups ran were playful, imaginative and creative in childlike ways, and enjoyed demonstrating their own ways of playing instruments, for example waving a rattle consisting of wooden prisms on a leather backing to imitate the movement of a snake. Jason, a mainstream boy, enjoyed making music himself using his imagination. He also seemed to accept what SEN children could and could not do. As it was the start of a new school term, mainstream members had just changed, and it was Jason's first time in the music therapy group. David, aged 10 years, with severe developmental delay and no spoken language, was the only special child in the session because the other two were absent. In a free improvisation section about half way through the 40-minute session, Motoko brought a long rain stick to David. She wished to see if it would enable him to maintain his attention longer than 1 minute, which was typically as long as he could keep his focus on any activity. As she started playing the rain stick for him, David paid attention to it, showing that the instrument interested him. After a while, she offered the rain stick to David, but Jason took it over and started playing it to David.

As Jason played, David held it at the same time to enjoy the sensation created by the falling beads inside. After a little while David stood up. After being briefly distracted by the keyboard which he was already familiar with, he immediately brought his attention back to Jason with the rain stick and moved to join him. When Jason banged the rain stick on the floor as he stood next to him, David gave a big smile and then wanted to walk. David walked unsteadily because of poor muscle control in his legs, so Jason immediately started using the stick as a walking stick which they both held and put his other hand round David's shoulder to stabilise him and support his walking. They walked together towards the drum which Motoko was playing to accompany their walking. Jason tried to let David hold the rain stick independently, but he was unable to hold it firmly enough owing to poor muscle control in his arm, so Jason resumed playing it with him. The activity which Jason came up with in this particular session evoked from David his longest-ever concentration of 6 minutes, and also the biggest smiles ever seen from him. Later in the session, Jason danced with David, this time supporting his body to help him to mirror his movements.

Because the other two SEN children were absent that day, it is not surprising that the two other mainstream children busied themselves with their own playing, paying no attention to each other or to David or Jason. What was notable was the clear contrast between these two and Jason who, rather than associating himself with his able-bodied peers, chose of his own accord to play for, and with, David as well as for himself. The SEN teacher who attended the session commented, 'Jason is born to be a therapist.'

After that individual 'inclusive' interaction, we now look briefly at a development which occurred during an inclusive group activity.

CASE STUDY: RACHEL (KEY STAGE 1 GROUP) – MODELLING

Rachel was 6 years old, non-verbal, with severe learning disability and visual impairment. She was specifically referred to music therapy by the school. At first she seemed to dislike all sounds and used to cover her ears for most of the session. She was unable to sustain playing in free improvisation, and she used to stop playing after a few moments of banging. In the 'Hello' and 'Good-bye' songs, which were sung with Makaton signs, she was rather passive, just watching Motoko and the group. However, after 19 months, as the 'Good-bye' song went around the group, repeating the same verse with different names, she suddenly completed the whole verse with Makaton signs, and took everyone by surprise, as until that moment she had only watched other people making the signs and had been unable to copy them herself.

Passive learning had clearly occurred over a long period, but she had only now gained the confidence and/or the motivation for active involvement. This might well have been impossible without other children to provide models.

The next example illustrates the valuable roles played by the teaching assistants and the teacher while the therapist was leading the session, such as:

- physically supporting SEN children to play instruments

- supporting activities by taking part as models

- helping with the organisation of activities

- encouraging both SEN children and mainstream children to engage in activities.

We have already seen from the previous two case studies that the first and second of these roles may also be played by mainstream children, but adult staff were naturally more biddable and dependable, with (in most cases) a deeper understanding of the children. Both teachers and teaching assistants were very engaged and willing to learn how to meet the children's different needs musically, thus becoming the therapist's extended hands.

CASE STUDY: ALAN (KEY STAGE 1 GROUP) – STRUCTURE

Alan was 5 years old with autistic spectrum disorder involving learning disability as well as communication and social interaction difficulties. He could not stay in one place for more than a few seconds and constantly walked round the room in a circle. Motoko started walking round with him, holding wind chimes and presenting them in front of his eyes. Finding that he showed an interest in touching and making sounds with this instrument, school staff quickly learned to stand in three different corners of the room where Alan was likely to walk past, presenting him with Indian bells or rattles.

Challenges of including mainstream child helpers

There are several challenges, such as:

- the mainstream children's own need for attention

- lack of interest in making the kind of music (simple, often improvised) which suits the SEN children

- the different balance of freedom and direction most appropriate to SEN and mainstream children in a group situation.

The mainstream children's need for attention is normal for their age, and not in itself a problem; however, difficulties could arise from the school's primary concern that the groups should provide therapy for the SEN children. The mainstream children were not all as resourceful and motivated to help their disabled peers as Jason, and encouraging them to do so could have conflicted with motivating them to play for their own enjoyment. They would sometimes, as in the case study involving Jason and David, make music most readily when left to their own devices for a while – even if that music bore no relation to what others were doing! This in turn created a degree of musical confusion which, though perhaps less distracting to the children than to the staff, reduced the clarity with which musical guidance could be given by the therapist, or dialogue perceived and developed.

One factor that may have accentuated some mainstream children's tendency to 'go off on a tangent' was the fact that the teaching assistants saw their role in sessions as primarily a continuation of their role in the classroom, where they would generally be concerned only with the children with special needs who most needed their support, and perhaps continuously assigned to a certain child. They thus largely ignored the mainstream children who may have concluded that how they spent the session did not concern the assistants, whom they also viewed as being interested only in the SEN children.

One further source of difficulty was that many of the SEN children responded best, or indeed only, to a child-centred approach, whereas many mainstream children required more structure and tighter boundaries in order to feel secure and to flourish. Rather than seeming inconsistent and unfairly restrictive of the mainstream children, the staff, including Motoko and John as therapists, found themselves relaxing boundaries for all the children in a way which possibly disadvantaged the mainstream children. It has to be said, however, that subjecting children with the level of disabilities seen in these groups to a mainstream regime of discipline and direction would neither have helped the special children nor developed the mainstream children's understanding of them. The gentler, if more chaotic, course we took avoided entrenching difference and division and undoing the school's progress in inclusion. Positive outcomes, such as those described in the case studies above (especially the first), which were by no means rare, vindicated the work. We found the staff consistently positive in their comments on the value of the groups, even on what felt to us as therapists like 'bad days'.

Inclusive music education

Many of the activities and experiences in these music therapy groups had an educational aspect, but music education as a subject in the curriculum is a different enterprise. Before 2013 the Music National Curriculum for English and Welsh schools divided the subject into three broad areas – composing, performing and appraising – thus maintaining a balance between emotional, intellectual and practical skills. The National Curriculum for England (Department for Education 2013) dissolves these distinct categories and distributes their component elements differently while still striving for the same balance. Few schools take up the option of 'disapplying' the National Curriculum for pupils with special needs, preferring to offer every child the basic National Curriculum framework, differentiated to an appropriate level. For the severely disabled, this entails a developmental and experiential approach rather than a didactic one, but the mainstream pupils in our inclusion groups were entitled to a music education clearly distinct from therapy. As we could not provide this, music lessons remained the responsibility of the school.

Inclusive music therapy as education for citizenship

Although the inclusive music therapy groups did not meet the mainstream children's *music* educational needs, some at least of the mainstreamers underwent considerable *social* learning. The groups gave them an opportunity, which many took, to learn more about the strengths and interests of the SEN children and become not only at ease but actively supportive when sharing activities with them. This must surely qualify as preparation for adult life in society, the aim of citizenship education. In the 1980s, during the period of consultation prior to the introduction of the National Curriculum, a draft of the music curriculum:

> …proposed the inclusion of music education in the compulsory curriculum because of its wider value in developing non-musical social skills of communication, co-operation and what has come to be known as emotional intelligence (Goleman 1996). Witkin (1974) had already argued for the teaching of creative arts in general on the same grounds. (Strange 2014, p.25)

The SEN pupils attending the inclusion groups were also prepared for adult life in society by the experience of positive, accepting behaviour from their mainstream peers, such that as adults they would be less fearful of bullying, ridicule or rejection for their disability, and more aware of the respect due to them as human beings. A consequence of such improved integration would be a reduced vulnerability to mental health problems, which despite some conflicting evidence tend to be more prevalent among the learning disabled (Smiley 2005).

As the school already actively promoted an educational and social climate in which inclusive experiences provided such benefits for both mainstream and SEN pupils, the role of our inclusion music therapy groups was to provide a particular setting, medium and approach ideally suited to furthering the school's inclusive philosophy.

References

Department for Education (2013) *The National Curriculum for England and Wales.* Available at https://www.gov.uk/government/publications/national-curriculum-in-england-music-programmes-of-study, accessed on 20 February 2016.

Elefant, C. (2010a) 'Action: Must We Really End?' In B. Stige, G. Ansdell, C. Elefant and M. Pavlicevic (eds) *Where Music Helps: Community Music Therapy in Action and Reflection.* Farnham: Ashgate.

Elefant, C. (2010b) 'Reflection: Musical Inclusion, Intergroup Relations, and Community Development.' In B. Stige, G. Ansdell, C. Elefant and M. Pavlicevic (eds) *Where Music Helps: Community Music Therapy in Action and Reflection.* Farnham: Ashgate.

Goleman, D. (1996) *Emotional Intelligence: Why It Can Matter More Than I.Q.* London: Bloomsbury Publishing.

Smiley, E. (2005) 'Epidemiology of mental health problems in adults with learning disability: an update.' *Advances in Psychiatric Treatment 11,* 214–222.

Strange, J. (2014) 'Improvised Music to Support Interaction Between Profoundly Learning-Disabled Teenagers and Their Learning Support Assistants.' PhD thesis, Anglia Ruskin University, Cambridge. Available at http://hdl.handle.net/10540/314588, accessed on 20 February 2016.

UNESCO (1994) *The Salamanca Statement and Framework for Action on Special Needs Education.* Paris: UNESCO.

Witkin, R.W. (1974) *The Intelligence of Feeling.* London: Heinemann.

Chapter 16

Building Musical Bridges in Paediatric Hospital Departments

Tone Leinebø and Trygve Aasgaard

Introduction

Experiencing being a hospital patient may be challenging for anyone. For children, a serious illness may interfere with the developmental process of extending their attention from dependence on the family towards the outside world and the opportunity to learn through play and interaction with other children. To live for long periods in a hi-tech hospital milieu poses additional challenges to the multiple physical and psychological stressors related to having a serious illness; this is a life situation that may also have a number of negative impacts on the child (Berríos-Rivera, Rivero-Vergne and Romero 2008). Sadness and loneliness can mark young patients' lives in hospital, although, interestingly, in a recent study of American children's emotional responses to hospitalisation, the highest mean among the emotional items identified was 'happy' (Kim *et al.* 2014).

For adolescents, long periods of sickness and hospitalisation potentially interfere with the healthy developmental tasks of establishing independence, autonomy, identity, peer relations and career goals (Neville 2005). Indeed, a condition like childhood cancer affects not only the young patient, but her or his entire family, parents, healthy siblings and others: socially, emotionally and at times even economically (Williams, Williams and Williams 2014). This is why music therapists frequently work with families, just as much as with individual patients. In many paediatric hospital wards, one or both parents accompany the sick child for long periods during daytime and occasionally sleep in the patient's room. Often music therapists are on friendly terms with the brothers or sisters of long-stay patients, children who are easily 'put in the shade' by the focus on the patients, but who, for various reasons, spend hours within the hospital walls.

The goal of this chapter is to show music therapy activities and interventions within various interdisciplinary and/or interfamilial contexts, demonstrating the usefulness of a therapeutic approach based on continuous cooperation and interdependency. Who is being assisted and who is assisting may change from one situation to another, but sometimes the music therapist is choosing or acquiring an assistant for a specified period. One musically gifted physician, not working in the paediatric department, once asked if he could be the music therapist's apprentice for some months. This was granted, and thereafter he regularly turned up at agreed times when the music therapist did group work with patients and parents. This 'medical' music therapy assistant did an excellent job and received positive evaluations from many quarters, not least because of his improvisatory stunts and good-natured humour. Occasionally, the music therapist has asked a young visitor to be his musical assistant for a couple of hours while their patient brother or sister is spending some time in laboratories or treatment rooms. Waiting in the hospital communal areas may be very boring for young (and even old) people. Working with the music therapist is seemingly far more enjoyable, perhaps taking part in a procession while steering a big animal string puppet, or starting a sing-song by three beats on a timpani she or he has tuned, without assistance, to a specified note.

A specific physical or psychological problem, or a wish to nurture resources, is often the point of departure for music therapy with young patients going through a very demanding period of treatment and care. In daily practice, however, we deal with both problems and resources more or less simultaneously, with the common goal of promoting health. This is also a core element of a widely used definition of music therapy where 'health' is defined as '...the process of becoming one's fullest potential for individual and ecological wholeness' (Bruscia 1998, p.84). Thus, if the music therapist wants to start from 'where the patient is' at a certain time, various contextual factors must be considered. 'Health' is not just something we *have*, but something we *are*, or are *becoming*, and are constantly *performing* throughout our lives. Health and illness are not a question of either/or, but rather dynamic, coexisting elements in every person's life. In the paediatric ward we see, again and again, children with serious illnesses who still preserve many healthy aspects of themselves. 'Ecological wholeness' means here '...conceived as consisting of society, culture, and environment...'

(Bruscia 1998, p.87). Equally, no musical element can be isolated from the many contextual elements in which it is embedded and experienced.

Specific aims of music therapy practices in medical settings have been related to easing emotional and physical pain and serving as an important outlet for self-expression. Music therapy may also help the patient to cope effectively during a hospital stay by offering opportunities for choice and control. It may normalise the child's experience of being in hospital by improving quality of life, improving or maintaining parent–child relationships and providing an opportunity for family sharing and enjoyment. All this in turn may promote good self-esteem, provide developmental input, increase tolerance for medical treatment and give the child an opportunity to play and have fun while maintaining and developing health-related roles (Hilliard 2006; O'Callaghan and Aasgaard 2012). Music therapists often share treatment goals with those of several other professions in the paediatric department, such as nurses, teachers and psychologists. When hospitals invite artists to perform, this is generally justified by the similar aim of enriching patients' lives in various ways through the arts.

Hospitals in transformation

At Oslo University Hospitals, music therapy is available to all children and adolescents from 0 to 18 years of age; it encompasses medical, psychodynamic and/or environmental approaches. Today, far more young patients are treated within a shorter period than just 20 years ago, and even if there has been a small increase in the number of patients diagnosed with cancer, the number of days in hospital for inpatients has not grown accordingly.

The National Hospital, one of the four main campuses of Oslo University Hospitals, consists of highly specialised wards, and children who are admitted to the paediatric department are often transferred from one ward to another. A patient with a brain tumour might be admitted to the oncology ward for chemotherapy, to the neurosurgical ward for an operation and perhaps also to the intensive care unit owing to complications. Medically, this provides an efficient approach to treatment; it might, however, pose additional challenges to both the sick child and her or his parents in having to relate to new places and people within short periods of time (Ærø and Aasgaard 2011).

The music therapist has the privilege of working across wards and clinics; in some cases the music therapist is one of the few professionals who is able to accompany the patient wherever she or he is in the institution. In addition to addressing individual goals in music therapy sessions regardless of geographic location in the hospital, the music therapist may help facilitate the transition for a patient by maintaining an element of predictability and trust if there are difficulties adjusting to new wards or routines (Ærø and Aasgaard 2011; Bower and Shoemark 2012). A relationship with a familiar music therapist who – as a permanent supportive musical companion – is able to focus on and nourish the child's resources and health-related roles may be experienced as a friendly alliance beyond the realm of sickness and the inevitable medical treatment procedures, not least during particularly demanding periods marked by discomfort and uncertainty. Events such as a weekly sing-along or Musical Hour in one of the common rooms of the paediatric department may be among the few regular pleasurable events to which families can look forward in the hospital milieu (Aasgaard 2004). The provision of some stable, positive elements in the overall plan for medical treatment, and in the care of patients *and* parents, serves as a buffer against potential negative effects related to unpredictability, lack of control and other unforeseen factors related to hospitalisation (Longhi, Pickett and Hargreaves 2013; Franck *et al.* 2015). In our own hospital practices it is our experience, time and time again, that well-functioning multidisciplinary teamwork is desirable if music therapy environmental activities and individual sessions are to be commonly appreciated as self-evident elements of the hospital timetable. Interprofessional communication and cooperation result in better understanding between the various professions, and the music therapist is responsible for finding ways of informing allied health staff about music therapy, what it offers and in what situations it may be used to benefit a single patient or within wider contexts.

Music environmental therapy

'Music environmental therapy' has been defined as a: 'A systematic process of using music to promote health in a specified environment inside or outside of institutions' (Aasgaard 1999, p.34). 'When music therapy was reinvented as a modern profession in the middle of last century…it was constructed as a treatment profession where the individual relation between a client and a therapist was foregrounded' (Ruud 2004, p.11). Gradually, music therapists have also been working with whole communities where individual problems, strengths and challenges are understood systemically, and where networking, empowerment and (simply) exuberance through musicking are central. The term 'musicking' was put forward by the musicologist Christopher Small, who claimed: 'Music is not a thing at all, but an activity, something that people do' (Small 1998, p.2). In music therapy theory and practice this concept is used in relation to musical *activities*, where 'musicking' is about specific ways of interaction and communication.

When children are admitted to hospital for a longer period, the hospital departments and wards become their temporary home, playground or school, and the arena for human interaction. A hospital often contains several different milieux. ('Milieu' is understood here as the immediate environment.) Professional musicians and, eventually, music therapists have a long history of 'musicalising' various hospital milieux. As early as the tenth century, Arabian musicians were employed by medical doctors of the time to play in hospitals; music was also present in some of the numerous European spas which emerged since. Florence Nightingale wrote about the potential beneficial effects to the sick of listening to wind or string instruments or singing in her *Notes on Nursing: What It Is, and What It Is Not* (1969), and later contributed to engaging professional musicians to play in large hospital wards, often having more than 30 beds in one room. Some kind of interdisciplinary cooperation was seemingly understood as a prerequisite for enabling such activities to take place, and basic knowledge of music's ability to enliven or calm should be part of every nurse's curriculum. Until the Second World War, singing lessons were also included in many European training programmes for nurses (Aasgaard 2006).

In 2014–2015, the organisation Live Music Now, founded by Yehudi Menuhin and Ian Stoutzker, delivered 766 performances for children and young people all over Britain by young, professional musicians (Live Music Now 2015a). This included several Musicians in Residence Projects within children's hospitals. These activities are not labelled music therapy but are similar to many other Arts for Health programmes: the focus is on relationships between art-based experiences and activities, health and well-being. While concerts have traditionally aimed at creating a beneficial institutional environment and meaningful individual listening experiences, we now register a stronger focus on interactions with the individual patient. The website of Live Music Now announced in 2015 that four musicians from the Royal Liverpool Philharmonic Orchestra '…will work closely with health care professionals to develop interactive music sessions for patients in four specific areas of the hospital' (Live Music Now 2015b).

Often, a music therapist plays a crucial role in administering and facilitating arts-based performances by visiting artists in the hospital. There is a fine line between a diverse and customised musical presence, and an overload of activities and 'entertainment' offered to persons who are also very sick or fatigued. The music therapist may be the one who draws this line of demarcation. Some artists are, seemingly, so much involved in their own performance that they pay too little attention to their audiences' reactions. When it comes to performing for hospitalised children, it is often far better to arrange a 15-minute concert or play than to present anything, even with a very high artistic standard, lasting twice that long. On the other hand, we must not underestimate the value of visits from selected distinguished musicians to the hospital.

Promoting a healthy hospital environment is obviously the shared responsibility of every staff member; it is, however, almost impossible to imagine just one profession playing the lead part in this process. Mental health professionals of many kinds have published literature in abundance on different approaches to developing a therapeutic environment in institutions. Very often this is also presented as an interprofessional challenge. The amount of available literature on systematic uses of environmental (or 'milieu') elements in medical settings is quite modest. Aasgaard (1999, 2004), however, applies the nurse theorist Suzie Kim's analysis (Kim 1983) of various environmental aspects to describe strategies of music therapy in cancer care. Here we find descriptions of ways of using music to influence temporal, spatial, physical, social and symbolic environmental elements. On the other hand, some artistically dedicated nurses have expanded the traditional repertory of nursing processes related to children with cancer to encompass artistic, not least musical, elements to create health-focused milieux, engaging in activities marked by fantasy and humour, and sometimes, hopefully, making tedious routines less boring (Bringager et al. 2014).

One part of the music therapy practices at Oslo University Hospitals, particularly focusing on temporal and social aspects, is seasonal musical celebrations and markings of other regular events, like birthdays. These activities are also ways of connecting to the outside world, perhaps even providing glimmers of normality for young patients who otherwise, in many ways, are defined by passive sick roles and isolation. Preparing for such events, music therapists often collaborate with teachers, preschool teachers and nurses: Who is responsible for decorations or costumes, who is deciding the menu and who is responsible for a sing-song and accompaniment? Hospital staff are used to working closely together when it comes to diagnostic procedures, treatment and care, but dealing with matters somewhat outside one's own individual professional platform is also a way of developing mutual goodwill and team spirit. Celebrations potentially serve as bridges from the patient's hospital room to the outside world, and from inactivity to activity, and strengthen feelings of togetherness and trust between all participants. A 'Grand Pirate Party' is an example of an annual event within the paediatric department where individuals from different professions and groups contribute to the preparation and implementation of the show.

This year's party begins with the music therapist walking here and there in the entrance hall with a large drum in her hands, inviting the young patients to 'shoot cannonballs' to show everybody what they are today: dangerous pirates! Almost all the children are dressed like pirates. They have also been equipped with painted scars and eye patches, and the noise produced when hitting the drum is often astonishing! Regardless of illness or bodily state, in that moment these children are now nothing but fierce pirates on a mighty ocean. Several children (and many parents) look surprised when realising how loud their own cannon sounded. Pirates' songs are yelled through the corridors, and the smiles and energy in the children's faces illuminate almost a whole department!

Aasgaard (2004) writes:

Regular, music-related events influence the rhythm in the paediatric ward and remind everyone present of other sides of man than sickness and disability. Many patients, as well as their parents, say that they are looking forward to taking part in scheduled musical activities. (p.161)

The weekly Musical Hour, arranged in one of the bigger open spaces in the hospital, is one example of planned 'happenings' where children, and occasionally also sisters and brothers of patients, sing, play and act, and sometimes even dance, together. The music therapists often invite staff from different wards and professions to be a part of the band of the day or a mini-choir, or to have a solo performance. One day a medical professor, also a very good pianist, accompanies the music therapist performing short classical pieces on a sackbut (baroque trombone) or treble recorder. On another occasion, a ward rock-and-roll band, 'Infusion Complete', consisting of three nurses and a medical doctor, performs a dramatised version of a song created by an 8-year-old patient in cooperation with the music therapist. 'Music in the Shift Change-Over' is also a regular feature at The National Hospital, with a particular emphasis on participation from busy staff who may have some time to spare around 3.00 p.m. Here, the house paediatricians often perform with their own jazz band, sometimes with a patient as soloist or together with the music therapist, who may be responsible for musical arrangements too. Arenas for musicking, like those described above, are seemingly highly appreciated by some of the staff, and give the audiences glimpses of sides of people they usually only see 'dressed in white' in more formal situations. This is also an opportunity for staff members to experience often unexpected, health-related, creative sides of their patients. Finally, communal musical events may also be used as a way of informing and presenting some aspects of what music therapy is to participating colleagues, not through words, but through learning-by-doing (Loewy 2001).

Music therapy to influence physiological parameters and as procedural support

Potential relations between musical interventions and respiration have been studied since the early 1940s (Ellis and Brighouse 1952). Today, music therapists collaborate with physiotherapists, nurses, paediatricians and parents in helping young patients to breathe more efficiently, slow down respiratory rate and boost deeper breathing. While the majority of research and practices in this field have been based on ready-made music, administered through loudspeakers or headphones, interventions may also entail listening to live music or even involving patients in singing or blowing selected wind instruments. A music therapist playing a guitar or similar instrument directly in front of a patient can observe behavioural signs and change tempo, loudness and style almost immediately. At Oslo University Hospitals, even infants dependent on oxygen are sometimes referred to the music therapist; listening and musical activities may improve oxygen saturation to normal levels of 95 to 100% after a few minutes.

Some of the most concrete forms of cooperation in a hospital setting are related to music therapy as a means of procedural support. Research in this field is done by medical doctors, nurses and music therapists and others – often in cooperation. Klassen *et al.* (2008) conducted a systematic review of 19 randomised controlled trials, involving 1513 subjects, on the efficacy of music therapy in reducing pain and anxiety in children undergoing clinical procedures. The authors considered the methodological quality as generally poor. Results, however, showed a significant reduction in pain and anxiety. The authors concluded by stating that music interventions are effective and useful as an adjunctive therapy in clinical situations with expected reactions of pain or anxiety.

The extent to which procedure-related cooperation in paediatric departments between music therapists and other professions is a systematic process probably varies between hospitals. At times, the music therapist's involvement may arise almost by chance, and only later does it result in more planned cooperative procedures. It is perhaps more common to involve music therapists in assessment or diagnostic procedures in child mental health care than in somatic paediatric medicine, but here too the music therapist may be able to create settings which allow the child to engage in a more natural way than if asked simply to perform some specific physical exercise.

The physiotherapist asks if she can study a music therapy session as she would like to assess Eric's ability to move his upper body and neck after a big surgical intervention. Eric wishes to play a drum kit during this particular session and demonstrates a wide range of upper body movements while playing his very own improvised drum solo. This skill has previously been unknown to the physiotherapist.

The following example illustrates how dynamic such a procedure can be and how the music therapist can take different roles during the course of treatment when cooperating with other health care professionals.

CASE EXAMPLE: ACTIVE MUSIC-MAKING AS DISTRACTION FROM AN UNPLEASANT PROCEDURE

Tom, a 12-year-old boy with Down syndrome, has an infected and complicated wound that needs to be assessed and attended to twice weekly. Every time, the boy experiences this procedure as very painful, resulting in a constant fear of going through the regular and inevitable agonising experience. At the time of referral to music therapy, his fear before the procedure is seemingly greater than the actual pain during the wound cleaning. At first, Tom needs to be held down by three adults, parents included, and is fighting and screaming the whole time while the doctor attends to his wound.

The music therapist builds rapport with the patient before the procedure is about to take place and learns about his love for One Direction, a typical teenage band. Then she engages the boy in drumming to one of their songs. Tom immediately starts to interact musically and expresses great joy doing this; he still needs to be held down by two staff, but he is now engaged in the music and keeps the eye contact with the music therapist between outbursts of discomfort. During the following week, the nurse and the music therapist work out a plan. It seems clear that Tom becomes sufficiently involved in the music-making to be distracted from the actual procedure. Gradually, after two more sessions, he is able to sit still, happily engaged in drumming to a song of his choice as the doctor dresses his wound. The nurse and the music therapist finally decide to develop the intervention further by adding a mobile phone to play the music video as a distraction. Tom gladly accepts this, and soon he is able to endure the procedure without any other support than watching and listening to music on the phone. The music therapist is no longer needed – at least not in relation to this procedure.

There is growing scientific evidence that music (activity) can help soothe paediatric patients during unpleasant medical procedures, mainly because of its anxiety-reducing properties (Hartling *et al.* 2013). But the example above also demonstrates the complex nature of many interventions. Which role did the actual musical vibrations from the drum and the melodies play? Which role did the music therapist herself play? Was the effect of her way of touching or her voice and body language different from that of the others present in making the procedure more or less stressful? Did the overall communication between the participants change after the music therapist arrived? Questions like these show how limiting and misleading it may be to reduce music therapy in interprofessional cooperative health care to one single variable. But it also shows how three professions interact successfully while collaborating to the benefit of a young patient.

Building bridges with other staff and families

In most forms of professional collaboration, basic mutual understanding of the different participants' roles and duties is mandatory. Sometimes this reciprocal understanding is present from the very start of a new project; perhaps more often, it is the result of an ongoing process developed through encounters, observations, discussions and numerous questions. Information about a new patient before a first session can be especially important. Music therapists in paediatric hospitals are usually dependent on information from nursing staff who, in most cases, have a broad knowledge of their patients, relating not only to their medical status, treatment and care, but also to their general family situation and their various strengths and challenges. The following example illustrates the necessity of building on each other's knowledge and resources in the interest of the patient. At times, it is the music therapist who knows the patient's hidden resources which have not been detected by other staff members.

CASE EXAMPLE: EMPOWERMENT THROUGH DIRECTING A COMIC MUSICAL ENSEMBLE

Clara is 7 years old and has been diagnosed with medulloblastoma (a fast-growing, high-grade brain tumour). A nurse asks the music therapist to visit Clara as she has been complaining of pain; she also appears to be scared and always sad. 'People dressed in white' are seemingly particularly frightening. The music therapist is familiar with the patient from previous sing-along sessions and quickly establishes rapport with both the patient and her parents. The nurse is also in the room and invited to participate in the session. It does not take long before Clara is smilingly engaged in a very personal version of her favourite song, bossing around both parents and the nurse to play on different instruments. The atmosphere is seemingly quite happy by the time the music therapist leaves the room. They all laugh and joke about how weird the nurse looked as a marching elephant.

Musical activities may, in some cases, act like bridges from problem-related focuses to more resource-related experiences and behaviour. We suggest that this may facilitate efficient coping strategies for long-term patients and families in the many inevitable battles with ill health and the negative aspects of hospitalisation.

With an acutely ill and hospitalised child, any family will face the challenge of how to readjust to the new situation. Parents are at risk of experiencing negative psychological reactions to having a sick child, regardless of the type of illness or length of hospital admission (Franck *et al.* 2015). Many parents also experience feelings of stress, depression and anxiety, which again might affect the child (Longhi *et al.* 2013; Muscara *et al.* 2015). By caring for the parent, we are also caring for the child, and vice versa. Sometimes we see parents who are feeling detached from their child because of the illness; perhaps the child is covered (disguised?) in unfamiliar hospital equipment that hinders normal closeness and familiar activities. In addition to this, parents sometimes feel there is an unwritten law in the hospital as to what is expected from them while spending days and weeks at the bedside. Parents are neither patients nor professional staff members, but they *are* responsible for keeping up a positive 'emotional climate' in the sickroom, as one father once said (Aasgaard 2002, p.114). In our paediatric practices, we often experience some mutual understanding with parents of the inevitable challenges that may accompany a (felt) obligation to lift the 'emotional climate' and how demanding it may be to play – continuously – a role marked by optimism, unconditional positive support and energy. Music therapists often assist parents in this struggle, temporarily taking over the role of the always optimistic entertainer; parents respond with gratitude for letting them relax or simply go away for short periods without having a bad conscience.

Close relatives may also assist the music therapist in many ways: informing her about the patient's likes and dislikes, resources and skills, being present at and reassuring babies or very young children in their first encounter with music therapy, and through their engagement in different musical activities with the child. Often parents are even able to follow up and develop music-therapy-initiated practices between sessions and after the therapist has left.

'Song Creations by Children with Cancer: Process and Meaning' (Aasgaard 2002) was one of the first well-documented research projects in music therapy demonstrating how creative activities, going far beyond scheduled music therapy sessions, could be meaningful, not only for the individual patients, but also in developing creative networks involving many people within and even outside the hospital environment. The processes of making, performing and using 19 songs by five patients were based on interaction and cooperation between a music therapist and young cancer patients, mothers and fathers, sisters and brothers, nurses and hospital (infant) school teachers. Very little of this was planned by the music therapist; different forms of cooperation evolved by accident or necessity during the approximately 3 years this project lasted: a mother was very inspiring to her sick daughter in writing lyrics, ironical and funny, but also related to the harsh realities of being sick and losing both her healthy blood corpuscles and her hair. A father had been allowed to bring with him his guitar into the isolation room of his child; he became an eager accompanist. A teacher helped a 15-year-old boy who had writing difficulties to write so that his thought-provoking texts could be understood. A 5-year-old brother heard a recorded version of his big sister's song about a suspiciously cheerful lady who is about to sting her with a needle in order to take a blood specimen; very soon he made his own 'farting' version of the lyrics and performed *his* song while playing air-guitar at home in front of his parents who almost 'died of laughter'. René, a 13-year-old girl, made a rap-like song about all her funny classmates. Because of very sore mucous membranes in her mouth and throat, René needed much support to be able to sing by herself. Her primary nurse stayed with her during the recording at the isolation unit of the ward, and eventually René managed to do the solo without any assistance while the nurse took the initiative to sing a riff between each verse.

It is impossible to decide beforehand that these things are going to take place. Obviously, a music therapist working in this way must be willing to let go of some control over activities he originally initiates. In the case of René, many different people were *taking part*, just as much as *assisting*, in the creative processes. Perhaps this resulted in (even) more good experiences for the young patients than simply being involved with making and performing their own songs together with just the one music therapist. But does this way of working potentially also endanger the more traditional concept of music therapy based on musical communication within a dyad between a patient or a specific group of patients and a therapist?

Ways of communicating the music therapist role

In this chapter, we have presented several examples of clinical cooperation, including staff education through participation. Interdisciplinary meetings are particularly useful arenas for establishing routines and meeting points for knowledge sharing. A paediatric department or hospital usually contains many different wards, and for a music therapist who caters for all of these, it is vital to be part of an efficient system of referrals – something not easily introduced overnight. But even today, how often does this system include a manual for how to prioritise music therapy referrals? A prerequisite for this to be well functioning is to have colleagues who know what the music therapist potentially can – and cannot – do.

One way of communicating our role is to be active at staff meetings where patients are presented, appropriate referrals are made and where challenges (and victories) are brought forward and discussed. At Oslo University Hospitals, music therapy sessions are documented electronically in the patient's clinical notes; however, even the best-written information still cannot completely replace verbal communication and exchange of thoughts between professionals.

The following case example illustrates how interprofessional meetings may be used to initiate and evaluate music therapy-related interventions.

CASE EXAMPLE: FOSTERING OPTIMISM, RESILIENCE AND RELIEF FROM RESPONSIBILITY FOR ILLNESS

Laura, an 8-year-old girl, has recently been diagnosed with leukaemia and admitted to the oncology ward. At a staff meeting, the paediatric oncologist outlines the comprehensive chemotherapy treatment plan that Laura needs. A nurse reports that Laura is overly well behaved in the ward, never protesting or asking for anything, always a little timidly doing what she is being told. The treatment team discusses different potential ways to strengthen this somewhat fragile girl during the scheduled long periods of strenuous treatment and hospitalisation, and music therapy is chosen as one potential element of adding health to Laura's life in the months to come. The music therapist asks for suggestions as to major goals for her interventions and the team eventually proposes a focus on self-expression and on fostering optimism and resilience.

The first musical encounter begins with free improvisation in a *hopefully* safe atmosphere. Laura appears quite withdrawn, staring at her feet when asked questions and seemingly mainly focusing on not doing anything 'wrong'. The music therapist is making no demands on her and continues improvising softly. Within 15 minutes, Laura relaxes and is no longer afraid of exploring different instruments or requesting songs that she knows. Would she perhaps like to make her own song? 'Do what you like – nothing can be wrong with this!'

At the next session, Laura proudly announces that she has made a song – all by herself! One afternoon her dad had been particularly upset about Laura's sickness; she had an idea of writing some lines about that and therefore she named it *Foreldresangen* ('Parents' Song'). The music therapist helps her improve the structure of the lyrics. Finally, the two of them try out melodic phrases, put them together, and all of a sudden Laura's first song is ready to be performed. During the creation of this song, Laura tells of how sad she is for her parents who are so anxious and troubled because of their daughter. At the end of the session, the music therapist and Laura talk about the question of responsibility for being ill, just why she has become ill and how to deal with her present feelings.

At the next multidisciplinary meeting the music therapist shares her account of the two sessions with Laura. Various staff members comment on the importance of keeping in mind this information. The nurses say that they will make sure every day that Laura has adequate factual information about her disease and treatment, and will also explain to her that the cancer she is now struggling with is not her own fault. She is also not responsible for her own recovery – or for looking after her parents; that is taken care of by the hospital staff. Some days later, Laura performs her song with great success for her parents and many others at the paediatric department's annual summer party. She has added to her identity by becoming a songwriter, composer and performer. Laura is showing the world that she is much more than just a patient; on the contrary: much of her is not affected by cancer at all. Perhaps, for a while, her parents are worrying a little less too.

Below is an English translation of the lyrics of *Foreldresangen* ('Parents' Song') (Figure 16.1).

It isn't easy being a parent
Making sure that nothing breaks at home
Making sure that no one falls and hurts their knees
Oohhh, it isn't easy being a parent
Ooh- ooo- aaaah
But luckily, sometimes it's easy too
It isn't easy being a parent
Making sure that no one eats sweets on a weekday
Making sure, no one's running away from home
When the children are behaving
It makes the parents happy
That is when it is easy to be a parent.

Foreldresangen

(parents' song)

Figure 16.1 The music and lyrics to Foreldresangen ('Parents' Song')

Conclusion: A more flexible interpretation of the music therapist's role

'Professionalism' is used as a word of honour to characterise desired qualities of music therapists' conduct and ethical concerns in relation to their clients, colleagues, the public and, not least, the interdisciplinary team. It has taken us some years of hard work, however, to be accepted as a professional discipline in the medical world. A medical superintendent often greeted the music therapist by saying, 'I notice you always have fun here!' More fun than the paediatricians? The music therapist was wondering, 'Would a more solemn look perhaps be helpful in gaining status and respect at the university hospital?' This theme is actually a concern for some music therapists who state that they simply do not want to work with ad hoc groups or with anything entertainment-like, nor to be observed by colleagues outside the music therapy office or individual patient rooms; they are seemingly afraid of losing their professional image in the open spaces (Aasgaard 2004, p.154).

A music therapist working with children and their families in a big medical hospital, especially if she or he also chooses to be present and initiate activities in the public spaces, must be ready to be called an entertainer, a music teacher or someone's musical pal, as often as a professional music therapist. Music therapy is still a young profession which is far from taken for granted in many paediatric departments, and the music therapists themselves are responsible for constantly looking for good tools for sharing knowledge and information as well as initiating new arenas for interdisciplinary projects. But we are lucky: our music is also our strongest force – a powerful means of communication affording an array of meaningful experiences. We have used the 'bridge' metaphor several times in this chapter to demonstrate means of connecting staff, wards, patients and parents, and of assisting our young patients across obstacles towards more enjoyable lives and contact with the outside world. One particular quality of a bridge is that it is open at both ends; you may walk alongside another person, you can lead the way or you may be the one who follows; these are among the shifting positions of any music therapist working in a paediatric department.

References

Aasgaard, T. (1999) 'Music Therapy as Milieu in the Hospice and Paediatric Oncology Ward.' In D. Aldridge (ed) *Music Therapy in Palliative Care: New Voices*. London: Jessica Kingsley Publishers.

Aasgaard, T. (2002) 'Song Creations by Children with Cancer: Process and Meaning'. Doctoral dissertation, Institute of Music and Music Therapy, Aalborg University, Denmark. Available at http://vbn.aau.dk/files/195251818/trygve_aasgaard_thesis_150909.pdf, accessed on 5 January 2016.

Aasgaard, T. (2004) 'A Pied Piper Among White Coats and Infusion Pumps.' In G. Ansdell and M. Pavlicevic (eds) *Community Music Therapy: International Initiatives*. London: Jessica Kingsley Publishers.

Aasgaard, T. (2006) 'Musikk i Helsefag: Fysioterapi, Ergoterapi og Sykepleie' [Music in Health Sciences: Physiotherapy, Occupational Therapy and Nursing]. In T. Aasgaard (ed) *Musikk og Helse*. Oslo: Cappelen Akademisk.

Ærø, S.C.B. and Aasgaard, T. (2011) 'Musikkterapeut på en Sykehusavdeling for Barn: Helsefremmende Arbeid for både Pasient og Miljø' [Music Therapist in a Paediatric Department: Health Promoting Activities for Patients and the Hospital Milieu]. In K. Stensæth and L.O. Bonde (eds) *Musikk, Helse, Identitet*. Oslo: NMH-publikasjoner.

Berríos-Rivera, R., Rivero-Vergne, A. and Romero, I. (2008) 'The pediatric cancer hospitalization experience: reality co-constructed.' *Journal of Pediatric Oncology Nursing 25*, 6, 340–353.

Bower, J. and Shoemark, H. (2012) 'Music therapy for the pediatric patient experiencing agitation during posttraumatic amnesia: constructing a foundation from theory.' *Music and Medicine 4*, 3, 146–152.

Bringager, H., Hellebostad, M., Sæter, R. and Mørk, A.C. (2014) *Barn med Kreft: En Medisinsk og Sykepleiefaglig Utfordring* [Children with Cancer: A Medical and Nursing Challenge]. Oslo: Gyldendal Akademisk.

Bruscia, K. (1998) *Defining Music Therapy* (2nd ed.). Gilsum, NH: Barcelona Publishers.

Ellis, D.S. and Brighouse, G. (1952) 'Effects of music on respiration and heart rate.' *The American Journal of Psychology 65*, 1, 39–47.

Franck, L.S., Wray, J., Gay, C., Dearmun, A.K., Lee, K. and Cooper, B.A. (2015) 'Predictors of parent post-traumatic stress symptoms after child hospitalization on general pediatric wards: a prospective cohort study.' *International Journal of Nursing Studies 52*, 10–21.

Hartling, L., Newton, A.S., Liang, Y., Jou, H. *et al.* (2013) 'Music to reduce pain and distress in the pediatric emergency department: a randomized clinical trial (report).' *JAMA Pediatrics 167*, 9, 826.

Hilliard, R.E. (2006) 'Music therapy in pediatric oncology: a review of the literature.' *Journal of the Society for Integrative Oncology 4*, 2, 75–78.

Kim, J.-S., Park, J., Foster, R.L. and Tavakoli, A. (2014) 'Psychometric validation of emotional reaction instrument-English to measure American children's emotional responses to hospitalization.' *Journal of Clinical Nursing 23*, 1541–1551.

Kim, S. (1983) *The Nature of Theoretical Nursing*. Englewood Cliffs, NJ: Prentice-Hall.

Klassen, J.A., Liang, Y., Tjosvold, L., Klassen, T.P. and Hartling, L. (2008) 'Music for pain and anxiety in children undergoing medical procedures: a systematic review of randomized controlled trials.' *Ambulatory Pediatrics 8*, 2, 117–128.

Live Music Now (2015a) *2014–2015 Annual Trustees Report and Audited Accounts*. Available at www.livemusicnow.org.uk/accounts, accessed on 5 January 2016.

Live Music Now (2015b) *Newsletter, Friday 27 February.* Available at www.livemusicnow. org.uk/lmn_news/item/68902/date/2015-02-27/title/ground_breaking_new_ music_residency_at_alder_hey_children_s_hospital, accessed on 5 January 2016.

Loewy, J. (2001) 'Building bridges in team centred care.' *The Australian Journal of Music Therapy 12,* 3–12.

Longhi, E., Pickett, N. and Hargreaves, D. (2013) 'Wellbeing and hospitalized children: can music help?' *Psychology of Music 43,* 2, 188–196.

Muscara, F., McCarthy, M.C., Woolf, C., Hearps, S.J.C., Burke, K. and Anderson, V.A. (2015) 'Early psychological reactions in parents of children with a life threatening illness within a pediatric hospital setting.' *European Psychiatry 30,* 555–561.

Neville, K.L. (2005) 'The Impact of Cancer on Adolescents and Their Families.' In T.O.B. Eden, R.D. Barr, A. Bleyer and M. Whiteson (eds) *Cancer and the Adolescent* (2nd ed.). Malden, MA: Blackwell Publishing.

Nightingale, F. (1969) *Notes on Nursing: What It Is, and What It Is Not.* New York, NY: Dover Books. (Original work published in 1859.)

O'Callaghan, C. and Aasgaard, T. (2012) 'Art Therapies Including Music Therapies.' In A. Längler, P.J. Mansky and G. Sifert (eds) *Integrative Pediatric Oncology.* New York, NY: Springer.

Ruud, E. (2004) 'Foreword: Reclaiming Music.' In G. Ansdell and M. Pavlicevic (eds) *Community Music Therapy: International Initiatives.* London: Jessica Kingsley Publishers.

Small, C. (1998) *Musicking.* Hanover, NH: Wesleyan University Press.

Williams, P., Williams, K. and Williams, A. (2014) 'Parental caregiving of children with cancer and family impact, economic burden: nursing perspectives.' *Issues in Comprehensive Pediatric Nursing 37,* 1, 39–60.

Chapter 17

Someone Else in the Room: Welcome or Unwelcome?

An Attachment Perspective

Eleanor Richards

CASE EXAMPLE: TOM, STEPH AND PAULA

A music therapist, Steph, seated at the piano, is working with Tom, who is 17 years old. Tom has profound and multiple disabilities and uses a wheelchair; he has no speech but occasionally vocalises. Because of his disability, he looks younger than his age. He does not use any instruments. Also in the room is Paula, a teaching assistant, who is present in case she is needed to attend to Tom during one of his occasional seizures. She normally sits quietly at a short distance from him and watches him intently, but she takes no active part in the session. Steph plays the piano and sings to Tom warmly and gently for a while. When she finds little active response, she moves a set of wind chimes close to one side of his chair, and although she encourages him, showing him what they sound like, he makes no move towards them. Suddenly Paula stands up and moves the chimes to the other side (her side) of Tom's chair and also encourages him to play. Steph responds by fetching a new instrument, a set of bells on a stand, and placing it where the wind chimes had been. There is now a symmetrical tableau with Tom at the centre, an instrument on either side of him and a female attendant beside each instrument. Tom reacts to this new situation with extremely agitated bodily rocking and high-pitched shouts.

One way or another, our attachments are always with us. In this chapter I consider this case example in terms of the issues that arise from it with regard to attachment, looking in particular at three areas of the therapist's experience: attachment to the patient, attachment to a preferred approach and attachment to theory.

Attachment theory

Since the emergence of the object relations school of psychoanalysis and subsequently the remarkable work of John Bowlby in the UK in the mid twentieth century, the significance and moment-by-moment implications of our relationships, past and present, internalised and not always consciously recalled, have been widely recognised.

> Bowlby...saw relationships as central from the start of life and strongly disagreed with the prevailing psychoanalytic view at the time of the infant as an 'autistic', unsocialised, self-absorbed creature, only gradually and with great difficulty learning about and accepting the existence of its fellow creatures. (Holmes 1996, p.205)

Here is Bowlby himself:

> What for convenience I am terming attachment theory is a way of conceptualising the propensity of human beings to make strong affectional bonds to particular others and of explaining the many forms of emotional distress and personality disturbance, including anxiety, anger, depression and emotional detachment, to which unwilling separation and loss give rise. (Bowlby 1973, p.44)

Bowlby also suggests that our sense of ourselves is articulated through the unconscious construction of what he called 'internal working models' through which we try to establish some unchanging, predictable patterns of how our life in relation to others will go. We derive these models from an accumulation of relational experiences, starting from the first moments of life. The term 'model' may sound a little mechanistic, but it also carries the implication that it is open to adaptation and change.

> Each individual builds working models of the world and of himself in it, with the aid of which he perceives events, forecasts the future, and constructs his plans. In the working model of the world that anyone builds, a key feature is his notion of who his attachment figures are, where they may be found, and how they may be expected to respond. Similarly, in the working model of the self that anyone builds, a key feature is his notion of how acceptable or unacceptable he himself is in the eyes of his attachment figures. (Bowlby 1973, p.203)

Many accounts of psychoanalytic theory share the view that recognition of anxiety and the defences that it may bring is central to our understanding of personality. In attachment terms, that anxiety is primarily related to fear of loss and thus to greater insecurity. That includes not only loss of human attachment figures, but equally loss of the frameworks, inner and outer, which give us a sense of who we are and where we stand in the world.

Attachment to the patient

In returning to our case example, that small episode, which lasted no more than a minute or two, raises issues on a number of levels related to attachment. I learned about it in my role as Steph's clinical supervisor; she described the events to me and found herself surprised by her strength of feeling in recalling them. I later saw the session on video.

So what happens if we look at this episode in terms of the ways in which existing attachment patterns are being played out, the ways in which they are challenged or disturbed by events, and the defences that may arise in consequence? When she started therapy with Tom, Steph, who was recently qualified, had had no experience of working with a carer in the room, but because she was anxious about Tom's epilepsy, she welcomed Paula's presence without very much reflection. But when Paula moved the wind chimes and started actively to encourage Tom, Steph felt what she recalled as 'a sudden surge of panic and irritation'.

She realised that her own feelings towards Tom, with whom she had been working for only 2 months at that stage, were warm and protective. She was moved by his fragility and always delighted when he looked up into her face or seemed to respond with pleasure to the music she offered. She began to value these small moments of connection within sessions in which Tom much more often appeared listless and remote. In supervision she spoke of how easily she could see him as a small child, full of needs, but also full of developmental potential. She also spoke of her deep conviction of the value of music as a therapeutic medium, and her pleasure in seeking to find 'the right sound at the right moment'.

Attachment-based thinking in therapy emphasises the two-directional nature of the working relationship in which the process of change may move in both directions.

> This has its model in early relating: as the child grows up, she may find security not only from learning that she has access to her carer's attentive and would-be empathic responses to her feelings, but also from the realisation that she is able to offer something of the same kind in return, and that it is that mutuality which allows for growth and new experience. Her repertoire widens and changes, and so does her carer's. Security comes not simply from feeling safe in the hands

of the stronger 'other', but more maturely from the recognition that partners in a relationship may sustain one another on equal terms, albeit in different ways. (Richards 2014, p.107)

In earlier discussions of her feelings about Paula's presence in the sessions (before the events described), Steph had said that if there had to be someone else in the room, Paula was ideal because she sat still and stayed quiet, and Steph could 'easily forget that she was there'. In due course we began to wonder whether Steph was in fact much more ambivalent about Paula and her potential for intrusion into the intimacy of the developing two-person process between Steph and Tom – easier, perhaps, to make her invisible and forgettable.

It seemed that Steph was strongly attached to two important elements in the work. First, she valued the developing relationship between Tom and herself. She spoke warmly in supervision about feeling that she was beginning more and more to perceive and respond to small gestures and reactions from him. Second, she felt that she was learning much about being a music therapist from the very fact of his relative reticence. She spoke of her pleasure in attending to his small sounds or to fluctuations in his breathing, and of how much she enjoyed what she believed to be moments of attunement through the music. She felt that she and Tom were gradually developing a shared repertoire and a way of expanding it together. All this is familiar territory:

> In providing the patient with a secure base from which to explore and express his thoughts and feelings the therapist's role is analogous to that of a mother who provides her child with a secure base from which to explore the world. (Bowlby 2005, p.140)

Just as mothers are (rightly) passionate about their children, this working relationship in therapy had for Steph an increasing feeling of intense two-person intimacy; at this stage, she had not begun to reflect on what might be the meaning of its deep importance for her in relation to her own attachment history. It is perhaps not surprising that she found it easier to become unaware of Paula's presence. When she could no longer forget it, because of Paula's intervention, she felt disturbed and angry. Her first response was shock: she and Tom had been intruded upon, as she experienced it, by a third person who herself knew Tom well and had a close working relationship with him at other times, of which Steph knew very little. Steph's rather competitive response, of immediately offering Tom another instrument, suggests the kind of straightforward rivalry that is a familiar dimension of triangular relationships. What was forgotten at that moment, however, was the potential impact of these actions upon Tom. He reacted with agitation and uncertainty, and the image on video of him flanked on either side by an instrument and an anxious professional represents clearly something of the confusion he may have felt and the emotional climate in the room. Here were two people, with both of whom he felt some security, now at odds with one another. To whom should he respond? Unable at that moment to find any security from another person, he resorted, in his rocking and shouting, to physically manifested patterns of solitary self-regulation; these were the kinds of behaviours which had brought about his referral to therapy in the first place.

We might speculate that Paula also felt a strong attachment to Tom. Whatever the nature of that, her intervention at that point might have come out of a genuine wish for him to be active and play, or a wish to outdo Steph in gaining his responsiveness, or simply from the fact that her tolerance of being the 'extra' person in the room had run out. All this serves as a reminder that management of the role of the third person in the room is far from straightforward.

The therapist's sense of the nature of her involvement in the work is all-important. It has to do with more than awareness of transference and countertransference perceptions and the clinical insights they may offer. In the relational model of working which is implicit in co-improvising music therapy, both participants are open to change and development; for that to be possible for the therapist, she must seek to bring together those various elements of herself, personal and professional, that may not always easily acknowledge one another, and in particular those aspects of experience which are difficult to accommodate. For Steph, her assurance in improvising with, and for, Tom, and her growing sense of her capacity to perceive and respond to his gestures, felt satisfying and valuable. It was much harder for her to acknowledge such things as her uncertainties about her therapeutic skills, her dependence upon the intimacy of her relationship with Tom and her desire to defend it from intrusion. 'Therapists…have to accomplish some deep internal processing before they can perceive in all simplicity what is going on inside them in the encounter with the patient in an analytic session' (Quinodoz *et al.* 2006, p.344).

Attachment to a way of working

There is also the question of Steph's attachment to a particular way of working and to the circumstances which led her to value it. At that stage she was recently qualified, and her experience of training had been predominantly exciting and inspiring. She had embarked on training with little direct knowledge of therapy practice. She found herself very drawn to all that she read and heard about boundaries, confidentiality and the intimacy of the two-person, relational model of practice. She was also excited by the thought of joining a professional community which included those who had trained her and others whom she admired. In supervision she spoke of having seen video of work with patients rather like Tom and described the sense of recognition she felt when she saw how other therapists approached such work. At the same time, her experience of training had brought quite ordinary disturbance and anxiety, and she had felt acutely aware of how often she found both clinical and theoretical material baffling and complex.

In her anxiety she found herself clinging to what she imagined to be correct procedures and methods of practice, which she had heard and read about in the course of her training and which seemed to her to offer at least some clarity in terms of what might be appropriate professional actions and boundaries. In the face of that, questioning and creative thought were less easy to find.

Attachment to theory

Theory can have many functions in the therapist's inner world. Main (2001) speaks of '…a certain kind of pleasure which comes, in part, from the replacement of feelings of helplessness in the face of a mysterious reality by feelings of power over it and competence at dealing with it' (p.2). Steph had found that her attention to boundaries and careful protection of the privacy of sessions brought her not only a sense of acting with proper professionalism, but also some emotional safety. She had also felt reassured by looking at music therapy literature which emphasised the capacity of profoundly disabled people to engage in intense one-to-one therapeutic activity.

We cannot suppose that we value ideas of any kind only for intellectual or logical reasons. Our attachments to them are much more emotionally rooted than that. Main (2001) puts it vividly:

The whole gamut of the feeling of which man [sic] is capable, from curiosity to loathing, from evangelism to competitiveness, always greets or becomes attached to ideas, areas of knowledge, theories, practices, and new facts. (p.4)

He also suggests that ideas or experiences which are unwelcome may have a blind eye turned to them, just as Steph tried to forget Paula's presence. He adds that if they are not ignored in that way, they may instead be swallowed but not digested (on some level Steph accepted Paula's presence but not its implications), so that sooner or later they need to be got rid of or, in mental terms, rejected without consideration. Steph's countermove with the set of bells has something of that.

If ideas or new moments of experience are pushed away or remain undigested in that way, they cannot be contemplated. Secure attachments, whether to people, ideas or identity, function as solid starting points from which it is possible to venture out to explore such new ideas or experiences, safe in the knowledge that they can be returned to at moments of anxiety, and that a central aspect of that return will be the opportunity to process and learn from what that exploration has brought. An outcome of that processing will be a shift in the relationship with the attachment object itself. A more anxious, dependent attachment, however, is one in which exploration feels more risky, and the object of attachment is used as an unchanging safe haven to provide protection from disturbance.

Among the greatest sources of anxiety is fear of loss. Steph felt security in her commitment to traditional guidelines about boundaries and confidentiality, and she took comfort from the knowledge that these guidelines had been promoted in her training. (Other approaches had been discussed, too, of course, but she found less interest in recalling them.) She also felt comfortable in the illusion that her relationship with Tom in the room was exclusive, in spite of Paula's presence. In due course she was confronted with a reality: Tom needed Paula in the room in the interests of his physical well-being. That reality collided with her own defensive need to work in a particular way. When her strategy of simply 'forgetting' Paula was rendered unworkable, she resorted to acting out by angrily introducing the bells. In that moment she could not reflect on her feelings; she simply needed to retaliate. Moments where the smooth process of therapy is disrupted, or the therapist's own satisfaction in her work feels threatened, may become moments where the patient is at risk of being on the receiving end of what Main (1957) has called 'primitive human behaviour disguised as treatment' (p.130). The chance was missed to work through it with Paula and Tom, modelling something about open, fluid communication; instead, she defended herself.

The role of professional training

There are implications here for training. The process of learning is itself one of potential loss: new ideas and approaches can only be engaged with if there is the intellectual and emotional space for them, and that means letting go of some fantasies and assumptions, and developing the courage to think openly and curiously. That depends on the student's development in other areas, of course.

> We can never be sure whether knowledge will form the basis of later initiative in thinking, learning and the growth of techniques, or whether thorough training, far from equipping the individual for independent work, will only increase dependence on the trainer and his or her appetite for further passive experience, and thus inhibit his or her own thinking. (Main 2001, p.5)

What Steph found difficult was to find a state of mind in which she could contemplate the reality of the situation – the necessity of having three people in the room – not as an impoverishment of her preferred ideal, but rather as a potentially interesting prospect which offered the chance to be imaginative and playful in exploring how it might best support the process of Tom's therapy and, by extension, widen her own thinking about approaches to clinical work. Anxiously attached children find it difficult to play; Steph's relationship with all that her training meant to her at that stage did not allow her to ask too many questions. These issues continue to face clinicians throughout professional life, and we go on needing to recognise the anxieties arising in the course of our work and to enjoy investigating them as openly as possible.

Attachment in music therapy

This is a book about music therapy, containing rich clinical material about work involving a wide range of patients and professionals.

Repeatedly it brings the reminder of the central part played by the music in the unfolding of clinical and interpersonal events. The experience of co-participating in music, improvised or not, may be one which brings to all those involved a sense, often outside conscious articulation, of the possibilities of inventive collaboration. There is plenty of existing evidence, outside the framework of this book, of the ways in which shared music-making can foster secure attachment. An example is to be found in the shared playing in analytically informed group work in music therapy which may be a means towards more attentive and deeper communication.

The question of the place of assistants in therapy sessions, and the fact that some therapists do not find such situations straightforward, has hitherto been much less readily addressed. This book demonstrates, from a range of perspectives, the ways in which clinical work may be enhanced by the presence of others, whether professional or non-professional, not simply through supporting patients in participation but in much broader and often less obvious ways.

Ming Hung Hsu, in his discussion of music therapy in care homes (see Chapter 7), writes of 'embedding music therapy in care practice'. That implies not simply that care staff may take some techniques out of the therapy room into other places, but that the spirit of the (music) therapeutic encounter may flourish in carers' dealings with residents. He adds, however, that this is a continuing developmental enterprise and that '...ongoing support should be available to help resolve difficulties and evaluate effectiveness'.

Anthi Agrotou also points to the value of music therapy participation in the personal development of carers, and the corresponding value of that for patients (see Chapter 8): 'The reduction of their carers' shame in exploring a new medium without previous knowledge brought the reduction of the patients' shame in doing the same.' That speaks clearly of the function of music in the emergence of an increasingly creative flexible group in which patients, care staff and the therapist together found the capacity to take on new knowledge through aesthetic pleasure in the music and in the process itself.

Tessa Watson echoes that in her account of the need for staff to have a space to consider experience (see Chapter 9). In a supportive atmosphere, in which they could begin to feel more secure with one another in their responses and speculations, staff and therapist were able to let go of some assumptions and anxieties about themselves and their patients (in Bowlby's terms, to adapt some of the limiting aspects of their internal working models) and so to go more boldly about the business of exploration.

Whether or not the role of attachment is spelled out or explored in individual chapters, this book illustrates that whereas decisions which unwittingly undermine the attachment relationships of client, assistant or therapist may threaten or blight the therapeutic enterprise, work which builds up secure attachments and exploits the opportunities they offer can lead to positive development and change.

References

Bowlby, J. (1973) *Separation*. London: Tavistock Press.

Bowlby, J. (2005) *A Secure Base*. London: Routledge. (Original work published in 1988.)

Holmes, J. (1996) *Attachment, Intimacy, Autonomy: Using Attachment Theory in Adult Psychotherapy*. Northvale, NJ: Aronson.

Main, T.F. (1957) 'The ailment.' *British Journal of Medical Psychology 30*, 3, 129–145.

Main, T.F. (2001) 'Knowledge, Learning and Freedom from Thought.' In L. Day and P. Pringle (eds) *Reflective Enquiry into Therapeutic Institutions*. London: Karnac.

Quinodoz, D., Aubry, C., Bonard, O., Déjussel, G. and Reith, B. (2006) 'Being a psychoanalyst: an everyday audacity.' *International Journal of Psychoanalysis 87*, 329–347.

Richards, E. (2014) 'Music, Attachment and the Group: Mainly Theory.' In A. Davies, E. Richards and N. Barwick (eds) *Group Music Therapy: A Group Analytic Approach*. London: Routledge.

Chapter 18

Valuing Human Resources

Training, Service Development, Research: The Way Forward

John Strange, Helen Odell-Miller and Eleanor Richards

Introduction

In this book we have surveyed a wide and diverse variety of situations in which assistance and collaboration in music therapy occurs, but the topic has by no means been exhausted. Our aim has been to demonstrate the important contribution which assistants and collaborators can make to music therapy. Some chapters have explored music therapy models and approaches where the role of an assistant or collaborator is fundamental, but we have also seen that where the role is perhaps less fundamental, or even unorthodox, it may nevertheless be highly beneficial.

We have not attempted to estimate the relative prevalence of work with and without assistants and collaborators, nor to draw comparisons between the work presented and other work with comparable client groups not involving assistants and collaborators. Clearly the approach which a music therapist working single-handed would take with the same clients would be very different, but we in no way wish to suggest that it would necessarily be inferior, or that a therapist working alone is at a disadvantage. However, to treat single-handed working as the norm risks marginalising collaborative work, for example, by failing, in workforce planning and skills development, to allow for it as a possibility.

We included only chapters featuring work with assistants or collaborators because such work has received less attention in the literature than its prevalence merits. This deficiency in the documentation of an extensive practical knowledge base is unfortunate for several reasons. First, it risks presenting a distorted picture of music therapy to those outside the profession. Second, it makes it hard for music therapy educators to point to models in the literature to guide trainee therapists who find themselves working collaboratively. Third, it makes it harder for qualified therapists to access information on collaborative approaches, with the result that they may fail to identify opportunities for such work when it might be clinically beneficial.

Several chapters describe work which was either genuinely without precedent or at least novel and pioneering from the point of view of the therapist concerned, and not reliant on existing literature. But for every therapist with the courage and insight to experiment and innovate, there may be several who, in their ethical concern to deliver safe and effective treatment, are more cautious. The development of the discipline of music therapy should not be left to the most adventurous. New initiatives can only be properly evaluated if they are adopted in a consistent manner by a substantial number of practitioners.

Equipping assistants and collaborators for their role

In some approaches with specific titles, for example 'Music and Attuned Movement Therapy' (Chapter 11), 'Music and Movement' (Chapter 12) and 'Triadic Support of Interaction by Improvisation' (Chapters 1 and 13), both the music therapist and the person(s) assisting or collaborating are expected to act in a very specific manner, involving new learning of the requisite skills. The proponents of these approaches do not, however, advocate formalising this new learning to create a specialist qualification. The role of the 'Interactive Music Maker' (Chapter 14) is a special case, where an accredited learning module was created to allow IMM practitioners to undertake safe and effective work autonomously, without direct oversight by a music therapist. However, a comparable 'musical carry over' beyond the therapy room is also a central aim of the work described in Chapter 4. In the case of the work described by Melhuish (Chapter 6), Hsu (Chapter 7), Agrotou (Chapter 8) and Watson (Chapter 9), what might be called a 'social carry over' is a central aim, as assistants and collaborators undergo a profound yet largely informal and experiential process of development.

A generic training?

If assistants and collaborators can become effective and safe exponents of many of the approaches described through practical mentoring on the job, would there be any value in creating a generic basic qualification upon which specialist skills could be built as required? This may seem a good idea, if the human and financial resources are available, but, at both the recruitment and the assessment stage, some who might have been effective assistants or collaborators in specific types of work would likely be excluded. It is, however, possible to lay down some general principles regarding training which will not risk replacing the present healthy diversity with a sterile uniformity. The first of these principles is that, whatever training is felt to be necessary in a particular case, quality is more important than quantity. The second principle is that the training music therapist needs time to assess the existing knowledge and skills of potential assistants, devise a training programme to correct any deficiencies, evaluate the learning achieved and modify her input accordingly. The third principle is that resources and a budget should be set aside for the therapist or therapy team to develop the training. Without this, time allocated for the assistants to receive training will be time wasted.

Provided assistants are adequately equipped for their role, in the ways described in many of the preceding chapters, the interest of patients will not be put at risk by involving in their therapy staff who are not subject to the statutory regulation governing professional music therapists. Apart from family members, whose involvement in music therapy is described by Kaenampornpan (Chapter 4), Strange, Fearn and O'Connor (Chapter 11) and Leinebø and Aasgaard (Chapter 16), those assisting or collaborating with the therapist in all other models described are already under contract in some other capacity (in a few cases it might be a volunteer's contract) and, as such, they are subject to both a selection process and enforceable codes of conduct. Some may also be under statutory regulation as members of another profession. In these circumstances, prescribing an additional formal qualification or registration as a pre-condition of assisting or collaborating in music therapy would be counterproductive. The workforce available for this important role might well shrink to include only those with the time, financial resources and academic ability to qualify and register.

Equipping music therapists for work with assistants and collaborators

Professional training in music therapy operates within financial constraints. It cannot price itself out of the market. Music therapy is not a conspicuously highly paid or even a secure profession, so tuition fees are unlikely to be seen as investment in the future. In the UK a small number of limited grants to support trainees are offered by charitable trusts, but no public money is allocated centrally for fees, although locally universities use public funds to resource MA programmes. Younger candidates are likely to have heavy student debts from their previous undergraduate course, and 'mature' candidates may have to sacrifice paid work to make time for study. There is, therefore, pressure to limit fees, which means limiting teaching hours. Masters-level courses rightly lay greater emphasis on self-directed study and research than do undergraduate courses, but this does not remove the need for taught elements of the training to provide a theoretical and practical basis for clinical work. It is the case, in trainings where supervision groups are run throughout the student's casework experience, that universities are already covering the issues laid out in this book to some degree, as most students at some point work with assistants in the room. In fact, this dynamic is often the focus of material in trainee supervision. However, we suggest that a module devoted specifically to working with assistants and collaborators, including questions about how to work with other professionals generally, in the therapy room and outside, would help to remedy a deficiency some students currently find in their training when they enter the workforce. We also recommend that attention be paid to this area in planning students' clinical placements, with at least one being in a situation where collaborative working is likely.

The question of whether or not to work with assistants present is not emotionally neutral; it is not simply a matter of deciding which approach will most benefit the patient. The presence of others beyond the immediate therapeutic relationship inevitably compounds the complexity of the dynamics in the room, and insufficient attention to that may put the therapy process at risk. A key aspect of training should be to encourage and enable students to find the security to look openly and with curiosity at their feelings in response to others; that may mean anything from awareness of rivalry or of a fear of being judged, to gratitude and pleasure in collaboration.

The additional cost of employing assistants and collaborators

Budgetary constraints have always worked against labour-intensive health interventions and will continue to do so. Situations in which a labour-intensive solution is found financially acceptable tend to be time-limited – a few hours in the operating theatre but not a few months in rehabilitation; at a multidisciplinary case conference but not when putting its decisions into action. Music therapy falls into the second category, being predominantly a medium- to long-term intervention. Is it sensible to advocate for the higher staff-to-patient ratio implicit in collaborative working if this can only be achieved by shortening the therapy?

There are, of course, situations in which, however long term the therapy, specific risks make therapy unsafe unless one or more professionals, in addition to the music therapist, can be permanently present, for example, in working with those with complex and critical medical needs or those presenting a high risk of injury to self or others, or of absconding. In these cases it may be possible to involve these others more productively in the music therapy process in ways that do not obstruct the primary role they are present to perform. This involvement could be an active one, as in much of the work we have explored, or it may be one of monitoring, recording and feeding back, both to the therapist and the multidisciplinary team. In either case, if the additional person is recognised to have a dual role, their presence is less likely to be seen as unacceptably costly.

The involvement of assistants and collaborators does not inevitably incur extra costs. We have seen in Chapter 16 that even those others who are only intermittently and briefly present, either in the course of their professional duties or as family members, may enhance music therapy if they are involved in simple ways, rather than being regarded simply as an annoying distraction for the therapist. Where the patient is undergoing a painful or stressful medical procedure or investigation, the music therapist themselves may seem to be the assistant or collaborator to the doctor or nurse, yet she or he is still a music therapist, and in relation to the music therapy the doctor or nurse is still a collaborator.

The role of research

Ultimately, the additional cost of most collaborative working must be justified by clinical outcomes. However, establishing the conditions for credible quantitative research into collaborative approaches is made more difficult by the expectation that the role of the assistant or collaborator as well as that of the music therapist be defined or even manualised. Moreover, to demonstrate the added value of assistants and collaborators, one would need comparable single-handed work as a control. However, as already noted, therapists working single-handed are likely to modify their approach accordingly. To attempt to replicate the collaborative approach without collaborators would be an unfair comparison and would not be in the clients' best interests.

These problems faced by quantitative research in this area highlight the value of qualitative research, even research such as that described in Chapters 1 and 13 where clinical outcomes beyond what can be immediately observed happening in the therapy room are not the focus. Detailed, credible, vivid and convincing descriptions of work with a particular collaborative approach can make it clear to the discerning reader that the assistants and collaborators are indispensable. Incorporating the views of service users, and particularly of the assistants and collaborators themselves, gives added weight to the benefits claimed by the therapist-researcher. A particularly compelling case is made by assistants' and collaborators' own testimony to ongoing enhancement of their skills, understanding and capacity to support clients beyond the therapy room.

As well as formal research, there is a need for more description and discussion of collaborative approaches in journal articles, conference presentations and the media. This could not only raise the profile of the work, as we hope this book will do, but also inspire others to explore the field in greater depth in writing and stimulate lively discussion, for which burgeoning social media now provide unprecedented scope.

Appendix

Guidelines for working in music therapy sessions with non-music therapists (Chapter 2)

Ensuring that staff have a basic understanding of music therapy
The biggest problem for music therapists appears to be the fact that people usually have many misconceptions and misunderstandings about music therapy. It is necessary to explain, for example, that music therapy is client led, that it is not just about having fun and that it is acceptable for *all* emotions to be expressed. Music therapists should remember that the different boundaries and expectations between the therapy room and other settings can be confusing, and staff will need some explanations.

If starting work in a new venue, consider arranging a brief presentation about music therapy, including video footage (if possible). Encourage discussion and find a common language for talking about music therapy work. Describe a range of tasks and roles support staff may be required to undertake. Give examples of good and not-so-good practice, for example the difference between taking a child's arm, making them play and 'hand-over-hand support' (Nordoff, Robbins and Marcus 2007, pp.276–277) to enable clients with physical restrictions to play, if this is their intention. Let staff know that there is no right or wrong way for clients to play instruments. Follow presentations with an experiential session. If possible, allow staff an opportunity to say if they *really* feel they do not wish to be involved in supporting music therapy.

Written guidance
Consider writing a basic information sheet for staff if there is to be a high staff turnover in sessions. It is likely that there will need to be a different information sheet specific to each venue.

Communication

Constant communication and liaison is vital, even if time is very limited. Affirm the value of all staff in therapy. Review and plan together on a weekly basis, if possible.

Learning from assistants

Use assistants' insight and knowledge about clients' history and day-to-day lives to inform the work where appropriate. This can give an added perspective and provide a more rounded picture of the client.

The spectrum of roles

Understand the spectrum of roles which staff may take on (see Figure 2.2): from being an observer, to an assistant, to a co-therapist, depending on the staff member's level of training, understanding and experience, the amount of time the music therapist has for joint working and, most importantly, the needs of clients. Staff appear to feel more confident if they are aware of what their role and task are to be. At the same time, flexibility is needed by both therapist and assistant, as roles can evolve over time. Indeed, in the course of one session, the assistant may be at times quietly watching and at other times participating in music-making. Reassure them that they will be guided by the music therapist. The therapist must accept responsibility for what happens in sessions.

The effect of assistants' presence

Be aware of inevitable changes to the therapeutic process due to another person being in the therapy room, but remember that this can be a very positive way of working, particularly for clients with autism, for clients with severe physical restrictions or profound needs and perhaps for very young clients. Assistants can be invaluable for practical help in group work.

Boundaries and confidentiality

Think carefully about boundaries and matters of confidentiality. For example, when working with clients who have experienced abuse, it will probably be necessary to insist on being supported by the same member of staff in order for the work to progress. Ensure that staff are fully cognisant about the confidentiality of sessions.

Assistant behaviour

Stress the importance to staff of being attentive at all times; just witnessing what the client is doing can contribute positively to the session. Even obvious points, such as avoiding interrupting sessions, are worth stating (gently). Encourage staff to play and sing when asked to do so – they are the role models for clients. Reassure staff that music therapy is not necessarily about singing in tune and playing the 'right' notes.

Interpersonal dynamics

Consider the dynamics which arise between yourself and the assistant. Sometimes assistants can feel envious of the new positive behaviours of clients seen in sessions or about the privilege music therapists have to work on a one-to-one basis. Equally, it has been found that therapists themselves can feel under scrutiny to prove the effectiveness of their work when they have an assistant in sessions. It is important to acknowledge and work through such issues, perhaps in supervision.

Reference

Nordoff, P., Robbins, C. and Marcus, D. (2007) *Creative Music Therapy: A Guide to Fostering Clinical Musicianship* (2nd ed.). Gilsum, NH: Barcelona Publishers.

Contributors

Trygve Aasgaard has established music therapy services in Norwegian paediatric oncology departments and in hospice care. His doctoral research investigated musicking with very sick young patients, their parents and hospital staff from a role-focused perspective. His special interests include music in medicine, nursing, physiotherapy and occupational therapy, practice and research. Prof Aasgaard has contributed chapters on case study research, songwriting, palliative music therapy and community music therapy to four previous compilations from Jessica Kingsley Publishers and co-authored chapters in *Integrative Pediatric Oncology* (Springer, 2012), *Oxford Textbook of Palliative Care for Children* (Oxford University Press, 2012) and *Oxford Handbook of Music Therapy* (Oxford University Press, 2015).

Anthi Agrotou qualified as a music therapist from the University of Roehampton[1] in 1987 and received her doctorate from the University of Sheffield in 1998. She is a registered supervisor of the European Music Therapy Confederation. Anthi has specialised in the psychodynamic use of music in treating people with learning disabilities and/or autism. Music therapy publications include a chapter in *Music Therapy in Health and Education* (Jessica Kingsley Publishers, 1993) and the multimedia documentary *Sounds and Meaning*, referenced in Chapter 8 of the present book. She is Professor of Music Therapy at the Arte Musical Academy in Nicosia, Cyprus, and sits on the Advisory Editorial Board of the online journal *Approaches: Music Therapy and Special Music Education*. Anthi has a private practice as a psychodynamic music therapist.

Jörg Fachner trained as a social scientist and graduated as an educationalist (M.S.Ed.) researching Nordoff Robbins Music Therapy.

---

1   For consistency, we have used this institution's current name throughout the section. Up until 2000 it was the Roehampton Institute of Higher Education, and from then until 2004, the University of Surrey Roehampton.

He has performed and recorded widely as a guitarist, singer and bağlama player. As an educationalist he has specialised in the use of music therapy as a treatment for clients with behavioural disorders in school and community settings. In 2001 he received his doctorate in medical science in Germany for a study of changes in neural correlates of consciousness during music perception. His research into states of consciousness, time perception, music therapy processes and the treatment of depression has been published in journals and books across the disciplines. Publications include music therapy conference proceedings and two co-edited books for Jessica Kingsley Publishers, *Music and Altered States* (2006) and *Music Therapy and Addictions* (2010). He was appointed in 2013 to the newly created post of Professor for Music, Health and the Brain at Anglia Ruskin University, Cambridge.

Mary-Clare Fearn qualified as a music therapist from the University of Roehampton in 1990 and has worked with a broad range of adults and children, both in education and the UK National Health Service. She is currently working in Dorset with children and young adults who have profound and multiple learning disabilities. She is particularly interested in working with other disciplines and has co-run many groups with a number of different professionals. This work has been presented at national and international conferences and in some cases published. Mary-Clare is a visiting lecturer on the MA professional programme at the University of Roehampton, a registered supervisor and a member of the British Association for Music Therapy's Supervision and Continuing Professional Development panels.

Sarah Hadley graduated in Music and Education from Christ Church College, Canterbury, and as a music therapist in 1986 from Nordoff Robbins, London. Sarah is the head music therapist at Oxleas NHS Foundation Trust and has nearly 30 years of experience as a clinician within the UK National Health Service and a 15-year involvement with the charity Music as Therapy International, which has demonstrated the benefits of delivering services in community settings, as opposed to clinics.

Motoko Hayata qualified as a music therapist from Nordoff Robbins, London, in 1999. She has worked with children and adults with a variety of needs in many different settings, and headed the music therapy team at Soundscape, Newham Music Trust, where she was a clinical placement supervisor for MA students from the Guildhall School of Music and Drama. She has presented her work at conferences in the UK, Australia, Argentina and Japan.

Ming Hung Hsu heads the Music Therapy Department at Methodist Homes (MHA), a charitable organisation providing care, accommodation and support for older adults throughout the UK. He qualified as a music therapist from Anglia Ruskin University, Cambridge, in 2007 and has since qualified as a Dementia Care Mapping user. His extensive interest in dementia and neuroscience has led to completing his current PhD project, funded by MHA, at Anglia Ruskin University. His research involves a clinical trial incorporating psychophysiological measures to investigate the impact of music therapy on the health and care of people with dementia in care homes.

Pornpan Kaenampornpan is a lecturer at the faculty of Fine and Applied Arts, Khon Kaen University, Thailand. She trained as a music therapist at New Zealand School of Music and recently received a PhD in music therapy from Anglia Ruskin University, Cambridge. Her research topic related to the involvement of families in music therapy sessions with their children with special needs in the context of Thai culture.

Tone Leinebø graduated as a registered nurse in 2006 and, after a few years of working at a paediatric rheumatology ward, went on to study music therapy at the University of Queensland, graduating in 2011. She has always had a keen interest in music therapy in the paediatric setting and is currently working with children and adolescents with a wide range of diagnoses at Oslo University Hospital, Rikshospitalet.

Ruth Melhuish graduated from Bristol University with a degree in French and Italian, and went on to study music therapy at the University of Roehampton, qualifying in 1991. Since then she has worked as a music therapist in the UK National Health Service adult and older people's mental health services in Bradford on Avon, as well as schools, homes and centres for people of all ages. She has a special interest in the role of music therapy in dementia care, and has experience of research, evaluation and staff training in this field.

Hannah Munro graduated from Edinburgh University with a degree in history and qualified as a music therapist at Queen Margaret

University, Edinburgh, in 2008. She then worked freelance before taking a position with Nordoff Robbins Music Therapy in Scotland in 2012. Hannah works with a wide range of clients in different settings, including a children's hospice and a UK National Health Service adult hospice. She provides training and experiential workshops for non-music therapists in Scotland. Her MSc research explored the experiences of music therapists working with assistants in sessions.

Rebecca O'Connor qualified as a registered nurse before training as a music therapist at the University of Roehampton. She has 25 years of music therapy experience in health and education, including a period as lead music therapist at Chelsea and Westminster Hospital, where she established and developed the music therapy service. Rebecca has been a course tutor in the MA programme at the University of Roehampton and is currently a senior lecturer on several music therapy programmes in the UK and Ireland. She established the music therapy service at the National Rehabilitation Hospital, Dublin, and has a Masters in research methodology. Rebecca chairs the Irish Association of Creative Arts Therapists and has published and presented at national and international conferences.

Helen Odell-Miller is director of the Music for Health Research Centre at Anglia Ruskin University, Cambridge, and a professor of music therapy. Before joining Anglia Ruskin University in 1994, she worked as a music therapist in the UK National Health Service, latterly with adults with mental health problems including personality disorders and dementia. As a clinician, researcher and leader within the profession, she has developed approaches and techniques which are embedded in professional practice, such as using improvisation with people with dementia. She gained degrees at Nottingham University, City University and Aalborg University, Denmark, for her PhD, where she examines and supervises in the international PhD programme. She co-instigated the NHS career structure for music therapists in 1982. She sits on the Council for Allied Health Professions Research Strategy Board and the International Consortium for Research in the Arts Therapies. Helen has published and lectured widely, and has been a keynote speaker at several national and international conferences in Europe, Australia, Asia and the USA. She has co-edited the books *Supervision of Music Therapy* (Routledge, 2008) and *Forensic Music Therapy* (Jessica Kingsley Publishers, 2014). Her research areas include dementia; links between diagnoses and music therapy treatment approaches in adult mental health; music therapy and personality disorders; psychoanalytically informed music therapy; as well as arts therapies and mental health. In 2016 she was awarded an OBE (Officer of the Order of the British Empire) for services to music therapy. She is currently actively involved as a singer in Cambridge Voices.

Eleanor Richards qualified as a music therapist at the University of Roehampton in the early 1990s and subsequently as a UKCP-registered psychotherapist at the Bowlby Centre, London. She is now a psychotherapist and supervisor in private practice, and a senior lecturer in the MA programme in music therapy at Anglia Ruskin University, Cambridge. Until 2013 she was a senior music therapist in the Cambridgeshire and Peterborough NHS Foundation Trust, specialising in working with adults with learning disabilities and associated mental illness. She is joint author/editor of *Music Therapy and Groupwork: Sound Company* (2002), *Supervision of Music Therapy* (2008) and *Group Music Therapy: A Group Analytic Approach* (2014), all for Jessica Kingsley Publishers, and has contributed to a range of other publications and international conferences. She is involved in the development of music therapy training and practice in India. In her continuing musical life she is active as a player and improviser.

John Strange qualified as a music therapist at the University of Roehampton in 1986 and worked from 1986 to 2010 with children and adults with learning disabilities in the education and voluntary sectors, supervising music therapy trainees on placement throughout that period. Since 1995 he has provided expert evidence to the courts in over 25 medical injury cases. From 1995 to 1998 he was chair of the Association of Professional Music Therapists (UK) and a delegate to the European Music Therapy Confederation. From 2002 to 2004 he was external assessor in clinical improvisation in the Masters in Music Therapy programme in Aalborg, Denmark. He received his PhD in 2014 from Anglia Ruskin University, Cambridge. John has contributed chapters to two previous books from Jessica Kingsley Publishers.

Catherine Warner has over 20 years of experience as a music therapist and leads the MA Music Therapy and MA Music Therapeutic Studies programmes at the University of the West of England (UWE).

She gained her PhD for participatory action research using music therapy with people with learning disabilities, and she has a strong interest in research into how music therapy can promote mental health and well-being. She has a number of chapters in books published by Routledge and Jessica Kingsley Publishers. She works as a cellist and her current clinical practice includes a multifaith women's music therapy group. In her work as senior lecturer at UWE she is responsible for setting up and supervising a wide range of student placements across the UK and abroad.

Tessa Watson is a music therapist and trainer with over 20 years of experience in various clinical settings. Currently convenor of the MA Music Therapy programme at the University of Roehampton, Tessa also has a clinical post in a UK National Health Service community team for people with learning disabilities. Previous experience includes work with the elderly and in forensic and community mental health. Tessa holds several roles within the British Association for Music Therapy. She is co-editor of the *British Journal of Music Therapy*, an Allied Health Professions Clinical Expert and a Health and Care Professions Council partner. Publications include *Music Therapy with Adults with Learning Disabilities* (Routledge, 2007), *Integrated Team Working: Music Therapy as Part of Transdisciplinary and Collaborative Approaches* (with K. Twyford; Jessica Kingsley Publishers, 2008) and a chapter in the *Oxford Handbook of Music Therapy* (Oxford University Press, 2015).

Lyn Weekes (retired) was a qualified further-education teacher and physiotherapist. She was for many years physiotherapy manager of three hospitals within Horizon NHS Trust and the multidisciplinary child assessment centre at Harper House, Radlett, Hertfordshire, also working at Great Ormond Street Children's Hospital in the Rett syndrome unit. She first co-presented 'Music and Movement' with the late Professor Tony Wigram at the World Congress of Music Therapy in Paris in 1983.

Subject Index

adult mental health settings
   assistant role in therapy 94–6
   family role for staff 89–91
affect attunement 202, 248
   see also Music and Attuned
      Movement Therapy (MAMT)
assistants
   definition of 13–4
   training for 23–4, 315–6, 320
attachment theory
   assistant's attachment style 33–4
   overview of 304–5
   PMLD patients 150–1,
      162–3, 166, 180–1
   secure attachment 267–8, 307, 310
   therapist's attachment to patient 306–8
   therapist's attachment to theory 309–11
   therapist's attachment to way
      of working 309
attitude of co-therapist 191
attunement
   affect 202, 248
   see also Music and Attuned
      Movement Therapy (MAMT)
autistic children, musical interaction
   therapy 24–5
auxiliary music therapists (PMLD patients)
   attachment style of patient
      150–1, 162–3, 166
   case studies 148–50, 153–4,
      157–8, 160, 161, 163–5
   dynamic matrix of group
      151–3, 159–60, 165
   envy of patient ameliorated 161–2
   foundation matrix 151
   free-discussion group 155–7
   manic defences 155
   participants 146–8
   self-confidence of 156

benefits of assistance 43–4
boundaries 46–7, 97, 171, 206, 322
brain area/function 231

care homes *see* dementia patients
challenges
   inclusion group (special
      educational needs) 281–2
   learning support assistants
      (PMLD students) 23
   staff present in sessions 45, 50, 304–13
   trainee music therapists 59, 64, 67
children as helpers *see* inclusion group
   (special educational needs)
citizenship education 283
co-therapist in NRMT
   attitude of 191
   background to role 186–8
   experience required 187–8, 197
   mediator role 190–1
   methodology of research study 189–90
   as music therapist 195–7
   problem areas 191–2, 196–7
   relational quality 192–5
   responsibilities of 190
   role in other therapy settings 188–9
   scope of role 190–2
collaborative teamwork
   importance of 254
   Interactive Music Making 264–73
   Music Therapy Home Programme 257–62
   Music as Therapy International 262–4
   Oxleas Music Therapy Service 254–62
   transient and constant practitioners 256–8
confidentiality 46–7, 322
constant practitioner *see* collaborative teamwork
containment 172–3, 178–82
contraindications for including
   family members 77
cost factors 177, 318
countertransference 91, 93, 188, 204, 217

dance movement therapy (DMT)
   100–1, 103–5, 112–7
   see also Music and Attuned
      Movement Therapy (MAMT)
debriefing the assistant 97, 206
deformities, fixed *see* 'Music and
   Movement' programme

dementia patients
    care plans 134–5
    carer learning from therapists' skills
        107–10, 115, 125–6, 131–2
    carer role around the therapy
        92–7, 132–40
    carer rotas/routines 113, 114, 121
    carer training 124–5
    distraction techniques 129
    emotion regulation 105–7,
        129–31, 136, 139–40
    emotional connections with
        staff 110–1, 112, 138
    Methodist Homes (MHA) 126–8, 133
    Music Therapy and Dementia Care in the
        21st Century conference 116, 117
    neuropsychiatric symptoms 121–2
    nursing home participants 101–2
    nursing home staff 102, 105–17
    person-centred approach 99
    psychosocial interventions 122
    referral for therapy 133–4
    research review 99–100, 112–7, 123–4
    skills of patient 105–7
    study procedure 102–4
    study results 105–11
difficulties
    inclusion group (special
        educational needs) 281–2
    learning support assistants
        (PMLD students) 23
    staff present in sessions 45, 50, 304–13
    trainee music therapists 59, 64, 67
dynamic matrix 151–3, 159–60, 165

economic factors 177, 318
education see inclusion group (special
    educational needs); learning
    support assistants (PMLD
    students); music education
ending the therapy 257

family members
    contraindications for inclusion 77
    influence of 75–6
    introducing music therapy to 78–9
    joining in session 79–80
    leading session 80–2
    mental health staff in role of 89–91
    Music Therapy Home Programme 257–62
    in paediatric hospital setting 287
    parents of PMLD children 178–9
    phases of developing relationship
        with 77–82
    primary carers 75
    research results 83–6

role in Thailand special
    education centres 71–2
subjects in Thailand research study 73
feedback/review to assistant 97, 206
financial factors 177, 318
fixed deformities see 'Music and
    Movement' programme
foundation matrix 151

gender differences 43

hierarchy of basic needs (Maslow) 74
history of music therapy in hospitals 289
hospitals
    history of music therapy in 289
    see also paediatric hospital setting

improvisational music therapy see triadic support
    of interaction by improvisation (TSII)
inclusion group (special educational needs)
    benefits of 278
    case studies 279–81
    challenges 281–2
    children in 277
    as citizenship education 283
    educational inclusion 275–6
    overview of 277
Interaction Guidance (McDonough) 26
Interactive Music Making 264–73

knowledge of the client, assistant's 61
learning support assistants (PMLD students)
    analysis of transcripts 29
    difficulties experienced by 23
    self-confidence of 26
    themes agreed by 30–2
    using TSII (triadic support of interaction
        by improvisation) 23–9, 247–8
    video clip analysis 27–9, 240–7
    see also inclusion group (special
        educational needs); staff present
        in sessions; triadic support of
        interaction by improvisation (TSII)

mainstream children as helpers see inclusion
    group (special educational needs)
manic defences 155
mental health see adult mental health settings
Methodist Homes (MHA) 126–8, 133
mother-infant internal model 237–8
multicultural practice 63
Music and Attuned Movement
    Therapy (MAMT)
    case study (PMLD child) 207–19
    case study (rehabilitation) 223–5
    development of 200–2
    movement facilitator role 202–3, 205–20

observer role 222
occupational therapist perspective 224–5
physiotherapist perspective 224
relationship in 206–7, 220
sensing movement intention 204
used in rehabilitation 221–5
music education 282–3
music environmental therapy
 (paediatric setting) 288–92
'Music and Movement' programme
development of 227–9
helpers' role 232–3
music therapist role 231–2
patients 229–30, 233
physiotherapist role 230–1
Music Therapy Home Programme 257–62
Music as Therapy International 262–4
music therapy and sensory interaction
 group (PMLD patients)
care staff physiotherapy exercises 173–4
carers' support 179–82
containment in 172–3, 178–82
reassuring the care staff 176
session structure 171–7
Soundbeam 169, 170, 175–6
waiting important in 172, 174–5

narrative inquiry method 56–7
non-verbal children 75
Nordoff Robbins Music Therapy see
 co-therapist in NRMT

observer role 40–3, 222
occupational therapist perspective
 (MAMT) 224–5
othering of assistant 62, 64
Oxleas Music Therapy Service 254–62

paediatric hospital setting
case studies 294, 295, 298–300
effect on family 285–6
effect on patient 285
flexibility of music therapist in 287–8
'health' in context of 286–7
music environmental therapy in 288–92
music therapy influencing
 physiology 292–3
music therapy as procedural support 293–4
parents in 295–7
referral to music therapy 297–8
regular musical events in 291–2
specific aims of music therapy
 practices in 287
parents see family members
physiotherapists in MAMT 224
 see also 'Music and Movement' programme
placement see trainee music therapists
professional status 301

profound and multiple learning disabilities
 (PMLD) see auxiliary music therapists
 (PMLD patients); inclusion group
 (special educational needs); learning
 support assistants (PMLD students);
 Music and Attuned Movement Therapy
 (MAMT); Music therapy and sensory
 interaction group (PMLD patients)
projection 66, 162, 183
prosodic acoustic cues 138
psychosocial stages (Erikson) 74

rehabilitation MAMT 221–5
relationship
client centred approach 75
close assistant-patient 91–2
in co-therapist role (NRMT) 192–5
mother-infant internal model 237–8
in Music and Attuned Movement
 Therapy (MAMT) 206–7, 220
staff presence and client-therapist 45–7
 see also attachment theory
responsibility
of co-therapist (NRMT) 190
remains with therapist 40–2
review/feedback to assistant 97, 206

safeguarding role 43, 55
secure attachment 267–8, 307, 310
self-confidence of assistant 26, 156, 176
self-determination 30
self-expression 30
sensory interaction see music therapy
 and sensory interaction
 group (PMLD patients)
situation selection 129
Song Creations by Children with
 Cancer: Process and Meaning
 (research project) 296–7
Soundbeam 169, 170, 175–6
special educational needs see inclusion
 group (special educational needs)
staff present in sessions
as assistant 40–3
benefits of 43–4
challenges of 45, 50, 304–13
as co-therapist 40–3
methodology of study 38–9
as observer 40–3, 222
previous research 37–8, 48–50
spectrum of roles 40–3, 48
 see also learning support assistants (PMLD
  students); trainee music therapists
status of assistant 61–4
supervision
co-therapist role (NRMT) 193
placement 60

Thailand special education centres 71–2
trainee music therapists
    challenges in working with
        assistants 59, 64, 67
    narratives by 58–68
    placement practice variation 54–6
    placement supervision 60
    strategies to enhance experience of 68
    training to work with assistants 317
training for assistants 23–4, 315–6, 320
    see also collaborative teamwork

transference 66, 91, 181, 188
transient practitioner see collaborative teamwork
triadic support of interaction by
    improvisation (TSII)
    case studies 243–7
    learning support assistants (PMLD
        students) 23–9, 247–8
    overview of 236–7, 249–51
    theoretical model of 237–9

video clip analysis 27–9, 240–7

Author Index

Aalten, P. 121
Aasgaard, T. 287, 288, 289, 290, 291, 296, 301
Ærø, S.C.B. 287, 288
Agrotou, A. 146, 156, 181
Aigen, K. 28, 170, 236
Aldridge, D. 99
Allain, P. 131
Allgood, N. 37
Alvarez, A. 153, 172
Alvin, J. 48
Ansdell, G. 38
Arigo, D. 131
Aylward, S. 134
Ayres, A.J. 225

Babb, C. 178
Baker, S.B. 79
Ballard, C. 99
Banerjee, S. 124, 133
Bannerman-Haig, S. 203
Banse, R. 138
Barrington, A. 180
Bartram, P. 183
Bateson, M.C. 56
Beadle-Brown, J. 179
Bender, M. 115
Berríos-Rivera, R. 285
Bick, E. 171
Bignold, K. 49
Blaustein, M.E. 177
Bowe, L. 115
Bower, J. 288
Bowlby, J. 148, 150, 151, 180, 238, 267, 305, 307
Bradley, M.M. 131
Bradshaw, S.A. 112, 115
Brighouse, G. 292
Bright, R. 100
Bringager, H. 290
Brotons, M. 100, 112
Brown-Wilson, C. 112
Bruce, E. 112, 178, 179
Bruinsma, M.S. 100, 123
Bruscia, K.E. 9, 38, 236, 238, 239, 251, 286, 287

Bunce, L. 37
Burland, K. 170
Burton, N. 128

Carr, C. 94
Carter, E. 22, 37
Cerejeira, J. 122
Chadwick, P. 24, 43
Chaidaroon, S. 79
Chanda, M.L. 130
Clair, A. 99, 100, 112
Clandinin, D.J. 56
Clare, L. 112
Clegg, J. 182
Coaten, R. 99, 112
Cockerill, H. 259
Cohen, A.J. 237
Cohen, L.J. 75
Collins, J.M. 48
Collis, M.-A. 182
Connolly, F.M. 56
Cooke, M.L. 123
Cooper, C. 99, 122
Corcoran, M. 265

Daley, S. 112
Darnley-Smith, R.M.R. 236
Darsie, E. 48
Davies, A. 13, 48, 188, 202
Davies, S. 112, 114
Daykin, N. 56, 57
De Backer, J. 236
Department for Education 282
Department of Health 99, 115, 179
Dickson, K. 123
Douglas, S. 99
Dugmore, O. 122, 125
Durham, C. 22

Ebberts, A.G. 100, 112
Edwards, J. 14, 202
Elefant, C. 276
Ellis, D.S. 292
Elman, N. 84
Emmanuel, L. 178, 182
Erikson, E.H. 74
Evans, K. 182

Fachner, J. 187, 188, 189
Fearn, M.C. 27, 174, 188, 201, 202, 203, 225
Fetters, M.D. 28
Flower, C. 14
Flowers, P. 29
Fonagy, P. 172
Forster, L. 48
Foulkes, S.H. 151, 152, 157
Franck, L.S. 288, 296
Froggatt, K. 114
Fusar-Poli, P. 130

Ganzarain, R. 160
Garred, R. 236
Geddes, H. 267
Gerdner, L.A. 123
Geyer, M. 188
Gilbert, M.C. 182
Gitlin, L.N. 123
Gold, C. 235
Goleman, D. 283
Goyder, J. 124
Graham, J. 49
Grant, E. 90
Grocke, D. 228, 230, 231, 232
Gross, J.J. 129
Guba, G.E. 39
Guetin, S. 123
Guzmán-García, A. 100, 112

Hadley, S. 265
Haj, M. 131
Hargreaves, D. 288
Hartling, L. 294
Health Care Professions Council 115
Henry, S.G. 28
Hewett, D. 24, 170, 173, 225
Hill, H. 100
Hilliard, R.E. 287
Hills, B. 48, 50
Holck, U. 25, 89
Holmes, J. 77, 305
Hooper, J. 178, 235
Hope, K.W. 133
Hornby, G. 78
Howard, R. 122
Howe, D. 180
Hsu, M.H. 100, 121, 123, 131, 135
Huberman, A.M. 47
Hughes, J.C. 100

Jacobsen, S.L. 89
James, I. 99, 100, 112
Jarman, M. 105
John, D. 57, 58, 63, 65
Jónsdóttir, V. 179

Kaenampornpan, P. 71
Kales, H.C. 123
Karkou, V. 100, 170
Kim, J.-S. 285, 290
Kinniburgh, K.M. 177
Kitwood, T. 99, 115
Klassen, J.A. 293
Klein, M. 155, 159, 160
Koelsch, S. 131
Kowarzik, U. 100, 114
Krabs, R.U. 131
Kverno, K.S. 99

Lagarto, L. 122
Larkin, M. 29
Lauritzen, S.O. 99
Lawrence, V. 122, 125, 133, 139
Ledden, T. 198
Lee, C.A. 236, 237
Levinge, A. 202
Levitin, D.J. 131
Lincoln, Y.S. 39
Linington, M. 181
Live Music Now 289, 290
Livingston,. G. 122, 123, 124
Loewy, J. 292
Lonergan, E.C. 188
Longhi, E. 288, 296
Loth, H. 79, 84
Loveday, B. 115
Lovell, E. 170
Lyketsos, C.G. 123

McDermott, O. 100, 112, 114, 123
McKinney, C.H. 89
Magee, W.L. 170
Mahoney, E. 63
Main, T.F. 309, 311
Marcus, D. 48, 186, 187, 198, 249, 320
Margallo-Lana, M. 121
Marti, P. 100, 112
Maslow, A. 74
Meadows, A. 228, 229
Meekums, B. 100
Melhuish, R. 116
Meyer, J. 114
Miles, M.B. 47
Ministry of Education of Thailand 72
Molyneux, C. 78
Morrissey, J. 182
Moss, H. 100
Muir, E.E. 49
Mukaetova-Ladinska, E.B. 112, 122
Müller, P. 37
Munro, H. 15, 36, 39
Muscara, F. 296
Music, G. 174
Mutthesius, D. 188

Nash, S. 24, 43
National Institute for Health Care Excellence (NICE) 131, 137
Nelson, V. 188
Neuert, C. 188
Neville, K.L. 285
Newman-Bluestein, D. 99
Newton, D. 112
Nicholls, T. 24, 25, 37
Nickson, B. 178
Nightingale, F. 289
Nind, M. 24, 170, 225
Nordoff, P. 48, 49, 74, 186, 229, 249, 320
Norman, I. 48
Nowikas, S. 28, 50, 187
Nyström, K. 99

O'Callaghan, C. 287
O'Connor, R. 27, 174, 188, 198
Odell-Miller, H. 92, 94, 100, 123, 128
Olazarán, J. 123
Oldfield, A. 14, 22, 37, 73, 77, 82, 89
Orrell, M. 112, 122, 124, 125
Osborn, M. 105
Ottesen, A.M. 99, 123

Packer, T. 115
Patel, B. 122
Pavlicevic, M. 37, 38, 49, 100, 112, 202, 236
Payne, M. 262
Payutto, P.A. 73
Perry, M.R. 222
Phan, K.L. 129, 130, 131
Pickett, N. 288
Pinney, A. 270
Playford, E.D. 112
Polichroniadis, M. 77
Pongsaksri, A. 73
Postal, V. 131
Pourtois, G. 138
Powell, H. 100, 112
Pratomthong, S.J. 79
Priebe, S. 94
Procter, S. 37, 49

Quin, A. 16, 265
Quinodoz, D. 308

Rabins, P.V. 121
Raglio, A. 123
Ragneskog, H. 123
Rainey Perry, M.M. 78
Riazi, A. 112
Richards, E. 13, 48, 64, 68, 188, 307
Ridder, H.M. 99, 112, 123, 128
Riessman, C.K. 56
Ritchie, J. 36, 38

Rivero-Vergne, A. 285
Robbins, C. 48, 74, 186, 229, 249, 320
Robinson, L. 123
Robson, C. 39
Rogers, C.R. 75
Roller, B. 188
Roman, T. 181
Romero, I. 285
Rowlands, J. 112
Royal College of Nursing 178
Ruud, E. 236, 237, 289

Salimpoor, V.N. 131
Sanderson, P. 170
Saul, B. 49
Scherer, K.R. 138
Schmidt-Robyn, B. 15, 37, 49, 50
Scholten, R.J.P.M. 100, 123
Schore, A.N. 267
Schubert, E. 239
Schultz, C.L. 178, 179
Schwabe, C. 188
Seitz, D.P. 123
Sekeles, C. 222
Sharma, A. 259
Shoemark, H. 288
Shustik, L. 114
Simpson, D. 181
Sinason, V. 159, 162
Skårderud, F. 202, 248
Slade, M. 112
Small, C. 289
Smeijsters, H. 236
Smiley, E. 283
Smith, J.A. 29, 105
Smyth, J.M. 131
Snaedal, J. 123
Snape, D. 38
Solé, C. 123
Sorel, S.N. 74
Spector, A. 122, 124
Speedy, J. 57
Spencer, L. 38
Sripada, C.S. 129, 130, 131
Stember, M. 255
Stern, D. 25, 33, 175, 202, 225, 236, 237, 238, 248, 259
Stewart, D. 25
Stone, W.N. 188
Storey, J. 182
Strange, J. 15, 23, 24, 28, 37, 236, 241, 242, 283
Streeter, E. 217
Sung, H.C. 123
Sutton, J. 22, 175, 236
Svansdottir, H.B. 123

Thompson, G. 74
Thompson, R.A. 129
Thompson, T. 114
Thorlaksdottir, E. 49
Trevarthen, C. 267
Tribe, R. 182
Trondalen, G. 10, 202, 248
Tubre, T.C. 48
Turry, A. 186, 187, 198
Tustin, F. 152, 174
Twyford, K. 14, 37, 48, 80, 180, 233

UNESCO 275

Van Den Bosch, I. 131
van den Broek, E.L. 131
van der Zwaag, M.D. 131
Vernooij-Dassen, M. 122, 125
Vickers, L. 22
Vink, A.C. 100, 123
Vorapanya, S. 73

Waddell, M. 180
Waite, M. 257

Wallin, D. 33
Walworth, D. 78, 80
Warwick, A. 37, 48
Waterman, H.A. 133
Watson, T. 14, 22, 37, 48, 49,
    80, 170, 180, 233
Weekes, L. 228
Westerink, J.H. 131
Wigram, A. 228
Wigram, T. 99, 123, 228, 230,
    231, 232, 235, 249
Williams, A. 285
Williams, K. 285
Williams, P. 285
Wimpory, D.C. 24
Winnicott, D.W. 9, 10, 273
Witkin, R.W. 283
Wonnacott, J. 182
Woodward, A. 37, 76

Yalom, I.D. 10

Zatorre, R.J. 131
Zuidema, S.U. 121